Praise for *Beso*

"BOOM! (This is one of the best books that I have seen come out in a long time!) *Besom, Stang & Sword* skillfully introduces the reader to important lessons in traditional witchcraft and sets them on a path of mastery. Orapello and Maguire open both their minds and hearts and guide us through a style of magic that has been intimately cultivated and thoroughly explored. This is a book that will quickly become a classic and a must-have for those who seek to discover the magic of the crooked path." —Devin Hunter, author of *The Witch's Book of Power* and *The Witch's Book of Spirits*

"When I first met Christopher Orapello and Tara-Love Maguire, I knew I was in the company of witches. Despite the commonplace setting, I could feel the stir of the wind between the worlds and smell the scent of deep earth and moonlight. Their book, *Besom, Stang & Sword,* fulfills the promise of that first encounter. They have performed the Great Work of witches and have made the old become new and live again. Chapter by chapter, they lay out the tools and the paths of their system of witchcraft. If you do the work described, you will claim your place in a broader reality filled with majesty and power. There are a thousand and one ways to be a witch. This may be your way, but if it is not, it will still be worth your careful attention. All the magicks of the world are intertwined, each a twisting path forming the weave of things." —Ivo Dominguez Jr., author *of Keys to Perception, Practical Astrology for Witches and Pagans* and other books of magick

"*Besom, Stang & Sword* details a beautifully wrought and immensely practical system of modern traditional witchcraft, born of personal insight, working experience, and dedication rooted deeply in the spirit of place. This is a book that offers the reader both clear guidance and the freedom to craft a path of witchcraft which is personal and meaningful to them and the landscape they live in." —Gemma Gary, author of *Traditional Witchcraft—A Cornish Book of Ways*, *The Black Toad*, and *The Charmers' Psalter*

"As an Appalachian witch, bioregional witchcraft is the only witchcraft that touches me, the only sort that reaches backward and forward, roving the spiritual as well as the physical landscape. This knotty and fine book is old and new, too—beautifully written, deeply researched and growing from the furrows of a genuine practice. Much to learn here and much to do. Bury yourself in *Besom, Stang & Sword's* evocative spirit. —H. Byron Ballard, witch and author of *Earth Works: Ceremonies in Tower Time*

In *Besom, Stang & Sword*, Christopher and Tara-Love have crafted an approachable yet artful guide to the practice of traditional witchcraft from a uniquely North American perspective. This in-depth handbook provides an inspired foundation with workable material in the form of rituals, spells, and explorations that both novice and experienced practitioners alike will find compelling and enlightening." —Laura Tempest Zakroff, author of *Weave the Liminal*, *Sigil Witchery*, and *The Witch's Cauldron*

"Orapello and Maguire's beautiful prose draws the reader into a modern take on traditional witchcraft. The craft as they present it is without pretension and strikingly elegant in its simplicity, and it stresses the practitioner's sovereignty and relationship with the spirits of the land. *Besom, Stang & Sword* is easily the most eminently practical book on traditional witchcraft available today." —Nicholas Pearson, author of *The Seven Archetypal Stones* and *Stones of the Goddess*

"With *Besom, Stang & Sword*, Chris and Tara open the doors to their own practices, laying out the materials of magic for all to see. The results drive home the central point that magic—specifically witchcraft—is available to anyone, but it requires time, effort, patience, and thought along with a dose of fate and a sizeable amount of risk. They build a hexagram of approachable practices that asks anyone picking up this work to root their magic in the land surrounding them and their own personal history, rather than taking secondhand sorcery from others. Chris and Tara reveal their Blacktree tradition without pretense or artifice, but instead with clarity, insight, and acid wit, which testifies to their talents as both seasoned occultists and engaging writers. This is a book that will reshape a reader's encounters with magic and the landscape around them." —Cory Thomas Hutcheson, author of *54 Devils* and host of the podcast *New World Witchery*

"*Besom, Stang & Sword* ensorcells witchcraft back to its primal roots, still hidden and alive beneath the surface of the dark soil of mainstream magickal traditions. The book reorients the Craft to return to the primordial forces, animism, baneful plants, folk magic, ecstasy, and hedgewitchery without gatekeeping, armchair pseudo-academia, pretension, or pomposity, making it incomparable to other books in its niche. The unclouded and grounded manner in which Orapello and Maguire write displays that they not only fully understand what they're writing about but that they are well seasoned, knowledgeable, and insightful regarding the cosmology and praxis contained within, which allows them to teach with crystal clarity." —Mat Auryn, author of *Psychic Witch* and blogger at *For Puck's Sake* on Patheos Pagan

"With *Besom, Stang & Sword,* Christopher Orapello and Tara-Love Maguire introduce you to the Blacktree path, a regional form of witchcraft which employs an inviting framework of practical magic aimed at helping you to discover the power of self and place. This immersive amalgamation of practice, rooted in traditional witchcraft, weaves together the essential components of folk magic, shamanism, animism, ancestor veneration, and the occult arts, while removing the excess pageantry. This leaves you with the blueprints for a more candid, modern approach to the craft. Invoke the power of your surrounding landscape, commune with the spirit that resides amongst it, and stir up the desire to reclaim your magical sovereignty as you tread the Blacktree path." —Hugh F. Carey III, founder of Eclectic Artisans Pagan Marketplace, and Sabbat Box, a subscription box service for Pagans

"*Besom, Stang & Sword* presents traditional witchcraft in a clear, easy-to-learn manner, and it does so within the context of a complete tradition that is nonreligious but filled with spirits. Most of us don't have a traditional witch living next door who can teach us her skills and traditions, but we can learn from Christopher Orapello and Tara-Love Maguire." —John Beckett, Druid and author of *The Path of Paganism*

"What an absolute treat to the senses it has been to delve into *Besom, Stang & Sword*! This text presents a cohesive system of practice, thorough in exploring the fundamentals of magic, yet unafraid to delve into the dimly lit corners of witchcraft. Christopher Orapello and Tara-Love Maguire offer their own meticulously curated system based on theory, history, folklore, and trusted praxis. They cover an astonishing array of topics in a refreshingly concise manner and offer clear instruction along with their own rituals and spell work. What they present to us is intelligent methodology and a powerful and spirit-fueled practice that reminds you that your tradition is a living creature to be respected and nurtured. Though a primer for their own magical system, there is no feeling of witchcraft-light here. This book encourages a deepening of your magic, a connection to your own bioregion, and a passion for the work you do with the land and your own spirits. This is sure to become a foundational text among magical practitioners. Orapello and Maguire have offered a treasure to their community with this tome. 'Magick is magick,' they say, and this book truly is just that." —Jen (Rue) Holmes, blogger and herb mistress at *Rue and Hyssop*

"Orapello and Maguire have done it; *Besom, Stang & Sword* is as comprehensive a guide to traditional witchcraft as one could ask for. Looking at the bark on their Blacktree, you can see the roots in 1734, Clan of Tubal Cain, and other traditions as the authors reach into the moonlight for future generations. From establishing yourself as a practitioner to reimagining the Witches' Pyramid, the book's sections are in-depth without leaving the reader feeling lost, and each chapter includes suggested titles for further study. It may take a few days to read but will keep you engaged for a lifetime." —Amy Blackthorn, author of *Blackthorn's Botanical Magic* and creator of Blackthorn Hoodoo Blends

"Thoughtful, incredibly practical, and rooted in reality: all of my very favorite things! In their book *Besom, Stang & Sword*, Chris Orapello and Tara-Love Maguire beautifully articulate everything I hold dear." —Deborah Castellano, author of *Glamour Magic: The Witchcraft Revolution to Get What You Want*

"There are some who would like their witchcraft to be of the kind that would be very comfortable sitting down for tea with the local vicar. There are also those who want to keep the teeth within the practices of the tradition. If you are of the latter persuasion, you're going to love *Besom, Stang & Sword*." —Damh the Bard, Pagan musician, poet, and storyteller, and pendragon of the Order of Bards and Ovates

Besom, Stang & Sword

A Guide to Traditional Witchcraft,
the Six-Fold Path & the Hidden Landscape

CHRISTOPHER ORAPELLO & TARA-LOVE MAGUIRE

WEISER
BOOKS

This edition first published in 2018 by Weiser Books,
an imprint of
Red Wheel/Weiser, LLC
With offices at:
65 Parker Street, Suite 7
Newburyport, MA 01950
www.redwheelweiser.com

ISBN: 978-1-57863-637-2

Library of Congress Cataloging-in-Publication Data available upon request.

Cover design and artwork by Christopher Orapello
Interior illustrations by Christopher Orapello
Typeset in Sabon

Printed in Canada
MAR
10 9 8 7 6 5 4 3 2 1

This book is dedicated with love to the enduring memory of
Sarah Elizabeth Lyter (1985–2018).

Bright daughter of morning,
Who knew your light would go so soon?

Contents

Introduction

For those who have gone before, and those who have yet to be.

In the spring of 2014, we began the journey that this book has grown to embody—the development of a modern system of regional traditional witchcraft. It sprang forth from our finally coming together as a couple to practice magick and ritual, after never having done so since we first met in the summer of 2001. This system, which morphed out of our individual paths and influences, came to be called *Blacktree*, a name that at first only reflected our fascination with the curious blackthorn tree. We later realized that this tree held a much deeper significance for what we were doing—specifically because of the Black Tree, which is our name and spelling for a symbol that we use in our practice. The Blacktree path became our unique form of traditional witchcraft. It distinctly reflects our individual North American upbringings, but is also inspired by the writings of Robert Cochrane, as well as those of Sarah Anne Lawless, Peter Paddon, Gemma Gary, Nigel Pennick, Paul Huson, Andrew Chumbley, and many others.

Traditional witchcraft initially caught our interest because of how it differed from the more common forms of Wicca that have been so prevalent over the past fifty years. The realization that people were looking to the past in a new way through the scholarly pursuits of Carlo Ginzburg, Jeffrey B. Russell, Emma Wilby, Claude Lecouteux, Éva Pócs, and others spoke to us. This was not myopic adherence to tradition for tradition's sake; it was the building of a strong, practical foundation with historical research, personal insight, and critical thought.

This knowledge invigorated our practice and confirmed what we had been feeling for many years—that many of the more commonly practiced paths of today's Paganism and the various offshoots of Wicca all contained elements that we felt were irrelevant to our lives. We sought to establish a system of witchcraft more in tune with our needs, as well as the needs of other witches like us. The Blacktree tradition—and this book—grew out of that budding desire.

Blacktree is a modern, nonreligious form of traditional witchcraft that is rooted in each witch's specific region. Instead of deities, it deals with the spirits of the land and the ancestors—*no gods, many spirits,* as we like to say. It is largely concerned with re-addressing what it means to practice witchcraft in the world beyond the tropes of modern Western Paganism. Rather than being based in ceremonial magick, the practices of Blacktree are more shamanistic in nature and differ in both method and intent from the fertility-minded, deity-based Wiccan streams of witchcraft. It is a modern approach to witchcraft that retains a keen awareness of the history and lore deep in its bones and blood.

In this book, we hope to provide seasoned practitioners with a new way to deepen their practice, as well as to introduce fledgling witches to the essentials of witchcraft. Our perspective anchors itself with one foot firmly planted in the lessons of the past and the other stepping into the boldest future, while staying focused on the natural evolution of the craft. Like the Fool card of the tarot, we are ever leaping into tomorrow.

This book lays before you a tool kit full of rituals, spells, exercises, and techniques that are steeped in a new perspective on practicing witchcraft in the modern day. It places witchcraft in a new light—one that shines brightly on a new era of praxis for neophytes and adepts alike.

Bendith (success and blessings), Chris and Tara

CHAPTER 1

Traditional Witchcraft

Traditional witchcraft is a wild beast with many parents and even more children. At its very core, it is a chimera of folk magic, shamanism, history, ancestor veneration, and respect for the land, but it can be a little difficult to pin down its actual definition. Essentially, traditional witchcraft splits into two main categories: magickal traditions and cultural practices. You can find a number of modern magickal traditions under its overarching umbrella—the Clan of Tubal Cain, Victor and Cora Anderson's Feri, 1734, and the Cultus Sabbati—all of which have been influenced by early modern witchcraft and personal gnosis. The traditions that fall under this banner also tend to eschew dogma in favor of symbolism and imagery steeped in folklore. These paths are magickal in nature and heavy in historical research and individual responsibility, with an emphasis on connecting with the environment.

On the other side of the definition, traditional witchcraft also encompasses widespread cultural practices like Seidr, Hoodoo, Brujería, and Curanderismo, which also involve the use of rituals, energy work, folk magic, divination, and close contact with spirits. These are all integral aspects of witchcraft itself, although individual practitioners of these paths may not actually refer to themselves as "witches" and we must be careful not to disrespect their individual self-identification when discussing them.

Blacktree witchcraft, the tradition behind this book, draws elements and style from both the magickal and the cultural sides of traditional witchcraft and blends them into a cohesive whole. It is generally North American in nature (after all, that's where we're from), but can easily be applied to any region. In addition, it owes a particular debt to the work of Roy Bowers, better known as Robert Cochrane (1931–1966).

It is simply impossible to discuss traditional witchcraft in any capacity without bringing Robert Cochrane's name into it. Cochrane emerged on the English scene in 1963, just when witchcraft was enjoying its modern revival in the United States and Britain. Despite his short three-year involvement, he made a lasting impression that echoes still. Whether this impression was good or bad depends on whom you ask. Cochrane was a firebrand who loved nothing more than stirring the pot, and he gathered as many enemies as friends. In his opinion, magick was a by-product of the search for truth, and he spoke of a witchcraft that was more mystical in nature—focused on the *realization* of truth, rather than its *illusion*.[1] In his opinion, magick grew out of the search for truth. He suggested a re-examination of all sacred cows to see if they still produced milk and sought a reinvestigation of past cultures and practices in order to determine if they held any useful truths.

Traditional Witchcraft, as presented in this book, takes Cochrane's notion of witchcraft a step further. Instead of basing our magickal practice on the past in an attempt to achieve authenticity, why not also look to the present? Or to our immediate surroundings? Why not contact the local land spirits? If witchcraft ever existed in the world, then it exists just as much in the here and now as it ever did in the past. The notion that witchcraft is solely a phenomenon of the past,

---

1   Robert Cochrane, "The Craft Today," *Pentagram* #2, November 1964.

or that it must be sought in far-off lands, or that it's only found by studying and embracing ancient cultures or deities ignores the very reality of the practice itself, as well as the power and connection we already have to our immediate surroundings. The substance, lore, and magick that we can acquire from our regional landscape are far more personal and substantial than any other connection we could ever hope to establish with any antiquated worldview or culture that is foreign to us.

This book contains a new approach to witchcraft. It brings you into a territory that may seem alien at first, but one that will swiftly begin to feel like home. Our approach bypasses all the romanticized New Age fertility rites, harvest festivals, and medieval role-playing that have become so persistently intertwined with modern Paganism and witchcraft, and emphasizes a deeper engagement with the land itself. Rather than enjoining you to commune with far-flung and aloof deities, this witchcraft leads you to interact with your ancestors, both nameless and blood-bound. We encourage you to make contact with the spirit of your own personal place in this world and to be unafraid of getting your hands dirty doing the work you aspire to accomplish.

What Is Witchcraft?

When we examine the history and cultural diversity of witchcraft, we learn that it is not actually a religion, but instead a practice. Cochrane might argue that witchcraft is not Paganism, although it retains the memory of ancient faiths.[2] Someone living in Europe several centuries ago might have described it in terms of sorcery, cursing, consorting with devils and demons, or performing necromantic acts. In those days, as now, many perceived witchcraft as a transgressive act, furtively performed in private and hidden from view. The terms

---

2   Robert Cochrane, "'Genuine Witchcraft' Is Defended," *Psychic News*, November 8, 1963, p. 8.

"witch" and "witchcraft" were not viewed as positive; instead, they were pejoratives used to denounce, demonize, and condemn folk practitioners—or anyone else for that matter—who were unfortunate enough to draw the wrong attention or upset the wrong types of people. While over the last century, a distorted and privileged view of witchcraft emerged, at least in first-world countries. Indeed, prior to its 20th-century revival, witchcraft wasn't considered a comfortable or safe practice. It was not viewed as a community faith tradition that was open and welcoming to the public, let alone one that came complete with children's groups, bake sales, and petitions for societal recognition.

It's important to understand that, outside the bounds of modern Neo-Paganism, witchcraft is not about *the* Goddess or *a* Goddess. It is not about *the* God or *a* God. It is not about seasonal celebrations commemorating the cycles of life, death, and rebirth. It is not about procuring a good harvest, literally or metaphorically. It is not about reliving the past or dancing in a cloak while drinking wine or wearing flowers in your hair. It's not even necessarily about being Pagan. Witchcraft is about sovereignty.

Witchcraft and Sovereignty

Witchcraft ties deeply into matters of personal governance and individual control. It addresses, with blood and sweat, the ills of life and society. In the hands of those who won't sit idle as life just happens to them, it's a tool for change. It's about magick and spells, herbs and spirits, flying and divining. It's about living in the world, for better or worse. It is raw. It is dirty. It is a skillset, a discipline. It is an art. Witchcraft is dwelling in the woods where people rarely go. It can be found right in your yard, in a nearby park, or in an undefiled and wild land. It is resting in forgotten caves and beneath silent trees. It even dwells in the endless bowels of the city, a living entity all its own. It is basking under the moon at night, breathing slowly beneath the silent stars. Witchcraft is all of these things and it has always been there, waiting to be rediscovered. It is a response to the fears lurking in the darkness and a means to deal with them. It is a weapon. It is a talent. It is an instinct.

Witchcraft is not *simply* about magick; that is why there are sorcerers. Witchcraft is not *just* about herbs; that is why there are herbalists. Witchcraft is not *only* about divination or contacting spirits; that is why there are psychics and mediums. Witchcraft is something wholly, entirely different. It is a lifestyle, a vocation, a liminal space defined by experience. It is a virtual crossroads where several paths meet and create their own space by virtue of their intersection.

Witchcraft is a methodology. It is a multifaceted practice that combines several skills and avenues of knowledge. The paths that comprise it sit squarely upon the landscape of history and folklore, individually distinguishable as magick, divination, and herbalism.

Magick leads to spells and exerting your will upon the cosmos to influence desired changes and effects. Divination is the act and process of divine seeing or foretelling the future. Herbalism is the knowledge and application of herbs for medicinal, culinary, and ritual use. The combination and interplay of these three streams of knowledge enable other practices like seership, soul flight, and necromancy to take shape. It is only when these various practices are blended together that witchcraft emerges as a distinct practice that uniquely combines history and folklore, magick, divination, herbalism, hedgewitchery, and necromancy into a unifying system that we refer to collectively as the Six-Fold Path.

Magick, divining, working with and growing herbs, having visions, flying out of the body, and consorting with ghosts of the dead. Witchcraft is *all* of these things. It consists of no religion or dogma. It has no need for clergy. It worships no deities. It celebrates no intrinsically holy days. Witchcraft is a practice that is focused on successful function, rather than being beholden to the aesthetics, symbols, and affectations of 19th-century occultism.

Witchcraft is secular and filthy—dirty, figuratively *and* literally. There will be times when you walk through your everyday life bearing the stains of some working you've performed. The evidence may be anything—the faint scent of scrying incense in your hair, a smudge of charcoal on your cheek, dirt under your fingernails. You will look at these traces of your craft and only you will know what they represent. And that knowledge will give you strength, a secret shield. You will look at them and think to yourself: *I did that.* And your face will flush briefly from the power of that knowledge. Your power.

The Devil and the Craft

We certainly cannot deny that the devil (or *a* devil) has been a key figure in many European accounts of witchcraft. He has been described as the witch-maker, the grand initiator. Indeed, he was the primary reason that witchcraft became synonymous with heresy from the Middle Ages through the Early Modern Period. It is from this association that older forms of witchcraft came to be labeled as "diabolism," as they were widely understood to involve working with or worshipping the devil.

It's no secret that the classic iconography of the devil—horns, forked tongue, goat legs, and pitchfork—originates in several Pagan deities or nature spirits. Images and lore involving Pan, Puck, Hades, Cernunnos, Herne, and others were forerunners of the iconic image of the Christian devil, who was generally depicted as a black-winged bat-like monster prior to the 19th century. This portrayal contrasted strongly with the typical imagery of white-winged angels, like that of Lucifer prior to his fall. Other stories about the devil are rooted in fairy lore, where he appears as a man in black, riding to the hunt with his hounds and the Queen of Elphame. His mutable appearance and developing role grew and changed alongside the imagery and lore of witchcraft, an evolution that continues to this day and into the foreseeable future.

To a Christian, the devil embodies sin and everything that good Christians should avoid. This implies, however, that, if you are *not* a Christian, there is no reason at all to avoid the "devil" or what he represents. However, many modern witches are distinctly (and quite vocally) *not* Christian, but still find themselves arguing defensively that this Christian devil has nothing to do with *their* Horned God. No doubt, this is an argument based in self-preservation. The fact is, however, that, while on the surface this may be true for many modern witches, the history of the devil and the Horned God—the Witch Lord or Witch Father, as some call him—are virtually one and the same. Moreover, this sameness is not actually a bad thing, nor is it something we should shy away from acknowledging or even celebrating.

Indeed, it can be tricky for traditional witches to turn their backs on the devil. In doing so, we run the risk of distorting the history of witchcraft as it developed in the Western world and missing what it can still reveal to us for use in our modern practice. By rejecting what the devil encompasses or represents, we condemn what it means to be completely human—a creature of the earth, including the wildness and carnality of nature. This further instills in us the dangerously romantic view of nature as a benevolent force that looks out for our best interests. In reality, nature is not our caretaker nor our friend. We must never forget this.

Nature is red in tooth and claw. The living modifications we have needed to develop just for basic survival reveal this to be undeniably true. Nature cares for us about as much as we do for a random hair found growing in a weird location. We cut it off or pluck it out without a thought. Just a momentary wince and it's gone. Nature is a monster, as well as a thing of beauty and wonder. It has teeth and bites the hardest those who attempt to make it pink and pretty gossamer. This is not to say, however, that we should not protect and value nature. Far from it. Nature requires our stewardship, the forging of a deep connection between animal and human. As humans, we now live outside of the wild, in a world of shoes and cars and condominiums. But still, we dream.

We now understand that the complexity of life is painted in shades of gray rather than black and white. We can see that it is time to tear down the tired, dueling archetypes of pure good and evil. As a representation of the wildness of nature, the devil reflects our own place in this complexity—human united with animal. Or go further and strip the devil of the many layers of myth and legend he has accrued over the centuries. Approach him as he truly is—nature itself in its most absolute form.

We embrace the devil as a symbol of humanity, as a creature of the earth, not as a trifling villain who encourages self-deception and self-loathing or a childish pawn employed by a narcissistic creator. There is no longer a need for that in this world. We have gone beyond such vanities. We have evolved and developed our own moral codes, an innate sense of the essential dichotomy of right and wrong. In our

craft, we call upon the devil as the Witch Lord, the Lord of Paths, and the Uniter of Worlds. He is the embodiment of nature itself. He unites the worlds within and without, Above and Below. He is like Eliphas Levi's iconic 19th-century image of Baphomet, a blended representation of the manifested world. Not good, not evil, but a duality—an integral part of the ebb and flow of existence.

Figure 1. Baphomet, the Sabbatic Goat, by Eliphas Levi.

As we make our way into these other realms, the Witch Lord is our guide, our contact, our touchstone. We do not worship him, however. He is not a deity. Instead, he is the primary spirit of place and a primordial force—the devil for a new millennia of practice.

Animism

Animism is a term coined by Sir Edward Tyler, known as the Father of Anthropology, during the late 19th century. In some ways, the term may be interpreted as meaning "doctrine of soul," as it derives from *anima*, the Greek word for "soul" and the Latin word for "life" or "spirit." The word "animated" also derives from this root. If something is animated, the implication is that it's alive, that it has a soul or some kind of consciousness.

Witchcraft thus exists quite well within an animistic worldview. Indeed, it almost demands it through its use of herbs and its interaction with spirits—especially the spirits of the dead. It makes sense that witchcraft is an animistic path, one that perceives everything as having a soul, including rocks, plants, trees, animals, the land, a field of flowers, the vast and wild forest, a waterfall, or the sea. On some level, all things are conscious and capable of interaction in an animistic world. By extension, all things in an animistic world must be treated as living beings because *they are*. This may sound a bit dogmatic, but it isn't. An animistic worldview is simply a different way to relate to the land and the cosmos—a fuller perception of the world that allows us to exist within it without making too much of a mess of things.

Animism views all things as distinct beings—each with its own consciousness and soul. *One is one, but within the all.* An animistic view does not collapse all things of the world into an overarching One; it implies no underlying monotheism or divine source. All things are connected, but still remain distinct. Thus individual beings or objects or places may possess unique and differing purposes and temperaments. This explains why some places may feel less welcoming than others, something you may have experienced in an old building or while walking in the woods. Beings gather where places are untouched or long abandoned, and personalities of places may change over time due to interaction with other beings or just through the natural progression of life. To animists, the world is most certainly alive and it sings, in a million voices, a singular chorus of life. To witches, the world is a complex interaction of animate beings with distinct means and ends. Part of becoming a witch is learning to cultivate those relationships to aid us in our craft.

Becoming a Witch

There has been much debate over the years as to what specifically makes someone a witch. Some believe a person is born a witch; others believe that only initiation can make a "true witch." If you do not already consider yourself a witch, but would like to become one, you have already taken your first step by simply reading this book. All witches who ever were became so through their own doing—by deciding to practice witchcraft.

To become a witch and walk a path so removed from conventional society requires that you actively seek the path. It is an act of free will, a demand for liberation and personal sovereignty. You have to desire this thing called witchcraft, against the pressures of society and against what so many of us have been brought up to believe. In doing so, you sacrifice conventionality for the mysteries and experiences that the Craft contains.

So you don't have to be *born* a witch to *be* a witch. Moreover, no one can actually *make* you a witch, despite any lineage or background they may possess. It is not up to someone else whether or not you become a witch. The decision is yours alone—like playing an instrument or reading a book. It is an active choice you make and it is a path you walk with intent. Although teachers and mentors may guide you on your way, the surest way to become a witch is by having an intention to become one and having the will to dare.

The following short ritual is designed to introduce you to the Witch Lord and the spirits of the land. Through it, your eyes will open to a different world. You will be changed forever. It will place you fully upon the witches' path, as long as you choose to walk it.

This ritual actually consists of four parts—stepping onto the path, creating a crossroads, hailing the Witch Lord, and creating the Cord of Sovereignty. The rite can withstand many variations, depending upon your location and living situation. Spontaneity is always a great catalyst for ritual, but the version shared here should be applicable no matter where you are or what you have at your disposal. Witchcraft does not require fancy tools and elaborate props to be successful. Farmers' markets are a great resource for locally sourced produce and other products, and are highly recommended for ferreting out what you need. Materials originating in your area help fuel your magick and infuse it with local energy, while also cultivating a connection with and personal alignment to the land. Supporting local farms and businesses helps inject life into your local economy and will assist you in your personal stewardship of the region.

You will need these items to perform the rite:

- An offering bowl (if you are working indoors)
- A navigational compass
- A bag of small, shiny objects, like glass beads
- A bottle of locally produced red wine or a reasonable substitute
- A small loaf of locally baked bread
- A pair of scissors
- A red cord roughly ¼ inch in diameter and cut 24 inches longer than you are tall. (Example: If you are 5 feet tall,

you'll need a cord 7 feet long.) Cut the cord to the proper length before you begin, so it's ready prior to the ritual.

STEPPING ONTO THE CROOKED PATH

Perform this rite on a full moon. The clearer the sky, the better. If possible, find a secluded outdoor location. If this is not possible, you can perform the rite indoors. If outside, wear dark clothes to take advantage of the cover of night. On your way to the space, see if you can find a suitable stick or branch about waist height and bring it with you. Do not remove the branch without asking permission of the spirit of the wood. Explain your need and wait for an answer. If you feel it is permissible, leave some of the shiny objects you brought with you—but don't lose your car keys! Verbally thank the branch and the space, and continue on your way with the branch. If you are unable to procure a branch or stick, or know in advance you will not be able to find one, bring a staff or cane with you. The stick/branch is not required to perform the rite and there's always a way to substitute any ritual component. Necessity demands creativity.

Once at the site, make peace with your surroundings and ask permission of the land and its accompanying spirits to proceed. If you are not welcome in that space, you will certainly know right away. You'll feel a disquieting dread in your heart and bones that will deepen the longer you stay. If everything appears fine and favorable, determine which direction is east using your compass. Facing east, sit in silence upon the earth for several minutes, feeling the solitude and embracing the local sounds of the night. If you are lucky enough to do this outside, ask yourself these questions: What time of the year is it? What do you hear? Are you surrounded by the manic chorus of deep summer crickets and cicadas? Or is this the thick of autumn, with tiny peeper frogs looking for love? Are you chilly? Is the ground hard or damp?

If you are inside, you can still listen. Listen and feel; search out any other living beings in your vicinity. Can you feel the spirit of the dwelling you are in? Sit on the floor and, if weather permits, open a window to foster a stronger connection to the outside world.

Now begin to center your mind and body through slow, relaxed breathing and quieting your thoughts. This will help to bring you into the present moment and create a buffer between your everyday life and the ritual you are about to perform. Breathe deeply and slowly from your belly to induce a relaxed state. With every exhalation, gradually guide yourself into a calm breathing pattern. While still seated, consider the following to help you come to a singular moment for the rite:

- Think about your immediate surroundings—the walls around you, or the trees and bushes. What is before you? Next to you? Behind you?

- Think about what exists around you in the distance—east, north, west, and south.

- Think about where you are in relation to those places and how long it would take you to walk to them.

- Think about where you are in your country with those directions in mind and the distant places surrounding you, located hours away.

- Think about where you are on the planet in relation to other countries.

- Think about the ground (or floor) upon which you are sitting and the earthen layers of the planet existing beneath you.

- Think about how the entire planet is currently rotating and moving through the vastness of space, even though you can't feel it.

Sit for several more minutes, experiencing this sensation of being a point in space. Once you have reached this point, stand up. If you have a branch or stick, bring it with you as you take a step and a half forward toward the east. Pause for several breaths before beginning the second part of the ritual—the Crossroads Rite.

THE CROSSROADS RITE

This is a short ritual to create a crossroads wherever you happen to be. Depending on why you are performing the rite, it can be modified to fit your intent and to fulfill a variety of functions. Here, the rite is being used to create an intersection to fulfill the role of an actual crossroads, a liminal space. It is also emblematic of the phrase "the Crooked Path," which is another label for witchcraft itself. The rite delineates a working area by heading in different directions and forming a Solar Cross. In other paths, this same symbol is also referred to as the Mark of Cain.

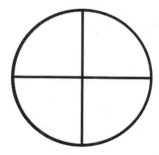

Figure 2: A Solar Cross, known in some paths as the Mark of Cain.

Standing slightly east and forward from where you were just seated, face the east. If you have a branch or staff, hold it in your left hand with one end touching the ground. Say the following aloud, addressing the space as you do so:

From the east, I go to west.

Turn and take three steps to the west, dragging the branch so that it inscribes the ground, marking a trail. If you do not have a branch or staff, drag your left foot as you move to create the same effect. Now, standing three steps to the west, turn right and say:

About to north.

Continuing to drag your branch or foot, walk one-quarter of a circle around to the north. Then turn right, face the south, and say:

And then to south.

As you take three steps, crossing the center of the space where you were originally seated in meditation, say:

Crossing roads as I go about.

Facing south, turn right and, continuing to drag your branch or foot, walk one-quarter of the way around the circle to the west and say:

Laying the ground for a witch's work.

In the west, turn right and walk three steps to the east. Say:

Down at the crossroads is where I vow.

In the east, turn right and, continuing to drag your branch or foot, walk one-quarter of the way around the circle to the south. Say:

To meet with she and he and they and thou.

In the south, turn right and walk three steps to the north. Say:

Upon this night, and in this hour.

In the north, turn right and, continuing to drag your branch or foot, walk one-quarter of the way around the circle to the east, completing the rite. Say:

I call upon thee to beseech thy power.

HAILING THE WITCH LORD

Once the crossroads is established, walk from the east to the center of the space. Knock or stomp three times upon the ground (or floor), then pause and call upon the Witch Lord using the following words (or something spontaneous of your own devising):

Hail the dread Lord of witchcraft, the wilderness and night!
I, (state your full name), call upon you,
To visit and recognize me as a wanderer,
And new disciple of the Crooked Path.

I stand before you of my own free will,
In silence and in secret,
To know the wonders of your ways.

Lord of Wild Abandon, Uniter of Worlds,
Grant me your passion, permit me your blessing,
As I embark upon this journey on this full moon night.

From this time forth, be my guide to the greater realms,
Throughout, about, above, and below,
As I desire—it is so!

Take out the bottle of wine you brought with you. Open it and say:

With this wine, the blood of the land—
May it fill me with your passion and thus—
It is so.

Take a drink of the wine, then pour some on your left index finger and anoint your forehead. Pour out the rest of the bottle onto the ground around you while turning clockwise. If you are performing this rite indoors, pour the wine out four times into the offering bowl instead. Then take out the bread you brought with you, hold it before you, and say:

With this bread, made of the land,
May it fill me with your blessing and thus—
It is so.

Eat a single piece of bread, then scatter pieces of it to the east, south, west, and north. If you are performing this rite indoors, break off four pieces of bread, hold up each in turn to its appropriate direction, then place them into the offering bowl. Once the offering is complete, proceed to the final portion of the rite—creating the witch's cord.

THE CORD OF SOVEREIGNTY

The Cord of Sovereignty is the witch's cord of initiation. It is made by tying knots along the cord, from foot to head. Once the last knot has been tied, the cord is cut. This ritual item is comparable to the "cable tow" found in Freemasonry, which symbolically delineates initiates' ability to give of themselves to their fraternity. The witch's cord also resembles the Measure often found in British Traditional Wicca. While the cable tow is purely symbolic, however, and is only meant to show initiates that they are in control of decisions about what comes first in their lives, the Wiccan Measure is a physical object (generally a rope used to measure candidates during their actual initiation) kept by the High Priest/ess of the coven that creates a spiritual link between initiates and their coven mates. In the Blacktree tradition, we prefer to return the cord to candidates directly after initiation, so they may freely conduct themselves in the world as witches who are in control of their own lives, with no spiritual Sword of Damocles hanging over their heads.

To begin, tie a knot in one end of the cord. Hold this knot under your left foot between your big toe and your index toe. Thread the cord between these two toes so that your foot is holding the knot to the floor. Once this is done, say:

With this first knot, may I always be grounded, walk a balanced life, and stand strong against any threat or tyranny.

Draw the rest of the cord up and tie another knot level with your groin. Say:

With this second knot, may I maintain dominion over my own being; I am my own person, now and evermore so.

From the groin, draw the cord up and tie a knot level with your belly. Say:

With this third knot, may I always be full of food and drink, as well as with knowledge, wisdom, and life.

From the belly, draw the cord up and tie a knot level with your heart. Say:

With this fourth knot, may I live joyously, but responsibly, with my emotions; and may I be passionate, reverential, and compassionate to those who need and deserve it.

From the heart, draw the cord up and tie a knot level with your throat. Say:

With this fifth knot, may I forever hold sway over my own speech and may I honor my oaths and any words that I speak henceforth.

From the throat, draw the cord up and tie a knot level with your third eye—a spot on your forehead between your brows. Say:

With this sixth knot, may I see and know beyond the veil and in life. And with this sight, may all be revealed unto me.

From your third eye, draw the cord up and tie a knot level with the crown of your head. Say:

With this seventh knot, may the Witch Lord and Witch Queen aid and empower me in all that I do.

Using the scissors, cut the cord an inch or so past the final knot and, while holding the cord, say:

With this Cord of Sovereignty, may I seize governance over my own self through wherever this path will take me. May I be empowered to pursue my dreams and to succeed in attaining them in accordance with my Will. So mote it be!

You can wear the cord as you see fit. Tie it around your waist, drape it around your neck and over your shoulders, or wrap it around your left arm—whatever is most comfortable and practical for you.

Once the cord is in place, sit down, close your eyes, and relax. Take a few minutes to allow this moment to sink in. During this time, you may receive information through mental images. Instead of trying to clear your mind, explore the random thoughts that present themselves. You may be visited by the Witch Lord himself; you may be given a new name; you may make contact with a familiar spirit, or with something more. These conversations and experiences, whether they occur mentally or verbally, are significant. So be sure to keep an open mind and be observant.

When the time feels appropriate, get up from your meditation and thank the Witch Lord. Knock or stomp three times upon the ground (or floor) and then depart. Be sure to take the empty wine bottle with you. Leave some glass beads as additional thanks and either leave the branch you found, thanking it for its service, or, if you feel an affinity for it, bring it home to turn into a wand or staff, depending on its size and shape. If it has any leaves, be sure to save them, as they will help you identify what type of wood the branch is. Different varieties of wood hold different meanings or associations, and all things have their own voice. So be sure to begin paying attention to these sorts of messages or directions, if you don't do so already.

If you performed this ritual at home, clean up the space and go outside for some fresh air. Re-engaging with the rest of the world outside your ritual space can be a little disconcerting, so it is always a good idea to reground yourself. Watch a film to help return your consciousness to your normal baseline. Hydrate and eat some food. If you keep a journal, write down your thoughts and experiences for later reflection.

For the next month, you may want to sleep with your cord under your pillow to further enhance your relationship with it. Witches' cords are powerful tools, as they embody the witches themselves and their will. After sleeping close to your cord for a month, keep it in a secret location and wear it whenever you do a working.

On Your Path

This four-part ritual is about introducing you to the powers and spirits of the world at large, rather than purely about initiation or dedication. It is really quite a simple ritual, despite how lengthy it appears in print. It is meant to establish communication and to begin a relationship with the spirits of your region. The Witch Lord is only one component of your local landscape. He should be viewed as a mentor and guide, rather than as a deity or being to worship. He may visit your dreams or be seen in the leaves of the trees on a breezy silent night, but he is most surely your first step into the world of the Craft.

SUGGESTED READING

Mastering Witchcraft: A Practical Guide for Witches, Warlocks, and Covens, by Paul Huson.

A Grimoire for Modern Cunningfolk: A Practical Guide to Witchcraft on the Crooked Path, by Peter Paddon.

The Original Folk and Fairy Tales of the Brothers Grimm: The Complete First Edition, by Jacob and Wilhelm Grimm.

A History of Witchcraft: Sorcerers, Heretics, and Pagans, by Jeffrey B. Russell and Brooks Alexander.

Children of Cain: A Study of Modern Traditional Witchcraft, by Michael Howard.

The Rebirth of Witchcraft, by Doreen Valiente.

IN VERITATE TUA

CHAPTER 2

Besom, Stang, and Sword

As you stepped onto the Crooked Path, you experienced firsthand what it's like to step sideways into a different world—into an unfamiliar landscape based in ritual, mystery, and magick. In this rite, you performed offerings, evocations, and proclamations. You ventured into a trance state and created a magickal space, possibly without even realizing it. The tools you used were simple and the rite was mostly dependent upon your actions, your will, and the words you spoke. In many ways, it was a small test to see if you dared to step into the shadowed unknown. After all, in order to practice witchcraft successfully, you must be prepared to step outside your comfort zone.

In the magickal system presented here, we use a blend of tools influenced by the practices of Robert Cochrane, traditional grimoires, and Early Modern understandings of witchcraft. These are by no means the only tools you may use during your practice as a witch, but they're necessary components for the system of witchcraft described in this book. Folk magic—and by default, witchcraft—is mostly comprised of simple methods and techniques that allow it to succeed under any circumstance or at any location. Unfortunately, witchcraft has been turned into something of a stage production over the last 100 years. While this type of witchcraft has maintained some of the beauty and significance found in some forms of ritual, the prevalence of this habitual production has encouraged the illusion (whether intentionally or not) that there are precious few other ways to practice magick.

The Tools of Ritual

Tools have a combined function in the performance of magick and ritual. In some ceremonial-based systems, like Wicca or the Hermetic Order of the Golden Dawn, ritual tools become a symbolic manifestation of the elements. They function as an extension of the practitioner and, like mundane tools, also serve to accomplish specific tasks. It's far easier to pound nails into a board using a hammer than with your fist. Also, far less painful! In the same way, there's a practical side to ritual tools as well as a symbolic one, and both help to unite conscious with subconscious.

This chapter discusses the besom, stang, and sword, as well as some more unusual tools and altars, as they are viewed and used in the Blacktree tradition. Additional tools that may be required in your rituals include saltwater, offering bowls, offering plates, incense, charcoal, incense tongs, candles, and a cauldron. These are all common in modern practice and shouldn't be difficult to procure. If you need any of these to perform any of the rituals presented here, they will be listed and briefly explained.

You may notice that, while there are formal methods for obtaining some of these items, there are no cleansing and consecration rituals recommended or provided. We feel that witchcraft is more literal in its execution than figurative. Thus your tools become sacred or special through their use, not because of any ritual performed to make them so. At the same time, it's also commonly recognized that tools set aside specifically for ritual should be used only for that purpose and should be treated with respect outside of ritual. After all, as a craftsperson, it's important to respect your tools. We suggest that, if a tool feels as if it needs to be cleansed and consecrated for some reason, you can run it through a purifying incense made of equal parts rosemary and thyme and seal it with a kiss. There is really no need for any pageantry beyond that.

The Besom

A union of earth and air. The word "besom" comes from an old word for broom. The besom is essentially a wand or staff with a cylindrical bundle of twigs or broom corn bound to one end. Because its shaft-and-bushel arrangement is symbolic of the union of male and female, it was used as a symbol in fertility rites and weddings. Newlywed couples jumped over it, symbolically consummating their union and insuring many squalling babies to come.

From a practical perspective, the besom also serves the common purpose of cleaning your work space and home. It also has an interesting relationship to the path of history and lore, as it can be turned into—or at the very least resemble—a torch, which also makes it symbolic of illumination and knowledge. The inverted besom resembles a thriving tree, in contrast to the clattering-bone appearance of the witches' stang.

You can make your own besom with traditional materials—an ash handle, some birch twigs, and willow strips used to bind the twigs to the handle (it's more difficult than it sounds). Or you can purchase a besom from a private craftsperson. The practical role that the besom (or any tool, for that matter) plays in witchcraft always supercedes the symbology of the materials from which it is crafted. In a pinch, even a fallen branch still adorned with fresh leaves can easily work as a substitute in any ritual that requires a besom.

In ritual, the besom resides in the north and is used for closing and ending the ritual by sweeping the space in a counterclockwise direction.

EXERCISE: MAKING YOUR OWN BESOM

For this exercise, you will need:

- A branch (see directions for sizing)
- A power drill with a ¼-inch diameter drill bit
- Broom corn
- Four 12-inch zip ties
- Jute twine
- One-inch x 14-gauge nail
- Wire cutters
- Stainless steel kitchen shears or utility knife

Select the handle of your besom from a local forest. Be sure to ask the tree or the land before cutting or removing it, and then leave a suitable offering of thanks. The thickness and length of the handle are entirely up to you. Just realize that about seven inches of the handle will be hidden by the brush end and that it should be at least one inch in diameter.

Drill a ¼-inch hole through the handle about one inch from one end, then drill another about one inch from the opposite end. One hole will be used to anchor the brush and the other will be used to create a means to hang your besom when it's not in use.

Determine which end of the handle will be used for anchoring the brush and thread your jute twine through the hole you drilled. Tie the twine using a good knot, but don't cut it. Tightly wrap the jute twine three times around this part of the handle.

Next, take your broom corn and tightly bind a suitable amount into a cylindrical shape, making sure that the bottom end of the bundle

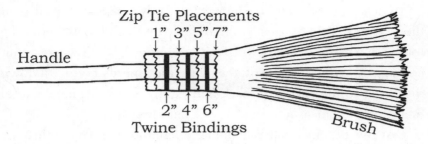

Figure 3: Making a besom.

is as even as possible. The overall thickness of the base of the brush should be at least twice the thickness of the handle when bunched together. Keep in mind that the base of your brush will condense a little during this process. Using one of the zip ties, loosely hold the brush together about seven inches in from the end of its base. Don't tighten the zip tie yet.

Slip the end of your handle to which you tied the twine about seven inches into the base of the brush, entering from the side so as not to misalign the shafts at the bottom. This should place your handle right in line with the zip tie. Shape the bristles of your brush evenly around your handle, making sure that it is as centered as possible within the base of the brush.

Take a second zip tie and wrap it around the brush, about five inches in from the base. Notice how this shapes your broom as you gently bind the zip tie. Don't tighten it too much; just make it snug. Using the two remaining ties, repeat this about three inches from the base, and then about one inch, working your way toward the bottom of the brush, each time checking how this affects the shape of your besom. Once all four ties are in place, tighten them gradually, until they are as tight as you can get them.

Now take the twine that is sticking out from the side of your besom and tightly bind this area of the brush together, wrapping the twine around several times to create a strong attachment. Again, don't cut the twine.

When you feel that you have sufficiently wrapped this area of the besom, spiral or weave your twine down the brush to about the four-inch mark and tightly wrap this area as well. Don't worry about crossing over your ties. Tie off the twine, then spiral or weave it down the brush to the two-inch mark and tightly wrap this area several times for good measure. Again, don't cut the twine.

At this two-inch mark, hammer a nail into the handle through the brush, avoiding the twine and leaving some of the head of the nail exposed. Loop some twine under the head of the nail and tie it down tightly. Cut the twine and hammer the nail down a little more so that it won't get caught on anything during use.

Once complete, carefully remove the four zip ties using your wire cutters. With your kitchen shears or utility knife, clean up the ends of your brush as you see fit, trimming any irregular bristles to create a nice neat edge. With some additional twine, tie a loop at the opposite end, through the other hole you drilled, so you can hang your broom when it's not in use. If you can't hang it, always store it standing with the brush end up to preserve the bristles and shape.

The Stang

The stang is an emblem of wood, an altar of the land spirits, and is closely tied to the paths of both herbalism and hedgewitchery. It is a tall, forked staff, designed to be reminiscent of a tree, uniting the Above with the Below. It is the *axis mundi,* or World Tree, found in Norse mythology, Russian folklore, and Haitian Vodou practice, as well as in many other diverse cultures and systems. It resembles a pitchfork, an important tool for countryfolk, and is also associated with images of the devil, as well as with the tools associated with Hades and his brother, Poseidon.

In ritual, the stang is emblematic of the Witch Lord and is placed in the southern quarter of the work space, because, for us, this represents the element of earth. After all, a tree is planted in the earth, not in the air! It can be seen as a wand with a forked end, in contrast to the wand-like besom, which stands opposite it in the northern quarter of the ritual work space. Once the Compass is laid, the stang is ritually raised to unite the worlds, Above and Below, and to permit us to travel between.

EXERCISE: MAKING YOUR OWN STANG

The stang is traditionally made of ash, but any indigenous wood can provide the direct connection to your surroundings that is required. Finding the wood for your stang in your own yard or a local forest is ideal. Be sure to ask permission of the tree spirit before removing or cutting anything, and always leave behind an offering of thanks. Glass beads, marbles, candy, sloe gin, and rum can all be used to show your gratitude, but, ultimately, it's best to learn what your individual land prefers.

Once you have chosen the wood for your stang, you must "shoe" the end of it with an iron nail to preserve its power. You can do this simply by pre-drilling a lengthwise hole in the bottom end of the stang and hammering an iron nail into the hole. (Pre-drilling helps to keep the shaft from splitting.) Shoeing the end of the stang in this manner locks in the energy and keeps it from dissipating during outdoor rituals. Indoors, we use a stand to hold the stang in place as we do our work.

You can decorate your stang however you like. To give it an added role in ritual, adorn it with the skull of a stag by tying the antlers to the forks of the stang with soft leather straps. You can also attach a crossbar to the stang's pole underneath the skull and drape a cloth over it to make it resemble a person standing just outside the ritual space. Depicting the stang in this manner permits the Witch Lord to be present in body, as well as in spirit.

The Sword

Forged of earth and fire, the sword resides in the east and is used to define the boundaries of the work space. The sword is the athame, or ritual knife, writ large. However, the athame—a common tool found in other modern traditions of witchcraft—is not used for cutting. Rather its function is just the opposite of what a blade is intended to do.

The sword is a symbol of power, dominance, and defense. It is emblematic of the plow and how it was used to define the borders of property in centuries past. In ritual, it defines the work space by scribing a boundary into the earth. The presence of iron and its application also help to keep troublesome land spirits at bay, mischief-makers who might otherwise make their presence noisily known or be obtrusive in other ways. Above all else, a sword is a weapon forged of earth and fire, and its use in ritual reflects this very nature. If you cannot obtain a sword, or if an actual sword proves to be unwieldy in your working space, a ritual knife can function as a reasonable substitute.

The Cord of Sovereignty

The Cord of Sovereignty is a red cord that contains eight carefully placed knots (see chapter 1). It symbolizes witches' dedication to their craft and their dominion over their own being. In some witchcraft traditions, this cord is called the witch's Measure and is said to be reminiscent of the cable tow described in Masonic ritual. However, the witch's Measure functions as an instrument of control, while the cable tow represents obligation and personal responsibility.

The Cord of Sovereignty, as used in Blacktree, is a symbol of personal empowerment, recognition, self-governance, and liberation. It is worn by witches in any manner they see fit during ritual and can perform double duty as a measuring instrument when they need to mark physical boundaries with the sword. Using the cord in this way makes the working space an extension of the practitioner, further connecting witches to their craft.

The Blackthorn Cane

The blackthorn cane—a witch's blasting rod—is used for protection, purification, grounding, clearing a space of any negativity, smiting, banishing, and similar types of workings. Blackthorn is a shrubby hardwood tree indigenous to the UK and the west coast of North America, but it is also cultivated in a wide variety of other locales. It grows along the edges of wild places and creates impenetrable boundaries when left untamed. Born in such liminality, it holds deep ties to witchcraft and it, along with its cousins the hawthorn and the rowan, frequently pops up in folklore beyond its indigenous European regions.

When the blackthorn drops its flowers and leaves in preparation for winter, its branches brace themselves black against the sky. The tree is associated with the dark half of the year and is covered in long needlelike thorns that can inflict wounds that run the risk of turning septic, so be cautious when working with it. The thorns themselves can be used in place of pins or nails for magickal workings, as their venom is sure to add another level of energy to such acts. In contrast to the thorns' dangerous nature, the bittersweet sloe berries the tree produces are added to gin to make the liqueur sloe gin. In Blacktree, we often use a good sloe gin as a land offering in our rituals.

Unless the blackthorn tree is indigenous to where you live, the easiest way to shop for a cane or wand made from its wood is most likely online. Alternately, you can also shop around for an Irish shillelagh—a traditional fighting or walking stick that is frequently made of this alluring hardwood.

Besides its other associated functions, the blackthorn cane can also be used to trace out symbols on the ground or in the air. You can drag it behind you as you walk about to define the work space—for instance, during the Crossroads Rite—to combine its powers of intent with those of purification, grounding, and banishing.

The Token of the Land

The Token of the Land symbolizes the contractual relationship between a witch and the land itself. Through that connection, it represents the power of the land and allows witches to tap into and unite with that resource during ritual. The token is an item of residency—meaning that it is a semi-permanent possession retained while a witch resides in a particular location. If and when you choose to move from that area, it should be returned to the place from which it was taken. The token can be a rock, a jar of soil or sand, a seashell, or a significant piece of branch or bark. For practical reasons, it should be no larger than what you can easily handle.

EXERCISE: OBTAINING YOUR TOKEN

To find your token, go outside and look around your space until you locate a suitable object that resonates with you. Ask the object if you may remove it from its home to serve as a representative of the land in your magick. If you sense that the object is agreeable to your request, announce your intentions to the surrounding area, saying that the item in question has given you its permission. If you feel that the local environment is compliant, remove the object and leave an offering of thanks. Glass beads, shiny coins, colorful candy, bread, or milk have all been used successfully in our area, but you should experiment to see what your local land spirits prefer. If the time ever comes when you need to return the token, thank it for its service, return it home, and leave an offering of thanks.

The Skull and Hearthstone

The skull and the hearthstone are the primary components of the ancestor altar (see below). The skull, in this case, should only be represented by a human skull. Although some traditions allow the use of an animal skull, we in the Blacktree tradition do not use animal skulls on the ancestor altar, as human ancestors are human spirits.

It is not necessary for this to be a real human skull, however, as there are a number of challenges in procuring one. Although it is not illegal to possess an actual human skull, they can be difficult to obtain ethically and, while a real human skull is ultimately preferable and certainly adds a level of sobriety and seriousness to any ritual that cannot be achieved otherwise, sometimes it's just not possible. Moreover, a drawback to working with a real human skull is that its personality may conflict with you and your work. Another obstacle is cost; human skulls can be quite expensive. If you are lucky enough to have the disposable funds to purchase a real human skull, we advise that you thoroughly research the vendor you are planning to purchase from to insure that the skull was obtained through ethical means. *Boneroom.com* and *skullstore.ca* are two viable online resources for human bones. With all of this said, a skull made from an alternate material like resin or crystal will suffice.

The skull represents our connection to the dead and serves as a home in which an ancestral spirit can reside for the duration of a rite. In Blacktree, we place the skull atop the hearthstone, which is symbolic of the hearth of the home—a gathering place of loved ones for warmth and familial bonding.

The hearthstone can be made of any stone that could be used to build the hearth for a fireplace. We use a brick-shaped piece of limestone with felt attached to the bottom to avoid scratching the surface of our altar. Whatever stone you choose, it should lend a sense of foundation, a feeling of solidity through which it can fulfill its role. And, of course, it must support the skull resting upon it.

The Message Box

The message box is simply a container used to hold messages written to the ancestors during visitations to the ancestor altar between each full moon. Ours is a small wooden box with a slot on top that allows us to drop in messages. The messages themselves can be notes of thanks, acknowledgments, wishes, or sigils—whatever you desire. On the night of the full moon, burn these messages in a cauldron to send them out into the ether.

The Trinity of Altars

In Blacktree, we define three separate places within the ritual space as altars—places that represent power centers related to the practice. These do not need to be actual altars, in the sense of being a holy surface or table. They can simply be places on the ground or the floor that are associated with three distinct locations within the working space. Their placement and relationship to the space, and to each other, will become more apparent as we discuss the working space itself (see below). It should also be noted that the first two altars discussed—the genius loci and the ancestor altar—also have a place and function outside the formal ritual environment for regular visitations and offerings to the spirits.

The Genius Loci Altar

The first altar in our trinity, the genius loci altar, resides in the south and is symbolic of the paths of herbalism and hedgewitchery. In the working space, it is represented by the stang. This altar is the embodiment of the Witch Lord, local folklore, and the spirits of the land. It is where they reside within the working space.

Outside of a ritual environment, this altar may reside in its own special location in your home. It serves as a place for communing with the spirits of the land and may actually be a specified surface. Place offerings of food, flowers, or found objects on this altar to honor the land spirits. Items typically found on this altar are your token (when not actually being used in ritual) and anything else you feel connects you to the land and your region's spirits.

The Ancestor Altar

The second altar in the working space is the ancestor altar, the place where we tap into our past and commune with those who have gone before. This altar is represented by the skull and hearthstone, which can be placed on a small, low table. Other items to include here are ancestral offerings, a piece of palo santo wood for burning, the message box, and any depictions of the deceased.

This altar resides in the west, with the setting sun, and symbolizes the element of Water, death, and the paths of divination and necromancy. This is where we venerate the ancestors and welcome them into the space during our rites. It also functions as a gateway, holding space for them in our world, and is connected to the Witch Queen. Outside of the ritual environment, this altar resides in its own special location—selected by the individual witch—to serve as a place of daily ancestral communion.

The Sacrificial Altar

The final altar of the trinity—the sacrificial altar—sits in the northeast corner of the space. Mind you, the name is not as gruesome as it may sound. It only reflects the function of the place where we put the Token of the Land during ritual, and where we leave any items we may be offering. The ritual salt and water for creating a fortified compass are also housed here.

The sacrificial altar unites the energy of the land and our connection to it with our ancestors via our offerings. In its most basic sense, it is represented by the token (outside of its general home on the genius loci), but it may also be accompanied by flowers and offerings of local bread and wine. With this duality in mind, this altar relates to both the Witch Lord and the Witch Queen, uniting their given realms and personal natures.

The Northern Quarters System

The Northern Quarters System is based upon the four *airts* (winds) of Celtic tradition. This system also appears in the work of Robert Cochrane and those influenced by him—for instance, the 1734 and the Roebuck traditions found in the United States, as well as the Clan of Tubal Cain in Britain. It differs from the more common system associated with the elements in that, instead of having Earth in the north, Air in the east, and Fire in the south, these three have been given new directional associations. In the Northern Quarters System, we have Air in the north, Fire in the east, Earth in the south, and Water in the west.

These associations relate to the unique way in which Blacktree views the world. Air is in the north because air is above us. Fire is in the east because that is where the sun rises. Earth is in the South

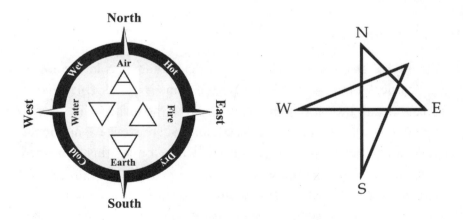

Figure 4. Northern Quarters pentagram.

because the earth dwells under our feet. And Water is in the west because water can be found to the west (or the distant west, as the case may be). Moreover, there are other reasons for Water's association with the west. The west is where the sun sets and is also the home of the West Gate, through which the dead are said to enter the Underworld. In Blacktree, we feel that the environment-based alignment of the elements in the Northern Quarters System represents a more land-based approach, one we prefer in our craft.

Placing the elements in this manner also aligns them with the four qualities attributed to them by Aristotle—hot, cold, dry, and wet—and sets them in direct opposition to one another, as shown in Figure 4. Air, which is hot and wet, sits across from Earth, which is cold and dry. Fire, which is hot and dry, sits across from Water, which is cold and wet. This system also gives us a variation on the shape of the pentagram (see Figure 4). It is awkwardly shaped, but strangely still very compass-like and has neither an upright nor inverted position that can be distinguished, emphasizing the dual/neutral nature of the Craft. Magickally speaking, however, it requires a different drawing method from what is found in the well-known Lesser Banishing Ritual of the Pentagram and other rituals that come from the teachings and practices of the Hermetic Order of the Golden Dawn or other similarly derived systems.

When tracing these pentagrams in a working, practitioners start at the element's associated point and make the decision of whether to draw the pentagram in a clockwise or counterclockwise direction based on whether they want to invoke or banish that particular elemental energy—clockwise to invoke, counterclockwise to banish (see Figure 5). These pentagrams can then be used during moments of evocation, banishing, blessing, and purification, depending on the work at hand. For example, the banishing Earth pentagram can be used to banish negative energy from a space, and the evoking Fire pentagram can be used to instill passion and power into an object during a consecration or anointing rite.

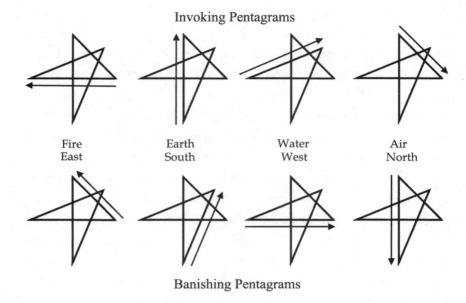

Invoking Pentagrams

| Fire | Earth | Water | Air |
| East | South | West | North |

Banishing Pentagrams

Figure 5. Invoking and banishing pentagrams.

Having elemental associations built into the framework of the Blacktree tradition serves to anchor other systematic components and symbolic ritual elements into the tradition successfully. Thus the elemental associations serve more as a foundational aspect of the tradition than a ritual one. We do not work with the elements or elementals, or even necessarily call quarters, as is done in other witchcraft traditions. Rather, we use the elements in a more subtle way that allows them to operate in their own manner without pulling the rug out from under the rest of the ritual structure and magickal system. The benefits of these associations will become more evident as your work develops.

The Working Space

As shown previously, the layout of the working space derives from the pentagram itself. The various tools and altars are placed about the space to represent specific points on the pentagram. The space itself is kept open to permit movement. As you can see in Figure 6, the trinity of altars creates a triangle that plays off the pentagram layout in a curious way. When we look at the pentagram, the ancestor altar and the stang (or the genius loci altar) are united by the sacrificial altar. It is interesting that these two altars also embody the two aspects of animism—the spirits of the ancestors and the spirits of the land. In

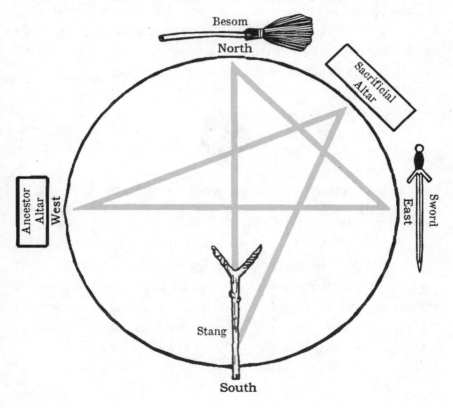

Figure 6. The working space.

the circle layout, they're joined by the notion of sacrifice, which is certainly something to contemplate. The stang and besom sit opposite one another, just as the ancestor altar sits opposite the sword, while the besom and sword sit along a diagonal, flanking either side of the sacrificial altar. This adds an interesting dimension when we take the Witch Queen into account, because she bears the besom and sword, which directly associates her with the sacrificial altar (see Figure 6). The beauty of this layout lies in the amount of threaded symbolism at play—a series of contemplative meditation exercises just waiting to happen.

The working space is also like a cauldron. Our actions fill it with ingredients and our movements stir it up. Therefore, in Blacktree, we have no concern about moving clockwise or counterclockwise in the space. Either one mixes up the energy as we work and doesn't restrict or confuse any dancing, chanting, or energy-raising.

EXERCISE: WORKING SPACE MEDITATION

Sit and meditate on the symbolic relationships within the layout of the working space. What does the placement of altars and tools reveal in relation to their elemental, directional, and symbolic qualities? What does it say about their relation to each other and how they exist around the pentagram? There is a great deal of insight and significance to discover by analyzing the symbolic relationships at play in this layout, which must be experienced rather than taught.

The Witches' Compass

No other aspect of traditional witchcraft has been more misrepresented or misunderstood than the witches' compass, a traditional witch's ritually created work space. Laying the Compass is often referred to as just another type of circle casting, but nothing could be farther from the truth. The method, intention, function, and reasoning behind laying a compass fulfill a role that is drastically different from casting a magickal circle.

Ritually created circles are common to magickal and divinatory practice; however, they have evolved over the years along with the systems that utilize them. When we investigate an older text like *The Lesser Key of Solomon* and other similar grimoires, we often find a layout for an elaborate magick circle that functions more like a workroom or sports arena than as a temple space. The methodical creation of these circles literally involves the elaborate drawing of lines, words of power, and symbols upon the ground using a variety of colored chalk or bloodstone, as prescribed in the *Grand Grimoire*. This mapping-out of the space is then sometimes followed by the recitation of specific blessings or prayers to finalize the circle's purpose and effectiveness. The interesting thing about this type of magick circle is that it is left in place on the floor between workings. The sorcerer and any assistants simply step into position and remain in place during a working until it is done. Then they leave when all the spirits have been thoroughly banished and the area is presumed safe.

With older magick circles, there is no ritual for circle deconstruction. This is very unlike late 19th-century practices in which the cast circle functions more as an erected temple space created primarily for worship and union with deity, but is also used as a protective space or container for ritual energy. This version of the magick circle is made through words, symbolic magickal tools, gestures in the air, mental visualization, and several circumambulations about the space, which is then more often than not ritually deconstructed after each use.

Unlike the cast circle, a compass is not necessarily a magickal temple, hallowed space, or container of energy. The compass is more of a physical, rather than an etheric, space. It has been cleared and oriented to the four cardinal directions and is anchored to the physical plane. Whereas a cast circle is viewed as a stationary magickal border that must remain unbroken during its use for fear of compromising its integrity and purpose, the compass permits movement in and out—at least while still on the middle plane—because it is not viewed as a barrier to energy. Instead, the compass is seen as a construct built to maintain a defined space and it allows witches to travel safely Above and Below, depending on the work.

To put it another way, the compass is an elevator; a cast circle is a fortress. This does not mean that a compass can't employ protective elements in its execution and function. Indeed, the presence of physical items like salt and iron certainly help to ward the space physically and, by default, magickally. But it should be noted that the inclusion of such protective elements doesn't instantly turn the compass into a cast circle.

This distinction between the compass and the circle may sound petty, but it isn't. It is one of the fundamental differences between Traditional Witchcraft and more ceremonial-based systems. Emphasizing this distinction is imperative, as it helps us understand these practices, because both techniques (compass and circle) have individual purposes that are separate and distinct. If you want to summon spirits, cast a circle. If you want to travel, lay a compass.

In a compass environment, nothing is necessarily evoked. Upon its establishment, the space is not typically filled with spiritual energy or deities. Instead of evoking spirits or deities, witches travel to them via the compass through movement, chanting, meditation, journeying, treading the mill, trancework, etc. It is during these times of travel that the initial compass serves as a place of departure and safe return—like a hotel lobby or a helicopter landing pad. The space defined and held by the compass is a fixed location on the physical plane—a touchstone you can depend on while visiting unfamiliar territory. Once you have left the physical plane, you shouldn't leave the compass space until you have returned. We will discuss more about traveling later.

If your home is already kept warded, then there is no additional need to secure yourself ritually from things that typically hang around at any other time of the day or night. After all, we all must leave the circle sometime! Many of us already have special jewelry, spirit helpers, or certain tattoos that fulfill this protective role—especially while we sleep—and the usual home warding helps tremendously in everyday life *and* magickal work. Of course, if you are working in a new environment, protective warding may be in order, or you may want to lay a fortified compass. Simple warding methods will be provided in chapter 3.

As you can see by now, the compass is *not* just another type of circle casting fancied up with a new name. It is uniquely different from a magickly cast circle in both concept and function, and will undoubtedly be a valuable addition to your practice.

LAYING THE COMPASS

To lay a compass, you will need:

- Your sovereignty cord
- Your stang
- Land offerings
- A navigational compass
- Quarter markers. These can be anything you like, providing they will stay where placed for the duration of the ritual. Iron spikes, lanterns, fist-sized rocks, torches, statues, flags, candles, etc. can all serve this purpose.

To create a fortified compass, you'll also need your sword, incense, salt/water, and your besom.

To begin, use your navigational compass to find magnetic north and determine which direction is east. Make your offerings to the land. Facing northeast, stand in silence for three or more cycles of breath. Then stomp upon the ground three times and state your intention aloud. Walk clockwise, drawing the space by dragging your left foot or the stang as you mark each direction, either by name or by placing an item at each appropriate point. Finish in the east.

Be sure to hold the stang in your left hand so that it scribes the space outside of where you will be working. As you go, say:

> *By east (place item)*
> *By south (place item)*
> *By west (place item)*
> *And north (place item)*

Now, anchor the stang in the appropriate place (in the center or in the south). At this time, if you feel the need for a more fortified compass, plow the space around you with the sword in a clockwise direction, purify it with incense, and bless it with saltwater. Then charge the space by dancing or moving about it counterclockwise, using the center as a pivot point while performing the following Compass Chant:

> *I take a step and travel forth*
> *To journey, beyond, up, and down*
> *From top of tree, to solid ground.*

> *To journey on through blackest night,*
> *To seek the chill and terror fright.*
> *To visit worlds and those be gone,*
> *Beyond horizons and through the dawn.*

> *I travel through, betwixt I know,*
> *Between the worlds and hedges go.*

Over the hill and down the way,
To claim the night and rule the day.
By east, by south, by west, and north . . .

Repeating from "I take a step and travel forth . . . ," continue until you feel the space is ready. You will feel a definite change in atmosphere when it is time. The chant is used to charge the space, induce an alpha trance, alert the spirits, focus you on the matter at hand, and transition you into a ritual mind-set. If you are working with others, it will also unite the group mind. Once you feel ready, proceed with your intended work.

When you are finished and have returned to the middle plane, sit silently with closed eyes for several minutes. Process what you set out to do and determine if anything was discovered or accomplished. Afterward, if you created a more fortified compass, sweep the area counterclockwise with your besom. Then remove your stang and your markers, thank the land, and clean up the space. This practice requires no additional closing.

More on the Crossroads Rite

You were first introduced to the Crossroads Rite when you embarked upon the Crooked Path and encountered the Witch Lord at the end of chapter 1. This rite is meant as an all-encompassing space-creation ritual that is defined by the intent of the practitioner. It can be performed purely to function as a compass or embellished to function as a magick circle. Its general purpose is to create a liminal space—a crossroads—within which you can work. It is a perfect ritual for witches who are pressed for time. It is appropriate for solitary work or for any spur-of-the-moment spell work, and it is especially useful for working outdoors under minimal circumstances. It can be tricky to perform in a group setting, however, because of the floor work involved, which is why it is ideal for solitary work.

When you perform the Crossroads Rite, you start in the east, then walk to the west (1), then the north (2), and finally the south (3), following the numbers in Figure 7. Use the numbers and arrows in the figure to guide you through the rest of the rite, making a complete circumambulation about the space and returning to the east (9). As you can see, this rite embodies the notion of a crooked path—one that meanders throughout, around, and about the working space. For practical reasons, it is not conducive to having physical objects or other people in the middle of the space. People must wait on the sidelines while the rite is performed, only entering the space once a circumambulation is complete.

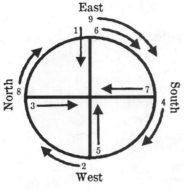

Figure 7. The Crossroads Circle.

To combine the Crossroads Rite with Laying the Compass, mark the space and perform the Crossroads Rite. Then say:

I call upon thee to beseech thy power.

Recite the Compass Chant. When you've completed the chant, do your intended work and conclude the rite as given in chapter 1.

To build the Crossroads Rite into a cast circle, as you return to the east (9), say the following as you define the circle with a visualized flame. Walk around three times, with each pass spiraling farther out from the one before it:

Around me I lay a flame,
Guarding against all those who dwell about.
A wall of protection, strong and true—
As I will it, so mote it be!

Then do your intended work and conclude the rite as given in chapter 1.

BESOM, STANG & SWORD

To Each Their Own

The rituals and tools presented in this chapter are meant to be viewed as a resource, not a standard of practice. Consider them as part of your witch's tool kit and use them as you see fit, interchanging and modifying them according to your intuition and your work. To maintain your own interest and growth, it is extremely important that you keep your ritual interesting and spontaneous. Witches should always grow—but grow with purpose, will, and intent. Stagnation equals death, and the first step to ritual death is ritual for the sake of ritual.

The formal design of the working space is intended to be used or dismantled as you see fit. Its firm foundation allows this, while at the same time providing you with a full-blown layout to use if your situation calls for it. A proper foundation and a good roof allow for all manner of witchy things to happen betwixt and between.

SUGGESTED READING

The Call of the Horned Piper, by Nigel Aldcroft Jackson.
Modern Magick: Twelve Lessons in the High Magickal Arts, by Donald Michael Kraig.
Encyclopedia of Witchcraft: The Complete A–Z for the Entire Magical World, by Judika Illes.
The Roebuck in the Thicket: An Anthology of the Robert Cochrane Witchcraft Tradition, by Evan John Jones and Robert Cochrane, edited by Michael Howard.

CHAPTER 3

Magick and Spells

Magick and spells are often used as a basis for fantastical films and stories, but they are much more than fictional creations. They are quite real and have a long and elaborate history flowing through the veins and arteries of every culture on the planet.

On its own, magick is not an inherently diabolic practice. Known and referred to as "theurgy" in centuries past—meaning the working of divine forces—magick was regarded as a benevolent practice and its application was more varied and common prior to the development of science and modern medicine. As knowledge of human anatomy and biology grew more widespread, healing prayers, spells, and chants faded, but were thankfully not forgotten.

Magick dwells at the outer edge of our scientific understanding of cause and effect. To quote Arthur C. Clarke: "Any sufficiently advanced technology is indistinguishable from magick." Yet despite the advances in science, mathematics, and the complexities of human knowledge, magick still remains and continues to be explored by people around the globe. Perhaps it enjoys a continued existence because of how easily it opens people up to an undeniable facet of the human experience. As it challenges and reveals aspects of human consciousness and reality, it shows that there is indeed much more to the world than what's visible to the ordinary eye.

Magickal Theory

Magick is primarily about influencing change. It is the art of influencing the results and outcomes in your life through the projection of your intent onto the cosmos. It can be executed through a variety of methods and techniques. Bathing, burning or extinguishing candles, burying statues, chanting, weaving, wearing jewelry, tying knots, and filling bottles are just some of the methods through which magick has been executed over the centuries. There are also various religious cosmologies under which magick functions perfectly well—despite the differences between them, and no matter which god or goddess is involved. There is such a varied list of magickal systems that have flourished throughout history that the only consistency found among them is that the practitioner's will is always central to their application.

Since there is no single system with which magick is solely associated, we have to consider the potential reality that the individual person is the greatest component of any magickal endeavor—not the technique, theology, or cosmology behind it. It's entirely plausible that all the symbolism, words, and tools found in relation to magick are simply useful props employed to inspire practitioners in the manner necessary to produce their desired result, thus enabling them to imprint their will upon the unfolding conditions of the universe in relation to their own lives.

One common misunderstanding regarding magick is the notion of its relationship to science. The misunderstanding persists largely due to Aleister Crowley's (in)famous definition of magick as "the science and the art of causing change to occur in conformity with will." The fact that science and technology often appear as magick to the less informed cannot be argued, and this may be part of what Crowley meant when he referred to science. Indeed, an understanding exists in which magickal rituals and spells are strikingly similar to scientific experimentation in their analysis of cause and effect. However, they are not "science" in a literal sense and differ from how science is perceived and applied in today's world. Magick was, however, no doubt a part of humankind's early pursuit and desire for control and understanding of how the world functions.

A full comprehension of how magick works will undoubtedly be forever out of reach because of the scope and breadth of human experience and the layers of reality magick embodies. After all, magick crosses the thresholds of time and space and moves into worlds beyond.

High and Low, Black and White, Darkness and Light

Essentially, magick is magick. It isn't black or white. It is not wholly good and it is certainly not intrinsically evil. If a color could convey magick's true character, it would most assuredly be gray—a color devoid of any ethical intention or moral implication. Every religion employs magick in some manner or another, whether in blessings, cleansings, holy water, or other practices. And anyone who has carried a lucky rabbit's foot or some similar totem, or made a wish by blowing out birthday candles or by dropping a coin in a well, has attempted to work magick as well. The working of magick is part of being human and of being self-aware. It is a natural tendency to try to impose our will and intent upon the world around us. The elaborate culture and history of magick are just examples of this tendency.

Like the rest of society, however, magick also suffers from a bit of socio-economic elitism. The magick familiar to many of us today developed centuries ago, as educated people sought an ultimate truth, or vast treasure, or nubile partners for lecherous exploits. These literate sorcerers worked with grimoires and other texts, writing and rewriting them until they had developed what would ultimately be referred to later as "high magick." This form of magick came to be labeled ritual, ceremonial, or temple magick. In many ways, magick in this form has contributed to the development of science through such arts as alchemy and astrology and the study of how natural things interact. High magick often involves elaborate execution, timing, costuming, and materials, and the lengthy recitation of invocations and prayers to carry out the intended work. This style and method of magick could be pursued by only those with enough education, resources, and time to procure and properly prepare the necessary items to carry out the work. This was a luxury not enjoyed by many.

In contrast to this elitist high magick, another magick developed that is often referred to as "low magick"—peasant magick, folk magic, or spellcraft. This type of magick reflects a more hands-on, less theatrical approach to workings and often employs everyday items, local herbs, and basic materials in its execution. It can certainly be much more spontaneous and simple than high magick, with minimal preparation and little planning required. Low magick can be done at virtually any time and without the need for a protective space. Indeed, it may simply involve the tying of a cord, the recitation of a prayer, the burning of charged candles, the keeping of lucky tokens, or the use of herbs in incense or ointments. This is mostly how cauldrons, broomsticks, and other household items came to be associated with witches and witchcraft. They were the tools and utensils of the common folk, the laborers of the land and home.

The Mechanics of Magick

Casting a spell is about aligning conscious with subconscious to carry out the intentions of individual witches. In turn, this is a restatement of the second rubric from the Emerald Tablet of Hermes: "That which is below corresponds to that which is above, and that which is above corresponds to that which is below, to accomplish the miracles of one thing." To work magick, you must unite your being in as perfect a manner as possible to send forth your intent into the cosmos so it manifests properly. Before you can do this, however, you must first understand the various aspects that comprise magick itself. The six components discussed below represent a theoretical breakdown of the spell-casting process, which also relates to the process of manifestation and the manner by which a spell comes into being.

Knowledge

Knowledge is a key component when it comes to working magick, because magick is like any other task. To practice it successfully, you have to be properly informed about why and how it's being performed, as well as its advantages and limitations. Magick is an art and must be internalized before it can be externalized. It must be personal enough to energize the intent and will of the witch or it will falter—much like an ill-prepared rocket.

To start, you must first determine what your magickal intent is. Without a fully formed intent on which to base your magick, you lose sight of what you want and may run the risk of performing ill-conceived magick.

Will

If knowledge provides the vehicle with which to work magick, then Will fuels the vehicle as it travels forth. Will is the expression of desire—our need to be known in the world. It is our tendency to come forth and be counted among the many. Will is how we reach into creation and the cosmos to manifest our wishes. It powers the formation of the world in our alignment. Will is the drive behind demand. In it sits the deepest sense of *knowing* that your magick will work and an awareness of when and how it's to be set into motion.

In the ritual presented in chapter 1, knowledge was exhibited by the planning and gathering of materials. Will drove that preparation, as well as the execution of the ritual itself. In every deed and uttered word, Will dwells beneath the surface, uniting the conscious with the subconscious, carrying out the rite itself. Will is also present in and applied through our intent, focus, and imagination—all of which go to serve the successful production of a magickal rite.

Action

Witchcraft is an art of action and any willed action can be looked on as an act of magick. Every magickal endeavor requires an action component to be successful. Action continues the goal of union by aligning conscious motor functions with subconscious symbolic acts, and this alignment lies at the heart of all magickal workings. By acting—by applying Will based on our knowledge—we engage with the world in a direct and deliberate manner. We make our presence known by acting. We let the world know we are here—that we matter.

Magickal action may include gestures, evocations, walking, postures, dancing, drawing symbols, chanting, crafting or destroying items, or cutting things apart and binding them together, among many other things. In spell casting, the action is a symbolic physical execution of the practitioner's Will, carried by knowledge.

Transcendence

The concept of transcendence in magick and ritual pertains to achieving and applying a trance state during a spell, which most often results from the primary method used. Trance states help to further unite the experience of drawing the body, mind, and spirit together. What once was a bodily pursuit (knowledge, will, and action) enters a mental phase (transcendence), enabling the magickal act itself to pierce the cosmos, to plant a seed into its etheric womb to grow and manifest. Trance states assist in accomplishing this feat.

Release

As a trance state develops and we sense that piercing of the cosmos, it is time to release our magick and embed its influence into the ether so it may manifest in our lives. This release is a moment of perfect mind/body union with the cosmos. There will be no official buzzer that goes off when this occurs, however. This union can only be sensed, and that sensing can only be recognized through personal practice.

This moment of union can also be referred to as a magickal climax or trigger point. It can be as dramatic as the apex of prolonged chanting, as minimal as a loud clap followed by perfect silence, or as slow as the guttering flame in a burning cauldron. When release has occurred, it is important to feel—and thus know—that the working was successful. Do not doubt its potential for overall effectiveness. The work is done. Reality will unfold as it should. So mote it be!

Manifestation

After release comes manifestation. Magick works in conjunction with the natural world; it will manifest itself only in a manner akin to the properties of the situation at hand and via the path of least resistance. In magick, there are no coincidences, just syncretic occurrences. To follow up any working, you have to cultivate the desired results through appropriate action. For example, a spell performed to acquire employment must be followed by submitting a proper application, cover letter, and resume for open positions. The desire for a healthy romantic relationship must exist alongside a robust social life. Follow-up actions after a magickal working lay the groundwork and opportunity for the desired outcome to occur. As in gardening, seeds will sprout only in well-tended soil.

Trance States

As a component of magick, trances help you merge with and communicate your Will to the cosmos. This allows your magickal intent to be planted, by means of a spell, into the cosmic ether. Trance states are simply altered states of consciousness achieved through techniques like chanting, dancing, rocking, swaying, pain, breath, and meditation, or through the use of any number of consumable entheogenic substances like incense, teas, smokable herbs, ointments, alcohol, and so forth.

You may be surprised to learn that trance states are intertwined with our everyday lives, even if we are not aware of them happening as we go about our daily activities. Being able to recognize trance states as they occur can help significantly in the application of your magick. Becoming accustomed to them can also make it easier for you to enter one at a moment's notice, which can be useful.

There are five different states, which represent the various levels of brainwave activity: delta, theta, alpha, beta, and gamma. Just as we shift gears while driving a car, we transition between different states of consciousness as we go about our daily routines, depending on what we're doing. Detail-oriented tasks that require more demanding mental activity involve one level of consciousness, while more menial tasks default to a relaxed state that doesn't involve as much higher thought. During these less active rest periods, we may be more susceptible to different forms of mental wandering, like ruminating over the past or wistful daydreaming.

The Five Levels of Brain Activity

Although the precise breakdown of brainwaves measured on the hertz scale differs between authorities, the approximate ranges most commonly given are as follows:

Delta state: 0.1–3 Hz
Theta state: 4–7 Hz
Alpha state: 8–15 Hz
Beta state: 16–31 Hz
Gamma state: 32–100 Hz

The levels of brain activity are measured in hertz—abbreviation Hz. A hertz represents one cycle of brain activity per second. Our brain activity normally occurs within a range of 0 Hz to over 40 Hz, although higher gamma states occur with frequencies of up to 100 Hz. The most common level of brain activity occurs in the beta range (16–31 Hz), and it can be recognized through conscious engagement in conversation with another. Those states that occur outside the beta range are what are commonly thought of as trance states.

Depending on what you are trying to accomplish, you can learn to shift into one of these levels of consciousness to aid in spell work, divination, meditation, spirit communication, soul flight, and journeying. Although there are five levels of brain activity, here we will focus on the alpha trance state, as it is relevant to spellcraft and divination, which will be covered in the next chapter. The other primary levels of trance occur in the delta, theta, and gamma ranges and will be discussed in chapter 9.

Alpha State (8–15 Hz)

This trance state is what we experience as our minds wander while doing mundane tasks, or during a light meditation. This is also the proper state for magick and intuitive-based work like divination and accessing or developing psychic abilities. Ritual, dancing, chanting, and grounding and centering are perfect catalysts for inducing an alpha trance state. Alpha states also help improve our memory and allow more inspiration and clarity of thought. One of the best times to mull over a problem is while sitting quietly in an alpha state.

EXERCISE: OBSERVING ALPHA

Try to take note of times when your thoughts drift away in a daydream or while doing a mundane task. What does this feel like? Examine your perceptions and bodily response.

EXERCISE: GETTING INTO ALPHA

Once you begin to have a sense of what an alpha trance feels like, try entering one intentionally. The easiest way to do this is to breathe deeply and slowly in a steady rhythm while relaxing your body and clearing your mind. This act is most commonly referred to as grounding and centering. Grounding here refers to a sense of releasing energy into the earth. Centering refers to a sense of bringing yourself into the present moment. This is usually done in silence and serves not only as a means to bring you into alpha, but also as a buffer between performing a ritual act or magick and what occurred a minute before. Was getting into an alpha trance easy? What made it easier or more difficult to achieve?

Spells

Spells are bits of magickal formulae designed to create a desired effect in the world, to help you manifest your Will. Spells come in myriad forms and employ a variety of materials, tools, and techniques. They can be as complicated or as simple as you need them be. Here, we'll give you some spells to add to your magickal tool kit. If you are new to spell casting, these can provide you with a good foundation on which to build. Remember, the fastest way to learn anything is to practice. Experience will always be your greatest teacher.

Binding, Banishing, and Hexing

Spells can be used to constrain and banish others, as well as to curse and malign them. Here are a few simple spells you can use to keep away those who mean to harm you or to send them on their way.

HOT FOOT

Are there people in your life you wish would just go away, but you don't necessarily want to cause them any physical harm? A Hot Foot may be exactly what you're looking for. "Hot Foot" is the name of a group of traditional American Hoodoo magickal formulas designed to help you rid yourself of someone while avoiding any blood on your hands. Some versions of the Hot Foot spell direct you to collect dirt from your targets' footprints or to sprinkle powders on their doorsteps. The spell given here is especially useful if you cannot get close enough to your targets to do any of these things or to procure anything they may have touched—all typical components of this type of spell. For this working, you don't even need to know your target's name.

To perform this spell, you will need:

- 1 bottle of hot sauce, the hottest you can find
- 9 straight pins
- Unlined paper

On the full moon, open the hot sauce and dump about a quarter of it out. You only need to make room in the bottle, so if you want to reserve this extra for non-magickal purposes, feel free. If you know it, write the name of the person you want to target nine times backward—from right to left—on the paper (see Figure 8). If you don't know your target's name, give a description—for example, "Rival for my lover's heart" or "Shithead in Accounts Payable."

Then turn the paper one quarter turn counterclockwise and write your name nine times over what you have already written—this time, forward (from left to right, see Figure 9).

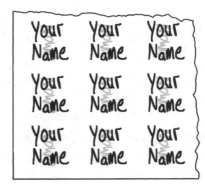

Figure 8. Hot Foot spell paper with target's name.

Figure 9. Hot Foot spell paper with your name added.

Roll the paper away from you into a tight scroll and drop it into the bottle, followed by the straight pins. Screw the cap on tightly, then shake the ever-loving hell out of it for about thirty seconds while saying:

[Name], as another day is gone and will never return, may you leave me be and never come back.

On each of the coming days as the moon wanes, at eveningfall, go back to your bottle and shake it again. Repeat the statement you made when you created the bottle. When the next dark moon comes, again at eveningfall, take the bottle somewhere with running water. Give it one last good shaking, then throw it in the water. Leave the scene and don't look back.

BINDING AND CONTAINMENT JAR

This combines the process of binding with the element of containment by using a bottle. It is good for controlling bad habits, people, or situations. You can use a photograph to represent what or whom you're binding, or you can design a sigil to represent the problem. If you are binding a person, that person's name or date of birth or any other relevant identifying information can also be used.

To perform this spell, you will need:

- A wide-mouthed jar
- A black candle
- A lighter
- Pen and paper, or a photograph
- Twine
- Salt
- 4 sharp pins

Cut the paper so that it will roll up and fit easily into your jar. If you are using a sigil, draw it on the paper. When ready, roll the paper up away from you, with the sigil or image inside. Insert one pin through the bottom of the rolled-up paper and say:

> *With this pin, I do bind*
> *[what or whom you are binding and why].*

Then take another pin and insert it above the first one, perpendicular to it, making a cross. Say:

> *With this pin, I do contain*
> *[what or whom you are binding and why].*

Insert the third pin through the rolled-up paper above and perpendicular to the previous pin and say:

With this pin, I will stop [what or whom you are binding and why].

Insert the fourth pin above and perpendicular to the third, along the top of your rolled paper, and say:

And with this pin, I will control
[what or whom you are binding and why].

Tie the rolled-up paper closed with the twine, going several times around. Say the following as you finalize the knot with conviction:

I bind [what or whom you are binding and why] and instead, I wish/want [what you want to happen]. So mote it be!

Place the paper in the jar so it stands upright within it. The pins should stabilize it while still allowing the lid to shut tightly. Begin filling the jar around the paper with the salt, as you say:

And finally, with the power of this salt, may I now cleanse, purify, and bury you from ever doing harm to me again.

When the jar is full, screw on the lid and draw a banishing Earth pentagram over it. Bring the energy down and say:

I banish [problem] and I instead invoke [draw an invoking pentagram] for [what or whom you want in your life instead].

Light the black candle and seal the lid of the jar with its wax to contain the energy. When finished, store the jar in an appropriate place—in a toilet tank or just behind the toilet is good, or in the freezer. You can also dispose of it in running water or bury it in a mucky bog or marsh.

STOPPING GOSSIP

This working, which is influenced by traditional American Hoodoo, uses a beef tongue (you can get one at your local butcher or grocery store) to stop all manner of unwanted talk. Gossip is its most common target, but it has also been used successfully to win favor in court cases.

To perform this spell, you will need:

- A fresh beef tongue
- Black string
- A heavy-duty sewing needle
- Unlined paper
- A black candle
- A knife

Write your target's name on the paper nine times, three by three, as shown in Figure 10.

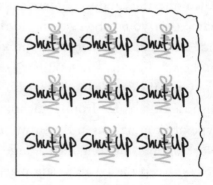

Figure 10. Stopping gossip spell paper with target's name.

Figure 11. Stopping gossip spell paper with "shut-up" added.

Turn the paper counterclockwise one quarter turn and write "Shut up" over each name written, as shown in Figure 11.

Turn the paper counterclockwise another quarter turn and write the following over all of it:

I command you now—Stop your gossip; stop it!
As this tongue is sewn shut, so will be yours.
Nevermore will you speak ill
Of me or any of mine.
Your tongue is bound and tied from here on,
Your mouth is stoppered and silent.
Your silence forever is what I command,
Your silence forever is what I demand.

Fold the paper in half, pointing away from you. Turn it counterclockwise one quarter turn and fold it in half again, still pointing away from you. Continue doing this until you can no longer fold the paper.

Take the knife and make a long, vertical slit in the center of the beef tongue. Tuck the folded paper inside. Thread the needle with the string and sew up the slit. While sewing, repeat your command over and over.

Carve your target's name into the side of the candle, vertically. Then turn the candle counterclockwise one half turn and carve your name over your target's name vertically. Turn the beef tongue on its side and make another small slit with the knife. Stand the candle up in the slit, light it, and let it burn down completely.

Once the candle is completely burned down, take the tongue and dispose of it as far from your home as possible, preferably in some type of running water. If you want to add additional *oomph* to the working, put the tongue in a large jar and add vinegar and pickling spices. Keep the jar in a safe place, taking it out every so often to give it a good shake and talk trash at it. When you feel your target has had enough, dispose of the whole thing as far from your home as you can—again, preferably in running water.

THE EVIL EYE

The evil eye is a spell that dates from classical antiquity. It can be performed by anyone—witches and non-witches alike. It consists of literally casting a scornful gaze upon a target that is so harsh that it transmits negativity and coats the person in ill will and bad luck. In Turkish, it is called the *kem göz;* in Italy, it is called *malocchio.* In Ireland, it is known as *drochshúil,* and the Germans name it *böser Blick.* Has someone done you dirty and you want to make them miserable for it?

To perform this spell, you will need:

- Just yourself
- At least one working eye

There are two main methods for casting the evil eye: direct and indirect. Proponents of the first believe that, for success, you must speak to your target. Go right up to the person and deliver the sweetest of honeyed compliments: "You have beautiful hair." Or "What a great sense of style you have." Or "Wow, you're so strong!" Don't go overboard with it, because, if you come off as creepy or leering, it's not going to work out well. You need to appear natural. And be careful not to compliment anything surrounding your target accidentally. Don't wax poetic about a pretty baby or a great dog.

As you speak your compliment, put the force of all your animosity for this person behind the words. Fill your body with it; release it at your target. But don't let it show on your face. Give some sugar, then walk away.

The second method for giving the evil eye doesn't require that you speak to your target. If you and the person are no longer on speaking terms, this is particularly helpful. You still need to be in the person's presence, however—at least, within view.

Wait until you catch the person's eye, then put all your animosity, derision, and antipathy into your gaze and shoot it right the hell at your target. Side-eyed glares are also quite effective, especially if you add in a good eye roll at the end of it. Throw that shade, then walk away.

Blessing, Cleansing, and Clearing

Spell work can also be used for blessing, cleansing, and clearing. Use the following spells to foster a positive atmosphere in your home and elsewhere.

HOME BLESSING FLOOR WASH

Floor washes are used as magickal workings in a wide variety of cultures and can be customized to suit your focus. This one is for blessing your home, whether you are just moving into a new place or if the place where you already live needs a quick top-up on its happiness and good luck.

To do this working, you will need:

- Peppermint (*Mentha x piperita L.*)

- Hyssop (*Hyssopus officinalis*)

- Bay leaf (*Laurus nobilis*)

- Cascarilla (powdered egg shell)

- Florida Water (an inexpensive version of Cologne Water)

- White vinegar

Create an infusion by pouring boiling water over the peppermint, hyssop, and bay leaf. Let this cool, then strain out the herbs. Pour the infusion into a bucket, then add a good two glugs-worth of both Florida Water and white vinegar, followed by a couple tablespoons of cascarilla. Stir it and then use to mop any of your floors, working from the back of the house to the front. When you get to the front, take the bucket outside and pour it in the gutter.

VERVAIN AND SAGE BATH

Just like homes, people can also benefit from a quick boost of happiness, luck, or blessings. Vervain, sage, and rosemary are all herbs associated with blessings and purification. Feel free to go through your favorite herbal correspondences and mix components to suit your purpose.

To create this bath mixture, you will need:

- Vervain (*Verbena officinalis*)
- Sage (*Salvia officinalis*)
- Rosemary (*Rosmarinus officinalis*)
- Salt

Pour boiling water over a good handful of each herb, either dried or fresh. Let them steep for fifteen minutes to create an infusion, then strain out the herbs. Add a tablespoon or two of salt to the infusion and stir to dissolve, then cool to a comfortable temperature. Take the infusion into the bathroom with you, undress, and get into the tub. Pour the infusion over your head and body, then allow yourself to air dry.

If you want to remove the influence of a specific person, while pouring the bath over you, focus on washing the person from your skin, out of your mind, out of your heart, and out of your life. Envision all your target's influence going down the drain. This simple shift in awareness can have tremendous mental and physical results that can be noticed immediately.

UNCROSSING RITE

Is nothing in your life going right lately? Do you feel as if you've been jinxed? When someone's put a working like the evil eye against you or has soured your life with a vinegar jar, it can feel as if every day is weighted down by a heavy, gray oppression. The slightest movements drag you down and despair clouds your heart. This Uncrossing Rite will clear these conditions for you, send the bad energy back to its creator, and restore your good luck.

To perform this rite, you will need:

- Rue (*Ruta graveolens*)
- Hyssop (*Hyssop officinalis*)
- Salt
- A pitcher to hold water (roughly two quarts)
- 2 white candles (glass-encased, if possible)
- A small piece of unlined paper
- A fireproof container in which to burn the paper
- Incense (If you don't specifically have Uncrossing incense, use something purifying, like sage or frankincense)

The day before you perform the rite, take one tablespoon each of the rue, hyssop, and salt and stir them into a pot with about two quarts of boiling water to make an infusion. Let it steep for fifteen minutes, then cool. Strain most of the infusion into your pitcher, but set aside about half a cup in a bowl for later.

On the day of the rite, rise at dawn. Do not speak to anyone (including pets). Write on the paper that you want the crossed condition undone and whoever crossed you struck down. Light your incense, then ignite the piece of paper with the incense charcoal. Drop the paper into your fireproof vessel and let it burn completely.

Bring the pitcher of herb and salt infusion into the bathroom with you. Light the two white candles and place one on each end of your bathtub, either on the floor or on the edge of the tub. Be careful to keep them away from anything flammable, like your shower curtain or the toilet paper, and remove anything from the area that could catch fire. Undress completely and step between the candles into the tub. Pour the entire pitcher of infusion over your head and down your body. Traditional Hoodoo practitioners recite Psalm 51 three times at this point. Because this ritual is heavily based on a Hoodoo working, you can also do that, or you can come up with a similar verse of your own.

Step out of the tub, again passing between the two candles, and allow yourself to air dry. Do not towel off at all—not even your hair. While you dry, recite Psalm 37 (or something of your choosing). Once your body is dry, put on clean clothing and snuff out your candles; do not blow them out. Take the bowl of reserved infusion and sprinkle it around your home from back to front, then out the door. You can also put the infusion in a spray bottle and spritz it about or use an aspergillum—branches of hyssop work well for this.

Love, Prosperity, and Protection

Spells are often used by witches to draw love and prosperity to them, and to provide protection from malign forces. You can use the spells below to protect yourself and bring love and plenty into your life.

HONEY JAR

Honey jars are fantastic spells you can use whenever you need someone to look favorably upon you. This spell is especially effective for an angry or straying lover, but can also be very helpful in getting authority figures to feel kindly toward you. A honey jar is really a gentle giant of a spell, but once it gets going, the results are undeniable. Honey jars (or sweet jars) are found in many cultures that practice any type of folk magic, but they are especially loved in American Hoodoo.

To perform this spell, you will need:

- A small glass jar with a lid

- Unlined paper

- A red pen

- Ground cinnamon (use cinnamon red-hot candies for a little added kick)

- Ground ginger

- Saffron (*Crocus sativus*)

- Patchouli (*Pogostemon cablin*)

- Honey

- Olive oil

- Your own hair or fingernail clippings

- Your target's hair or fingernail clippings, if possible

- A small pink candle (birthday candles are excellent)

On a Friday night, tear the paper down until you have about a four-inch square. Write your target's full name on it three times (see Figure 12).

Rotate the paper a quarter turn clockwise and write your name across your target's name three times (see Figure 13).

Figure 12. Honey jar spell paper with target's name.

Figure 13. Honey jar spell paper with your name added.

Around this, write a short sentence of intent—for example, "Look favorably upon me"—over and over, without lifting your pen from the paper so that the words are all connected to one another. Write it as many times as it takes to encircle the names, but be mindful of your spacing so the circle does not connect in the middle of the sentence. You may need to practice this a couple times before you get the hang of it; it's surprisingly difficult to do when muscle memory forces you to lift the pen from the paper at each word's end. Being mindful and concentrating on each letter of each word as you write will help.

Add the spices and herbs and the hair and fingernail clippings to the center of the paper, then fold the paper in half toward you. Speak your intent aloud. Turn the paper a quarter turn clockwise, fold it toward yourself again, and repeat your intent aloud. Keep turning, folding, and speaking until you can no longer fold the paper. Drop the packet into the empty glass jar.

Eat three spoonfuls of the honey, each time saying:

As this honey is sweet to me, so I will become sweet in the eyes of [Name].

Pour honey over the packet until the jar is almost full, then screw the lid on tightly. Put a little bit of olive oil on your fingertips and dress the pink candle from the root to the top. Heat the candle base until it is soft, then affix it to the top of the lid. Light the candle and concentrate on the flame, repeating your sentence of intent. If you are using a birthday candle, let it burn down entirely. If you are using a larger candle, burn it for fifteen minutes. For the next four weeks— on Monday, Wednesday, and Friday nights—burn another candle on the jar and speak your intent to the flame. After that, keep the jar somewhere safe and burn a new candle on the lid every so often to keep the sweetness flowing.

LUCKY NUTMEG

We originally learned the lucky nutmeg spell from Appalachian witch, author, and forensic folklorist H. Byron Ballard. This is our adaptation of her traditional spell. Nutmeg has long been considered to bring good fortune to those who carry it. A wide variety of cultures use nutmegs in spellcraft, despite the fact that they were grown only in the Banda Islands (the Spice Islands) up until the mid-19th century. This made them quite expensive, and may even be why you were thought to be incredibly lucky if you had possession of a nutmeg.

To perform this spell, you will need:

- A pinch of dirt from the land on which you reside
- Vervain (*Verbena officinalis*)
- Chamomile (*Matricaria chamomilla*)
- A 4-inch square of unlined paper
- A red thread
- Something small and shiny
- A whole nutmeg (if you can't get one, you can certainly use some ground nutmeg, but this spell works better with a whole nutmeg)

On a full moon, pile the dirt and herbs into a hillock in the center of the paper square. Give it a stir with the index finger of your non-dominant hand, while thinking about how very lucky you are. Put the small shiny object and the nutmeg on top of the mound, then tightly gather the paper up around everything into a neat package. Tie the package with the red string, winding it around from all different angles until the paper is completely covered. Keep thinking about how lucky you are and how lucky you will continue to be. Carry the package with you every day, in a pocket or your bag. Each full moon, take it out and place it in the moonlight for the night.

WITCH BOTTLE

A witch bottle is used to thwart negativity and counteract any magick directed at a person or household. It serves to distract the negative energy. The urine, hair, or nail clippings inside the bottle identify the members of the household, but are also combined with defensive and reflective elements to deal with any negativity coming at the home and its residents, including pets.

To create a witch bottle, you will need:

- A bottle or jar
- Dirt and dust from around the home
- Hair and nail clippings of the people and pets in the household
- 3 razor blades
- 3 nails
- 3 pieces of broken glass
- 3 pieces of a broken mirror
- A black or red candle
- A lighter or matches
- Your own urine and 3 drops of your own blood

Add the dirt, dust, and any hair and nail clippings to the bottle. Then, add the three razor blades and say:

> *May these blades protect me, my home, and those I love*
> *from harm and negativity.*

Add the three nails and say:

> *May these nails protect me, my home, and those I love*
> *from harm and negativity.*

Add the three pieces of broken glass and mirror and say:

> *May these pieces of glass and mirror confuse and diffuse all harm*
> *and negativity that may come to me, my home, and those I love,*
> *and return it to its sender.*

Fill the bottle with your urine and add three drops of your blood, then replace the lid. Using the candle, seal the bottle with wax. When finished, draw an invoking Earth pentagram over the bottle and bring the energy down. Then say:

As I will it, it shall be done!

Dig a hole eight inches or more deep outside your home, as close to the front door as you can, and bury the bottle upside down. If your bottle is freezer-safe, you may not need to worry about burying it below the frost line. If it is not, the bottle may shatter when the ground freezes, negating the working.

LAYING WARDS

Wards are apotropaic magick (from the Greek word *apotrepein,* meaning "to ward off," derived from *apo* ("away") and *trepein* ("to turn"). Their function is purely to turn away harm. One of the easiest ways to protect your home and those who reside within is through warding. This working can be as elaborate or as simple as you like.

To lay wards, you will need a small bowl with something purifying in it (water and salt, home blessing oil, etc.) or a small plate and sage bundle.

Start at the first opening (window, door, fireplace, etc.) to the left of the front door of your home. If you are using water and salt or some type of blessing oil, dip your finger in the bowl and trace a protective symbol on the window sill, pane, or frame. We prefer to draw a unicursal hexagram, but feel free to use any invoking Earth pentagram. If you are using a sage bundle, light it, blow it out, and trace your symbol in the air with the smoke. Hold the plate under the bundle as much as possible to catch any ash or embers.

After you've warded the first window, move to the next opening in a counterclockwise direction. This may be another window, a door, a vent, or a pipe. Be sure not to miss any bath and sink drains in your bathroom and kitchen, as well as any laundry facilities. At each opening, trace your ward and then move to the next, making your way through each room until you reach the back of your home. Then continue back around until you return to your front door.

Once back at your front door, trace your final ward and put every ounce of protective energy you can behind its force. Lay your hand on the surface of the door and say:

> With these wards, I grant protection
> From all who would seek me/us harm.
> With these wards, I lay defenses
> Around all who live within these walls.

Periodically, you may feel as if your wards need refreshing. Your household may not be running as smoothly as it normally does, or there may be a lot of bickering and small illnesses present. Take the time on occasion to redo your wards, but particularly when the harmony of your home starts to go pear-shaped. It may be just the natural course of events, but small things going wrong can be indicative of workings laid against you and can lead to bigger issues down the pike. It's always better to be proactive.

SUGGESTED READING

Liber Null and Psychonaut, by Peter J. Carroll.

The Black Toad: West Country Witchcraft, by Gemma Gary.

Encyclopedia of 5,000 Spells: The Ultimate Reference Book for the Magical Arts, by Judika Illes.

Staubs and Ditchwater: A Friendly and Useful Guide to Hillfolks' Hoodoo, by H. Byron Ballard.

The Elements of Spellcrafting: 21 Keys to Successful Sorcery, by Jason Miller.

Black Magic: Religion and the African American Conjuring Tradition, by Yvonne P. Chireau

Mojo Workin': The Old African American Hoodoo System, by Katrina Hazzard-Donald

CHAPTER 4

Divination

D ivination is one of the core practices of all the magickal tools and rites that flourish beneath the banner of witchcraft. Gaining a firm foundation in its diverse methods and uses is, therefore, imperative to your later success on the Crooked Path. One way to understand how magick and divination coincide is to realize that magick is about enhancing your *influence* over your life, while divination is about enhancing your *awareness* of your life. In other words, magick creates and alters outcomes, while divination gives an idea of what those outcomes could be. Foretelling the potential results of a situation is useful in that it may help you decide whether magick should be performed to alter or enhance your future.

Divination can be accomplished either through systems of symbols, a ritualized methodology, common observance, a developed intuition, or all the above combined. The word itself comes from the Latin *divinare,* meaning "to foresee" or "to be inspired by a god." Divination is, thus, the art and practice of divine seeing. The most common and recognizable systems of divination are probably astrology (in the form of horoscopes) and cartomancy (card-reading).

As a tool, divination helps you develop a better understanding of what may lie on the road ahead or any decisions that may need to be made. When combined with spirit work and magick, divination begins to cross into the art of necromancy as corpse divination, or the art of divining with the dead. Aside from raising the dead to gain answers or knowledge of lost treasures—a favorite ancient pastime—necromantic divination in its most basic form is used to contact spirits and petition the ancestors for aid. In modern times, we find an example of this practice in the Spiritualist religion or in the mediumship of psychics. Mind you, neither Spiritualists nor psychics necessarily regard themselves as practicing witchcraft, but they still contact the spirits of the dead for insight.

Prophets, Oracles, and Soothsayers

What would the world be without its prophets, oracles, and soothsayers? After all, centuries ago, soothsayers and court astrologers were used to determine the ideal time for coronations or battles to assure the favor of the heavens. What would Queen Elizabeth I have done without John Dee working as her personal astrologer and advisor? Julius Caesar might have lived a little longer if he had heeded the words of the soothsayer in Shakespeare's play. Even former US First Lady Nancy Reagan was known to consult an astrologer on occasion, especially when it involved the life of her husband. Indeed, most religions would have no teachings, doctrines, or influence if not for their prophets and the messages they conveyed. And if receiving messages from the divine was considered so valuable in times past, why should it be any different now? So why is divination often looked down on in today's world?

One of the primary reasons that divination was denied or deemed heretical by many religions—beside the opportunities it gave to charlatans—is the potential threat it poses to existing theology and dogma. After all, it was the presence of some later prophets that enabled religions like Mormonism to come into being during the early 19th century. Indeed, prophets and their role in society continue to manifest even in the 20th century, as occultist and sorcerer Aleister Crowley demonstrated as the prophet for the New Aeon of Horus, which began in 1904. Further, in keeping with the human need for escapist fantasy, the 21st century has had more than its fair share of failed Rapture prophecies, whose epiphanies continue to be rescheduled, even if God never gets the memo.

Depending on the witch, any form of divination can function as a form of prophecy. However, it's important to understand that prophecy is more about receiving knowledge via an individual speaking for a deity than it is about actively seeking knowledge, which is what an act of divination typically is. Prophets are generally people who are or have been in direct dialog with a higher source. In these situations, there is no concrete basis for the information they receive, as there is in a system of divination like tarot, in which a particular card alludes to a potential outcome. In prophecy, the source of intuitive understanding is much more subjective, but it is not any less meaningful because of this—especially if the prophet and the message are both trustworthy.

Of course, it would be ignorant of us not to acknowledge the damage that prophets and charlatans can do, as history is full of manipulative and damaging cults based on revelations made by allegedly divine representatives. The Jonestown Massacre (1978), the Branch Davidians (1993), and Heaven's Gate (1997) are just some examples of well-known cults from recent history that claimed the lives of entire communities because of a megalomaniacal misuse of prophecy.

As a practice, prophecy utilizes trance in conjunction with seership. In the act of prophecy, individuals open themselves to receiving information at random or under ritually controlled conditions like mediumship, invocation, or journeying while in a magickal space such as a compass or circle. Prophecies can also occur at random— for instance, while you are daydreaming or doing mundane tasks, or during an unusual yet relevant encounter with a stranger or coworker that seemingly has no other basis in reality. To achieve the best results possible, you must be open, observant, and fully present in your daily life. Divinatory observances can be recognized and received only in the moment. If you are too busy thinking about tomorrow, you run the risk of missing the messages of today. Two great ways to open yourself up to prophecy are through dream work and meditation.

EXERCISE: DREAM DIARY

Upon waking, document your dreams in a diary used for this specific purpose. Take note of any details, thoughts, or feelings that you immediately recall when you wake up so you don't lose any valuable information. Not all dreams are prophetic or divinatory (oneiromancy), but all of them tell a tale. Documenting them will not only help you develop your prophetic accuracy; it will also help train your brain to remember your dreams better.

EXERCISE: PROPHETIC TRANCE MEDITATION

If you have trouble remembering your dreams, meditation may work better for you. Sitting in a cross-legged position, get comfortable, relax, and still your mind. Work in silence or, if you like, play some ambient or space music to help you detach from your surroundings. Once comfortable, take three deep breaths and begin to sway back and forth slowly and subtly to help induce a floating sensation. As you sway, continue to relax until you enter a deep alpha trance state. While you drift, either allow a situation you are curious about to dwell in the back of your mind or just allow any insights to come to you freely. To return, stop swaying, move your fingers and toes, and begin to breathe more deeply and with more intent.

Document your findings for later reference. This technique can be combined with the Crossroads Rite given in chapter 1 and with burning mugwort, provided that neither you nor anyone in the household is pregnant or trying to conceive.

Divination Theory

Divination plays heavily off divine communication and the law of cause and effect. We are always in contact with the universe, in a constant dialog as we go about our lives. When we are able to recognize and interpret the world around us, we can decipher what the universe is revealing.

An old example of this is the study of how the behavior of animals and plants may indicate future manifestations in the weather. These types of insight—the observation of natural patterns and occurrences—are generally referred to as *omens*, which are defined as natural or seemingly natural occurrences that foretell a possible future incident or outcome. Obviously, science has given us more accurate methods to "read" certain natural conditions, so we are less dependent today upon obscure superstitions or achy joints to predict local climate conditions. But it is also true that other types of omens—the actions of some animals, as well as atmospheric, celestial, or other life anomalies—can reveal more than simple weather phenomena and often even hint at more hidden realities if we are observant enough and able to decipher them. For example:

- Solar and lunar eclipses are often viewed as portents of destruction. Doom!

- If a bee flies into your home, it is a sign that you will shortly have a guest. However, if you kill the bee, the visit will be a negative one (probably because you shouldn't kill bees).

- If a bird flies into your home, this may be an omen of death soon to come.

- Bird droppings landing on your head are said to be a sign of good luck, despite how unpleasant the reality is.

- Blood on the moon, or a ring around the moon, is a sign of trouble not far ahead.

- A double rainbow is a sign of transformation in some Eastern cultures.

- Seeing three butterflies together is good luck.

- If your cheeks suddenly flush, someone is talking about you.

- Rain on your wedding day is said to be cleansing and a sign of a happy marriage, as well as fertility.

- Having an unknown black cat cross your path is bad luck.

- Sighting a mysterious black dog is a portent of death to come.

Granted, some of these omens (for instance, the celestial phenomena) are generally predictable and have minimal implications in certain areas of the world. We give this list only to indicate the various ways in which everyday phenomena may be useful for gaining insight into and information about life and the future. Moreover, you can also apply these concepts to other areas of life that aren't as easy to control. For example, the way drivers act on the road is a telltale sign of the current collective mental state of the region. A large amount of reckless driving means the local community may be angry or stressed over some bit of news or recent event. Calm and considerate driving reveals less stress and a generally happier culture. This may not sound all that mystical, but divination is about reading signs and gaining insight from the world around you. Even observing the body language of other people can be a source of knowledge and personal awareness that can help you decipher a situation.

Systematic forms of divination, such as the tarot or runes, can also be employed to interpret the outcome of a question or to provide a perspective on life. Any system or act of divination combines the factor of chance with a decipherable symbolic language (of some kind) to allow for interpretation and understanding. The idea of chance in such a method is what allows the cosmos to intervene. In tarot, shuffling, selecting, and distributing the cards into a specific layout combines chance (chaos) with order. Virtually any similar combination of elements can be used to perform an act of divination. Purposefully breaking an egg into a glass of water with the goal of obtaining hidden knowledge or pouring cream into your morning coffee with the same intent can produce startling imagery relevant to your daily life.

The list of known divinatory systems and styles is staggering. It ranges from reading cards (cartomancy) and the heavens (astrology), to reading entrails (haruspicy) and excrement (scatomancy). There are literally hundreds of methods of divination found throughout world history and there are no limits to how you can obtain answers. Indeed, the more you look into divinatory systems, the more you may find.

Divination as a Present Practice

Does divination foretell the future? And if we know the future, can it be altered? These issues are probably the trickiest aspects of dealing with divination's role as it begins to touch upon magick, reality, fate, destiny, and even time itself. In all reality, mindfulness has its effects and limitations on how certain situations develop, manifest, or change as time goes on. Magick helps to temper, guide, and influence life's developments, but, since we're not alone in the world, those around us also have an impact on how life proceeds and develops. Divination provides us with the opportunity to place our ears to the ground while receiving insight into our surrounding circumstances. It expands our awareness of the present and potential future events.

Divination also causes us to consider and realize things that we might otherwise inadvertently overlook. The thoughts, shifts of understanding, and considerations that a reading may induce are profound justification for the role of divination in our lives. A tarot spread revealing an ending or another person at play in a situation can shed new light on your understanding and ultimately influence how you approach an actively brewing scenario. Therefore, while the future is always in flux, divination offers you the opportunity to glimpse its direction and steer its development.

Types of Divination

Divination can take many forms, but what you may come to realize over time is that these forms all employ just a few different methods. In most systems, you interpret either symbols or patterns, or a combination of both. In some cases, even though two systems may differ in execution and aesthetic, the actual act of divination varies little. Throwing runes and reading tarot have very similar approaches and variations, and the art of scrying conveys an ability that translates into many different mediums, each of which is known as a specific type of divination. Here, we'll begin with seership to give you a brief and well-rounded introduction into divination. Then we'll touch on a form of cleromancy, followed by the arts of oomancy and cartomancy. We'll conclude with a firm foundation in the myserious art of scrying.

Seership

Seership is seeing beyond the veil and involves divining through one of your five developed senses or through your intuition. A purely intuitive reaction is more of a gut reaction and can be looked on as an unchecked talent or a flash of sudden clarity. This same clarity can also be developed and deliberately induced via the feelings or information you get from an object, person, or place, or in the experiencing of visions, lucid dreaming, scrying, spirit communication, etc. Any information acquired through the five senses, combined with a developed psychic awareness, can be extremely revealing and valuable. For example, breathing in through the nose helps you gain insight from your surroundings on an olfactory level, but also contributes on a psychic level. The impressions embodied by the breathing in of air from a particular location can serve as one of many valuable psychic gateways to unseen knowledge, as the air we breathe fills not only our lungs, but also our hearts and minds through the circulation of blood.

EXERCISE: TAKE A WALK

Visit an unfamiliar location like a forest, park, hospital, or historic building. What do you experience as you move about the location? How do different areas feel in comparison to one another? Do they feel inviting? Or do they feel threatening and seem to push you away? What are you feeling? Extend your senses outward and see what you pick up—even subtle feelings or sensations.

EXERCISE: VISIT AN ANTIQUE STORE

Visit an antique store and, in a sense, go shopping for insight. Experience how different items feel and the impressions they give you. Do they feel tired? Sad? Happy? Warm? Cold? Do they speak to you? Be sure not to allow the actuality of the object itself to color your impression of it. A wedding gown, for instance, may not automatically represent a happy day in a person's life.

CLEROMANCY (CHARM BAG DIVINATION)

Cleromancy, or charm-bag divination, uses twenty-four picture tiles that are either tossed or selected from a bag. To construct these tiles, use small-ish, flat tiles of wood or any other material of a decent weight that can be painted or inscribed in some fashion. Avoid making your tiles circular, as they have the tendency to roll. When marking your tiles with images, keep them simple, with as little detail as possible. Working on the small area of the tiles can be more difficult than you think and the potential for your lines to bleed and get blurry is stronger when you attempt fine details. These symbols need to be clear and crisp for ease of reading.

The following list of images can be altered for your personal use, but it can offer a broad vocabulary for initial use in a reading. We recommend that you devise your own representations for the items below. Also, consider placing the white and black crescent moons on the same tile, one on each side. Start with single tile draws until you're comfortable with the language of the symbols.

- Acorn: potential, new beginnings, fresh start, budding opportunity

- Bee: the heavens, spirits of the divine, soul flight, hedgewitchery, the need to perform journey work

- Bone: death, endings, structure, illness

- Butterfly: change, transformation, a new ability or talent, reaching new heights, transgression, elevation, ascension

- Button: mending, union, cooperation, secrets

- Cat: the underworld, the dead, the ancestors

- Coin: money, inheritance, good luck, good fortune, employment

- Crow: history and lore, a demand to know your roots (so to speak), core of the problem

- Crystal: clarity, unlimited potential

- Eye: sight, vision, psychic powers, intuition

- Feather: flight, freedom, travel, new horizons, escape

- Flame: new insight, an idea, an awakening

- Hare: herbalism, fostering, speed, agility, quick action

- Heart: love, support, friendship, compassion, happiness

- Key: unlocking, ignition, opening, initiation

- Leaf: shedding, growth, embarking on your own, breaking away

- Moon (black crescent): introspection, shadow work

- Moon (white crescent): growth, new light

- Ring: oath, obligation, marriage, union, a contract or agreement

- Seashell: prosperity, shedding, new home, creativity

- Serpent: magick (you may need to start compiling spell components)

- Stone: solidity, manifestation, foundation, earth

- Teardrop: worry, concern, fear, guilt, nightmares

- Toad: divination regarding a specific issue, perhaps the need for more or a different method, seeking outside advice

- X: conflict, crossroads, intersection, change of direction, opportunity

Create a circle nine inches in diameter and mark it like a compass. Each directional quarter relates to one of the four elements, which, like the suits of the tarot, pertain to different areas of your life. Orient your circle so the quarters align with the cardinal directions and sit so the element directly pertaining to your question is opposite you.

- East (Fire): passion, creativity, will

- South (Earth): money, finances, career

- West (Water): love, emotions, relationships

- North (Air): intelligence, ideas, mental state, wisdom, invention

Shake the bag to mix up the tiles. While holding some or all of the tiles, ask your question, then drop the tiles from roughly nine inches above the center of your circle. Observe the shape of the tile formation within the circle. Is the cluster vertical? Horizontal? Cross-shaped? More circular? Vertical tile formations tend to indicate the present, while horizontal tile layouts may show more of a past, present, and future timeline. Tiles in a cross pattern should be read from east to west, then from north to south. If your tiles are in a circular pattern, what do they surround? Which tiles are face up? Central tiles are more in line with the question, while the more peripheral tiles play less of a role the farther away they are.

Primary tiles are those that are fully exposed. Secondary tiles are those partially covered by other tiles. A secondary tile covered by a primary tile reveals a combined message and they should be read together. Layered tiles should be read from top to bottom, starting with the primary and moving down to secondary and/or tertiary tiles to determine the message. It's important to be aware of overall tile placement and relationships, but individual tile clusters can be messages unto themselves.

There are varieties of approaches to reading a system like this. Determining a personal method through experience will make your readings more accurate and useful for your craft.

OOMANCY (EGG DIVINATION)

Oomancy, or egg divination, is one of the easiest forms of divination. It requires just a few household items and little preparation on the part of the witch. Here is a simple divination you can use to answer your question.

To perform this divination, you will need:

- A raw, unbroken egg still in its shell

- A pushpin

- A clear bulb-shaped drinking glass—like one used for wine or beer—filled halfway with warm water

To begin, anoint the egg's surface with an invoking Water pentagram, using either saliva, water from the glass, wine, or a special divination oil. Holding the egg close to your mouth, whisper your question to it. Then pierce both ends of the egg with the pushpin to create two holes that are each about 1/16 of an inch in diameter. Place one of the pierced ends of the egg to your lips, creating a firm seal, and gently blow into the egg while leaning over the glass of water, forcing the whites of the egg out and into the glass.

Mentally ask your question again as you focus on the flowing egg whites. Once the yolk begins coming out, stop blowing into the egg and observe what shapes the egg whites have formed suspended in the water. Your question will be answered by interpretating these shapes and by the thoughts or feelings they induce.

CARTOMANCY (TAROT)

One of the more popular and appealing divination systems in the world is the tarot, which is a form of cartomancy. The artwork and creativity of various tarot decks go a long way in adding to the already alluring and mysterious nature of this centuries-old art. There are so many good books available on tarot that this section is not going to go into very much detail about the tarot itself. Instead, we will share one of our favorite five-card spreads with you. It is inspired by the widely used Celtic Cross and the even more basic three-card single-line spread (past, present, and future).

After determining your question, shuffle the deck you're using at least five to seven times to assure that the cards are properly mixed before dealing them out. While shuffling, focus on your question and allow the sound and routine of it to permit you to slip into an alpha trance. When you feel you have shuffled your deck enough, deal out your spread with the cards face up (see Figure 14). Look over the spread and see if any patterns are present—card suits, a majority of major/minor arcana, number patterns, etc. Also, take note of which way the images face. Not every reader reads reversals in their cards, but a reversed card's placement may be of importance to the overall spread. See if the artwork tells a story. Are certain cards looking at each other? Are any groups of cards looking at other groups? Are any cards looking to the past or the future? Take notice of these types of patterns and determine their significance.

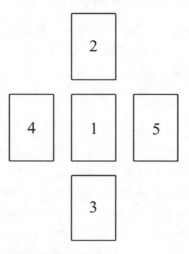

Figure 14. Five-card cross tarot spread.

Here's how to interpret this spread:

- Card 1—Present: Pretty self-explanatory. This card represents the present moment of the spread and is the card through which the others pass their influence and energy.

- Card 2—Above: This card is a part of the present column (cards 1, 2, and 3) of the spread. That which is above you, out of your control, or on your mind. It's up to the individual to determine what this card indicates, as this card and the Below card (3) are some of the greater revelations gained through this spread, providing deeper context to the situation at hand.

- Card 3—Below: That which is below you, under your control, weighing you down, or that on which you're currently focused. Similar to the Above card, it is up to the individual to determine what this card indicates.

- Card 4—Past: What particular component from the past is affecting the present? Where do the events from the present find their root? Is there an unresolved past issue?

- Card 5—Future: This is how events from the present will eventually transpire. Things to be mindful or aware of; things to look for.

Scrying

Scrying is the art of divinely inspired seeing and, as such, is also associated with clairvoyance. As a specialized technique, scrying is probably one of the most crucial skills for any diviner because of its versatility in magick and ritual. Scrying is the art of softening your gaze so you become open to observing what the universe—your subconscious, spirit, deity, etc.—chooses to reveal to you. As a technique, it is used primarily for divination and communication. However, it can also be used to aid in trance work and journeying.

Tools that are helpful for scrying include a candle flame, a campfire, running or still water, a black mirror, a dark bowl, a crystal ball, a piece of obsidian or labradorite, cloud formations, leaf-covered trees, and incense smoke. As with divination in general, when you consider the known scrying methods, you begin to notice that there are three essential approaches to it—the use of increased light, studying patterns, and the use of decreased light.

In scrying, you alter your sight so you can look through and into life, not at it. When you "see," in a normal sense, you are looking *at* life. When you look *through* life, you allow your gaze to soften and become privy to other knowledge. Looking through life can also be described as allowing your focus to shift to something insubstantial—like empty air—by relaxing the muscles in your eyes. Mirrors, candles, and smoke can help block distractions and give you something unobtrusive and ambiguous to gaze upon. What you see is not necessarily within the mirror, candle, or smoke; rather it is a part of your own vision.

As in experiences you may have had while working in an alpha-state trance, information obtained through scrying may be glimpses or realizations that occur in your mind's eye. At times, shapes and forms may appear directly in whatever material or surface you are using for focus, but not always. The shapes may help to inspire a narrative or trigger other thoughts, which, in turn, help you to obtain answers. In the case of spirit evocation, the material substance (like incense smoke) may serve as a direct visual interface with a summoned spirit, as lines, gestures, and forms are observed in the billowing smoke.

Part of learning to scry is discovering how you, personally, engage with the practice. This includes determining the techniques that work best for you, as well as how you tend to receive information. Not everyone scrys in the same way and if you are not successful with one suggested method, that does not mean you cannot scry at all. It may only mean that a particular method does not work for you. You should also consider the possibility that you may be overlooking success by not recognizing it as such—something that can happen if you are anxious or over-eager.

Success in scrying is mostly dependent upon your being open and unbiased enough to allow information to present itself in whatever manner it chooses. It is important not to make assumptions until you learn what works best for you. Everyone is different. You may see things that appear as actual images or as abstract objects. You may hear things with your ears or in your head. You may get pictures in your mind. You may just feel emotions. You may experience all of these or nothing at all. You may also be successful with only one form of scrying, but you'll never know unless you practice regularly to develop your ability. Any ability must be nurtured, and it is only through regular practice that your brain can begin to form new connections to help you with this art.

If you feel so inclined, burning an incense specifically developed for scrying can be helpful. There are any number of herbs you can burn that either correspond with particular magickal acts or are just downright entheogenic.

You can create a scrying incense using this simple recipe:

½ part wormwood (*Artemisia absinthium*)

1 part mugwort (*Artemisia vulgaris*)

1 part marigold (*Tagetes patula,* or any other common marigold variety)

1 part angelica (*Angelica archangelica*)

Burn the combined herbs on an incense charcoal prior to scrying, or use it for the actual scrying itself if you like, by gazing into the shapes and patterns the incense smoke makes in the air.

The Risks of Scrying

The risks that may exist in scrying are akin to those found within any other means of divination. Scrying is no different. But, just to be clear: Nothing can come through a black mirror or a crystal ball—despite Hollywood's best efforts to embed this notion and superstition in

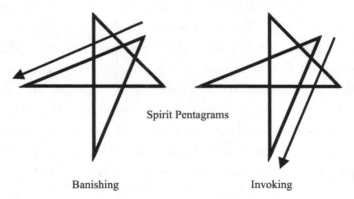

Spirit Pentagrams

Banishing   Invoking

Figure 15. Spirit pentagrams.

our modern psyches. If you remain concerned about this issue for personal reasons, there are sigils or gestures that you can use to help put your mind at ease. For example, try using the spirit pentagrams given in Figure 15. To get rid of a troubling sensation or vision, trace the banishing pentagram. To summon love, blessings, or protection, trace the invoking pentagram.

EXERCISE: THE GAZE

The first trick to scrying is the gaze. You want to use a relaxed gaze, one that isn't focused on any one thing, but is still aware and observing all things at the same time. The scrying gaze is similar to how we view 3-D stereograms. If you've never experienced these images, hold a finger up halfway between your nose and this book. When you focus on the book, anything between the book and your finger will blur out of focus and you'll see an optical illusion composed of two fingers. When you focus on your finger, the book goes out of focus. Switch focus back and forth between finger and book a few times. Get a sense of what this feels like.

When you think you have a good handle on how to make this adjustment with your eyes, focus on the point in space where your finger would be, but without actually having your finger there to look at. Focus on that empty point in space. This is the same visual sensation you need to scry. You aren't focusing on anything in particular; rather you are allowing your eyes to rest and your mind to relax into trance.

EXERCISE: INCREASED LIGHT SCRYING

Some of you may find increased light scrying to be more successful than simple gazing. This type of scrying is usually done with fire—for example, a campfire, a fireplace, or a candle. You can use incense to help with the trance effect and even soft music, if need be. Use methods that will help get you into a relaxed frame of mind. Determine what you want from the session. Are you scrying for insight? For communication with a deity or spirit? Or is this just a simple meditation? When you know why you're scrying, light your incense and candle (or draw near your campfire or fireplace), get comfortable, and gaze upon the flame for five to ten minutes. Record your results.

EXERCISE: PATTERN SCRYING

Determine your intent and prepare your environment as you did for the last exercise, but instead of gazing upon a flame, use the smoke from your incense as a means to scry. Focusing on the constant movement of the smoke may be a bit difficult at first, but the trick is actually *not* to focus on it. Instead, gaze upon the smoke as a general mass, billowing and transforming in the air. Anything that produces variable shapes can become an option for you to use with this method—clouds, blades of grass, the shifting leaves in the trees. Relax your gaze and look upon the mutable patterns created before you.

EXERCISE: DIMINISHED LIGHT SCRYING

Determine your intent and environment as before, but turn off all the lights. Fill a clear or dark bowl halfway with water and add several drops of ink to the water to blacken it. The inky water creates a void, allowing you to stare easily into the darkness. Determine whether you want any candles present and if you want them to be visible. You can use a shroud or large cloth to block a direct candle flame but still permit ambient light to illuminate an area. Just be careful not to place it too close to the flame.

Instead of a bowl of inky water, you can also use a scrying mirror. These are simple to make. Just take a clean piece of glass and paint one side of it with matte black spray paint. Then view it from the unpainted and shiny side. Or you can be creative and make an attractive version of your own by painting the glass from a photo frame, allowing it to dry, then putting it back in its frame.

The Crystal Ball

What is more instantly recognizable as the tool of a diviner than a crystal ball? Indeed, because crystal balls are so effective in such a wide variety of methods, they are a sound investment for any witch and are widely available in many sizes, colors, and depths of clarity.

Don't get hung up on the differences between real quartz crystal versus a crystal ball made of lead crystal, reconstituted crystal, or optical glass—unless of course, you prefer inclusions and other imperfections in your crystal ball. If that is the case, an inexpensive quartz crystal ball may be perfect for you. Just keep in mind that the material the ball is made from is not important and won't enhance or diminish your ability to scry. Essentially, the ball is just something to look at—that's it. Its cost won't determine how successful it is for divinatory purposes, and any inclusions or imperfections may actually help you, as they provide a depth of field to observe and gaze into. Lead crystal, reconstituted crystal, or optical glass—all fairly inexpensive, but man-made—are also very effective for scrying as they provide a neutral surface to work from, but one that creates wild visual distortions that can also be useful.

The reason we are making a point of all this is that real quartz is expensive and the bigger or clearer it is, the more expensive it will be. You will never find a quartz crystal ball as perfect or as large as a lead crystal ball without paying an astronomical amount of money. Lead crystal balls are perfectly clear and create wonderful optical effects when used in conjunction with candles or incense. A 100 mm (four-inch) ball is sufficient for personal use, while a 150 mm (six-inch) ball is good for coven use. Both are comparatively inexpensive and come in a variety of colors, which may also help. Size does not matter, as long as the crystal works for you and you are comfortable using it. Whether your ball needs a stand or is small enough to fit in your palm doesn't really matter either, as long as it is suited to your practice. Getting results with your scrying is what's important. No amount of fancy flash or witchy aesthetics will make up for a lack of ability or practice.

CRYSTAL BALL TRIPOD SETUP

This arrangement works well with a clear crystal ball and is suitable for general divination, as well as for spirit evocation and communication, which we will discuss in chapter 8.

To set up your tripod, you will need:

- A clear 100 mm crystal ball or smaller

- 3 wood dowels approximately ½ inch in diameter and 12 inches long

- ⅛-inch-wide black suede lacing

- A small incense burner, incense charcoal, and tongs

- An incense blend of wormwood and angelica, or something else suitable

- 2 taper candles

Gather up your three dowels so that the ends line up. With your suede lacing, tie them tightly together about three inches from one of the ends, wrapping and tying the lacing around the dowels several times to create a strong hold. Be sure to knot the end of it nice and tightly. Then fan out the longer ends of the dowels by twisting them slightly. They should pivot and spread apart at the place they are knotted together. Make sure that the legs are evenly spaced and create the shape of an equilateral triangle, with the long part of the legs at the base of the triangle. Each leg should be at about a 60° angle in relation to the others to insure stability.

Once your tripod is standing securely, carefully place your crystal ball on top of its short ends. If all feels stable, position your incense burner directly beneath your crystal ball on the same surface. There should be plenty of room underneath the tripod. While you're seated before it, position your candles on either side of the tripod to help illuminate the crystal ball enough so you can see the incense smoke swirling around it. Finally, light your incense, dim the lights, and scry. The combination of ambient light from the candles and rising smoke from the incense moving about the crystal ball creates a powerful effect that can produce some interesting results as you let your gaze soften and sink into the depths of the ball. Ask your questions aloud as you scry. Record your results.

To Keep in Mind

Divination does not need to be restricted to a set system of rules or to a specific method, though methods of divining are already so varied that it is tough to do anything that has not already been done. Get comfortable with as few or as many methods as you like; you don't need to become an expert in all of them. Also, understand that one method may just not be the one for you and that it may take some time before you hit upon the right one. Be patient and continue to practice, no matter what. It will come to you.

SUGGESTED READING

Keys to Perception: A Practical Guide to Psychic Development, by
Ivo Dominguez, Jr.

Tarot for One: The Art of Reading for Yourself, by Courtney Weber.

*Practical Astrology for Witches and Pagans: Using the Planets and
the Stars for Effective Spellwork, Rituals, and Magickal Work,*
by Ivo Dominguez, Jr.

*The Complete Book of Fortune Telling: A Comprehensive Survey of
Every Method of Looking into the Future,* by J. L. Smythe

CHAPTER 5

Herbalism

Within a witch's garden, there are a host of different personalities, all growing and thriving. There are healers—those helpful spirits with their enormous hearts that seem to be designed purely for ridding us of illness. There are also beautiful flowers—brief and tiny lives turning their pretty faces to the sun and joyously calling for any available pollinators to come love them. An impolite rabble of weeds will always make themselves known as well—rumbling and raucous, and appearing to have no purpose other than to grow, annoyingly, where they are least wanted. It can be most tiresome to see them suddenly sprout in the middle of your radishes or push their way through the cracks in your garden path. Weeds, however, are just plants that happen to be growing where you don't want them. There is no specific botanical category called "weeds"; it is only a word that denotes a particular opinion.

Medicinal herbs, coquettish flowers, and unwanted weeds can all be the same plant. *Perspective* is what changes what you call them. Weeds are not a species; they are a point of view. Most plants have some sort of medicinal or culinary value and many plants will produce some sort of bloom if left to their own devices. Any plant that is growing somewhere you didn't plan for it can be a nuisance. Green is green is green, however. When we look further into what each plant actually is and what its purpose may be, that's where the real fun starts.

It would be foolish to believe that we could discuss the whole of herbalism in a single chapter—or even attempt such a feat in one book alone. There are myriad books and reference texts available that do the subject far more justice than we could ever hope to do here, each one more interesting than the next. What we hope to accomplish here is to form a solid foundation on which you can base your own work with plants—specifically, within witchcraft. In this chapter, we'll give you a concise list of the more commonly used or most interesting plants, as well as some of their folklore and the best ways to steward them.

Technically, the botanical definition of an herb is "any seed-bearing plant that does not have a woody stem and dies down to the ground after flowering." However, the more common use of the word denotes any plant with seeds, flowers, or leaves that can be used for flavoring food or drinks, or for medicine or cosmetics. This is a very broad definition, however, so we're going to break it down for you just a bit.

It is a common misconception that herbalism is one of the more straightforward disciplines to learn. After all, it's just a bunch of plants, right? Throw them at the ground or in pots and they'll just grow. Isn't that how it works? This couldn't be farther from the truth. We don't expect any witch reading this book to become a master gardener by any means, but you really should know your *Mandragora officinarum* from your *Podophyllum peltatum*. It could mean the difference between an enlightening journeying experience and three hours of painful vomiting. Here, we'll look at two broad categories of the more interesting plants and herbs that witches should become familiar with: the baneful and the non-baneful.

Baneful Plants

Baneful plants are those that have any sort of poisonous or toxic component. They are everywhere. They're not carefully cultivated behind lock and key in fancy botanical gardens, *verboten* to the general populace, under tight regulation. Poisonous plants can be found anywhere—in your yard, in your wedding bouquet, in your grandmother's flowerpots. They grow wild along highways and lurk in drainage ditches; they're planted in landscaping arrangements. They're even commonly available for sale at big-box hardware stores, garden centers, and online retailers. Indeed, procuring a baneful plant is ridiculously easy. Cultivating them and making a responsible connection with their innate spirit is an entirely different matter. These plants do not suffer fools gladly, and anyone seeking easy legal highs should look elsewhere.

The Nightshades

The banes are primarily made up of the plant family *Solanaceae*—the nightshades. Within their ranks, one finds an incredible assortment of life ranging from the completely benign (tomatoes, eggplant, potatoes, peppers) to the incredibly toxic. They are an extremely prolific plant family that grows wild on every continent with the exception of Antarctica and exists within just about every type of ecosystem imaginable. The subfamily *Solanoideae* is where most of the more dangerous baneful plants are found, and these will be our primary focus here. In this group, you will find deadly nightshade, European mandrake, datura, and henbane, as well as *Nicotianoideae* (which houses the insidious *Nicotiana tabacum* which has enslaved and murdered millions of people). These banefuls sing a beauteous song only a few hear; it is lure—bait, provocation, and temptation laid out prettily for those burning a particular flame deep within their hearts.

If you choose to dance with these banes—the witching herbs and beyond—you will be placing your very life in their hands. They are a cohort of deeply dangerous entities, most of them naturally running thick with tropane alkaloids—that triple-headed wicked beast of atropine/hyoscyamine/scopolamine—all perfectly constructed to either stop a beating heart, rattle it back to life, or grant everlasting sleep. When you approach them, do it with humility, respect, and reverence—no bravado or boastfulness is acceptable. Don't ever turn your back on one of these plants or think you have the best of them, for they will steal the breath right out of your lungs with elegant green and purple fingers before you even realize it's happening.

We have not given dosage information for working with any of the nightshades (and will not). Nonetheless, it is established knowledge that they can be very beneficial allies for an informed witch when taken judiciously through some form of ingestion—eating, drinking, absorbing, or inhalation.

Deadly Nightshade (Atropa belladonna)

Our Lady of the Violet Veil is one of the most iconic baneful plants. She is named for Atropos, one of the three Greek Fates. As the one who cuts the thread of life, Atropos shows you the inevitable with every snip of her shears. Each part of this plant is poisonous to humans and to many animals as well, and it is widely considered by botanists to be one of the most toxic plants in the Western Hemisphere. It is wildly unpredictable and, although many may recommend various amounts as safe for ingestion, you should always exercise extreme care when working with it.

Belladonna has bell-shaped flowers, tinged purple and green, like tiny teacups of toxic poison. The blooms wither away after their time has passed, as all flowers do, but these blossoms ultimately give way to glossy berries that gleam almost black—much like the skin of an eggplant. Belladonna is a hardy perennial that thrives in areas with moderately long and warm growing seasons. It can sometimes be finicky about how much sun or heat it likes and thus really does best in partial shade.

The leaves, roots, berries, and flowers of deadly nightshade are all full of atropine, with the root being the most toxic. Atropine affects the nervous system. Specifically, it interferes with the activity of the parasympathetic nervous system, which controls involuntary actions of the human body (salivation, sexual arousal, tears, digestion, defecation, and urination). It's an anticholinergic chemical that works by blocking the mechanism of acetylcholine in the nervous system, thereby impacting the actions of the stomach, intestines, certain glands like the salivary gland, and the heart. Ingesting any plant that contains atropine causes increased heart rate, blurry vision, dry mouth, nausea, dizziness, dissociative hallucinations, inability to sweat or urinate, and convulsions. It is indeed quite toxic, and children have died just from eating the berries.

When applied topically in a lotion or salve, belladonna is good for pain and relieves inflammation. Taken in other manners—for instance, when smoked or eaten—it can induce a dreamlike state that feels like flight (perhaps leading to the notion behind witches' flights on broomsticks and flying ointment). Those using belladonna through any internal mechanism should definitely know what they are doing and must be fully mindful of the associated risks.

*Mandrake (*Mandragora officinarum*)*

While deadly nightshade may be the best known of the baneful plants, mandrake is certainly the one with the most folklore and mysticism surrounding it. Native to Mediterranean countries, the mandrake is said to sprout from the blood and semen spilled upon the ground under a hanged man as he swings from the gallows. It's a simply gorgeous plant, with great green leaves and golden fruits. When it blooms, the flowers can be either purple (for black mandrake) or white (for white mandrake). The star of the show, however, is the root.

Mandrake roots can grow quite large and tend to fork off in different directions, giving the impression of having limbs. Harvesting the root is said to be incredibly dangerous. Folklore tells us that, when it is wrested from the earth, it lets out an ungodly shriek, killing everyone within earshot. The solution to this was to tie the plant to a dog, plug your ears with wax, and then make the dog run off. The root is pulled from the ground, its screams fill the air, and the only victim is the unlucky canine you enlisted in your work.

Horrid mistreatment of animals aside, mandrakes are considered tokens of good luck, fortune, and fertility. Families kept mandrake roots as heirlooms, wrapping them in soft cloth and feeding them drops of wine or blood once a year. The roots have hallucinogenic and narcotic qualities. Due to its tropane load, however, ingesting mandrake directly in any fashion can also induce uncontrollable delirium. Taking too much can cause unconsciousness to the point of coma or death.

There are a few other species within the genus *Mandragora* that are similar to the *officinarum* variety:

- *Mandragora autumnalis*—largely recognized as a separate species, but with different circumscriptions. Many botanists claim that autumnalis is simply a variant of the *officinarum* species.

- *Mandragora turcomanica*—on the verge of extinction in its native areas of Turkmenistan and Iran.

- *Mandragora caulescens*—native to Nepal, parts of India, parts of China, Bhutan, and Myanmar.

These species, with the exception of *autumnalis*, are even more difficult to procure than *officinarum*, so for clarity and cohesion, when we refer to mandrake here, it is always with *officinarum* in mind.

All of the *Mandragora* can be difficult to find, partly due to how difficult they are to grow. The seeds can be pricey, finding already established seedlings for sale is next to impossible, and the roots are seldom offered for purchase. When they are, they are quite expensive. That being said, you can sometimes find enormous bags of cut "mandrake root" or "powdered mandrake" available for purchase in your local health food store or New Age shop. Be wary of anything like this, however, as this is invariably not actually *Mandragora* mandrake, but one of the two pretenders to the throne—American mandrake (*Podophyllum peltatum*) or English mandrake (*Bryonia alba*). Neither of these plants is within the nightshade family and they are completely different from *Mandragora* mandrake, despite what some unscrupulous sellers may tell you.

American mandrake, commonly called mayapple, is a gastrointestinal irritant and a liver stimulant. It's quite toxic and, if ingested, will produce nausea, vomiting, and stomach or intestinal inflammation. English mandrake, also called white bryony, is in the same family as cucumbers and squash (*Cucurbitaceae*). It's highly poisonous and, if ingested, can be a violent purgative.

When you see these three plants growing, it's easy to see how their leaves differ or how the fruits and flowers they bear are dissimilar. When they are dried, chopped, or ground and placed in a bag or some other type of preparation, however, it can be nearly impossible to tell them apart. Unless you absolutely trust your suppliers (and their suppliers as well, if they don't grow their own), avoid being ripped off by just not buying mandrake in any type of preparation, regardless of who is selling it. Your best bet is either to buy the seeds and grow everything on your own, or buy a whole root, if you are lucky enough to find one. It's the only way to be sure.

Devil's Trumpet (Datura stramonium)

Devil's trumpet is also known as thorn apple, devil's snare, and jimsonweed. It is sometimes incorrectly called moonflower because of its superficial resemblance to that particular flower and its similar vespertine nature. Datura is native to North America and, if left unchecked, can move so invasively that a few states in the United States will send out a health department official to destroy the plants. It grows wild in any moderate to warm area and, even though it is considered an annual by nature, its seeds are so prolific that it will come back in the same place year after year with little to no effort.

All parts of the datura plant contain atropine, hyoscyamine, and scopolamine, making it highly toxic and dangerous. (Are you sensing a theme among the nightshades yet?) Uninformed, recreational users of the plant frequently wind up in the emergency room when they realize that datura is, to be quite blunt, a nasty bitch. Datura intoxication results in delirium, hyperthermia, and tachycardia, so fatal overdoses are a definite risk. It is also a spectacular-looking plant, with long and graceful stems bearing jagged, deep-green leaves. The flowers are large and generally a velvety white, although other varieties occur in different colors, like gold, peach, purple, and white.

Datura blossoms open only at night and last until the sun hits them directly, then they wither. Once they fall, a small seedpod begins to form where the flower was attached to the stem. Over time, the pod grows larger and produces many little spikes all over its circumference. If left on the plant, the pod will eventually rupture and spill tiny seeds on the ground to start the growing cycle anew. While the blooms last only a short time, datura will flower repeatedly throughout spring and summer, extending even into autumn in more moderate climates.

In addition to *stramonium*, there are eight other species of datura within the genus:

- *Datura metel*—of which some cultivars have double or triple corallas

- *Datura ferox*—with longer spines on the seedpods

- *Datura wrightii* (known as "sacred Datura")—native to northern Mexico and the adjacent southwestern United States

- *Datura innoxia*—native to Central and South America

- *Datura ceratocaula* (originally from Mexico)—prefers to

grow in shallow, swampy areas; its toxicity travels up the food chain to the meat of animals that eat it

- *Datura quercifolia*—known as oakleaf thorn apple

- *Datura leichhardtii*—the only datura without showy, ornamental flowers; its flowers are yellowish white and rather unassuming

- *Datura discolor*—the desert thorn apple; this datura likes the sun a bit more than the others and has the largest flowers of all nine species

Henbane *(Hyoscyamus niger)*

Also known as black henbane or stinking nightshade. The dead in Hades are crowned in stupefying henbane, perhaps so they lose their memories of loved ones and life above more quickly. This plant has long been associated with magick and prophecy, and with necromancy itself. The priestesses of the Oracle of Delphi burned it to induce prophetic visions and it was generally thought of as an herb that witches used to bring down storms and blight the crops of their enemies. It is sacred to Hekate, the Greek goddess of witchcraft—she of the crossroads and liminal places. Hekate's ritual implements are passed through the smoke of burning henbane for consecration and dedication.

When you look at it from a botanical perspective and beyond the filter of folklore and magick, henbane is one of the more unassuming nightshades. It has small, cup-like yellow flowers, luridly shot through with greenish-purple veins and a dark purple center in black henbane, while the slightly less common pallid henbane (*Hyoscyamus albus)* has only buttercup-yellow petals. Both varieties are equally toxic. The leaves of the plant are long, prickly, and jagged, with the entire plant standing one to two feet tall, and multiple plants growing close together in clumps. The seedpod is a tiny marvel, resembling an elegant vase, complete with a lid that pops off to allow the seeds to escape for germination.

Henbane is not fussy to grow, although insects will attack it mercilessly—particularly snails, leaf-mining flies, caterpillars, and other pests that generally go after the nightshade family. It can be susceptible to powdery mildew, so avoid getting the leaves wet when watering and only water it in the morning so that any stray droplets of moisture have time to evaporate in the sun.

Like the other baneful nightshades, all parts of henbane are toxic to people and animals. It has effects similar to those of belladonna and datura, but is far milder in nature. It brings a tranquil feeling to the body, with a pronounced heaviness that belies its historical use in flying ointments. Compared to other nightshades, it has smaller amounts of atropine, but don't let that knowledge allow you to drop your guard. Henbane is still toxic and can kill a person or an animal who ingests it improperly.

Other Baneful Plants

Beyond all of the languid wisdom one may learn wrapped in the arms of a nightshade lover, there are other plants found in the witch's garden that are certainly as powerful as the nightshades, and it's vital that you learn about them. These other banefuls are just as powerful and full of Mysteries as the nightshades, but they must be approached in a very different fashion.

All of the banes have the potential to be deadly if carelessly approached. The nightshades are not exempt from this, but if they are prepared responsibly, you can still work with them. There are other banes, however, that you should never ingest. Not in any fashion. Not for any reason. Make no mistake, there are very successful modern medicines that are derived or synthesized from these plants, but the average witch or herbalist doesn't possess either the skills or the proper equipment to manufacture these medicines. Please do not attempt to do so under any circumstances. Instead of singular acts of simple ingestion, these types of banes make their connection with a witch on a different level. Approach building a rapport with them only through careful stewardship and cultivation and you will be rewarded.

Why include such deadly plants at all? All witches—and gardeners, for that matter—should be aware of what may lurk in their gardens; they should understand the associated risks and know how to take appropriate precautions. You must know proper comportment in the presence of these powerful plants—how to identify them, handle them properly, and care for them. There is so much misinformation out in the world, with so many silly and careless people advising others on practices that can ultimately cause harm or even kill. As witches, we must arm ourselves against this, so we can move, as light-footedly as possible, through our communities and protect ourselves from falsities.

How many times have we heard the old adage: If you're not afraid, you're not doing it right? How often have we been told that taking risks is a part of witchcraft? Mind you, these are definitely true statements. Witchcraft is certainly not for the faint of heart, but there is an enormous difference between risk-taking and foolishness. We may walk the lines of transgression and open our eyes to worlds that cause others to flee in mortal terror, but we should not act irresponsibly. This information on the most baneful of the banes is meant to help guide you as you search responsibly for further knowledge.

Monkshood (Aconitum napellus)

The beautiful blue-faced Queen of Poisons. There are few families (or subfamilies, for that matter) that are more collectively toxic than the *Solanoideae*. However, the genus *Aconitum* is one of them. Found within the family of *Ranunculaceae* (where buttercups are also found!), this genus contains plants that are much more individually dangerous than the nightshades. Among them is monkshood, a perennial that grows on long spikes (sometimes up to three feet tall), with palmate leaves and dark-blue helmet-shaped flowers. There are other cultivars, in white, pink, and yellow, but the blue is the most common.

Just as the nightshades have their deadly trio of chemical compounds, the tropane alkaloids, all of the plants within the *Aconitum* family are full of aconitine, a norditerpenoid alkaloid. Not to put too fine a point on it—aconitine is deadly. Within twenty minutes of ingestion, the first symptoms appear—paraesthesia (pins and needles), nausea, and profuse sweating. Shortly thereafter come violent vomiting, severe diarrhea, and excruciating pain, followed by muscle paralysis. This all leads to life-threatening arrhythmia (irregular heartbeat), tachycardia (rapid heartbeat), and ventricular fibrillation, rendering the heart simply incapable of pumping blood. Death is sure to follow, particularly as treatment for monkshood poisoning is only supportive and the poisoning action is so quick.

You must always take great care when dealing with monkshood, or with any of the other *Aconitum*, as the poison occurs throughout the plant—roots, stems, leaves, seeds, and blossoms. Even handling the plant without wearing gloves can cause the poison to be absorbed through the skin, which happens quite easily. Whenever you are working with any part of the plant, be sure to wear latex or nitrile gloves and dispose of them carefully when finished. To avoid accidental poisoning, never use tools used to cut any part of the monkshood plant to cut any other plant that you intend to ingest in any form. A good piece of advice, if you choose to cultivate monkshood in your own garden, is to keep a pair of dedicated garden shears clearly marked as being only for the aconitum plants—just to be on the safe side.

Monkshood should never be ingested in any way, whether by eating parts of it, inhaling any smoke from burning it, drinking decoctions or infusions made from it, or adding it to any salves or ointments.

Despite how terrifyingly poisonous our beautiful monkshood is, it is still very much a strong plant ally to have. It has a vigorous spirit from which you can learn quite a lot, particularly on the subject of transition or adaptation. The plant is found all over the world in various cultural folklore and mythologies. It's said to have grown from the drooling spittle of the three-headed Cerberus, the watchdog at the gates of Hades, and has ever been a plant sacred to the Greek goddess of witchcraft, Hekate. In Nordic tales, it is sacred to Thor and is known as Thor's Hat due to the shape of its blossoms. The Indian God of All Poisons, Shiva the Blue-Throated, was choked by his wife, Parvati, in an effort to stop the aconite he had swallowed from reaching his stomach—hence the blue throat.

Monkshood is intrinsically representative of death, the ultimate liminal state, but is also widely associated with shapeshifting, a liminal state all its own. Wolfsbane, the common name for *Aconitum lycoctonum* or *Aconitum vulparia*, was used to kill wolves with poison-tipped spears and arrows, and has long been connected with treatment for lycanthropy. (The Danish cure of simply scolding a werewolf is vastly preferable.) Monkshood and wolfsbane are not the same plant, however, despite how often their names are interchanged. Anyone working with any of the plants within the *Aconitum* genus should be aware that there are 250 distinct varieties, and you have to know which one you are working with. Some of the more common varieties of *Aconitum*, beyond the already mentioned *Napellus* or *Lycoctonum/Vulparia*, are *Aconitum carmichaelii, Aconitum ferox,* and *Aconitum fischeri.*

Foxglove *(*Digitalis purpurea*)*

Tiny gloves to hide the approach of vulpine chicken thieves. Foxglove also bears the names goblin gloves, folk's glove, dead men's bells, bloody witch's hat, and fairy thimbles. The origin of this beautiful flower's name is forever shrouded in the past, although the word *digitalis* itself is derived from the Latin *digitanus*, meaning "finger." Since time immemorial, however, foxglove has been associated with witches' cottages and fairy folk.

Foxgloves belong to the family *Plantaginaceae*—a very large group that, strangely enough, also contains plantains. While plantains live in the genus *Plantago*, foxgloves are found in the genus *Digitalis*, along with twenty other different species. The most common variety in this genus is *Digitalis purpurea* (common foxglove), but the group also contains *Digitalis grandiflora* (yellow foxglove), *Digitalis thapsi* (Spanish foxglove), and *Digitalis lanata* (Grecian foxglove).

Foxglove grows quite well as a tall and stately ornamental. It's a biennial plant, meaning it blooms in its second year. The bell-shaped blossoms rise on stalks from a rosette of large green leaves and occur in a variety of colors, including pink, purple, yellow, peach, white, and cream. They thrive in full sun and are hardy in areas with moderately long growing seasons and winter temperatures that don't frequently drop below zero. They like a little shade in the hottest parts of the summer for optimum performance and require well-drained soil. They will bloom all summer if you cut their stalks down after the blossoms have gone to seed and will spring back anew after winter's cold has left.

Foxgloves are surrounded by an enormous amount of fairy folklore, but what sort of friend are they to witches? In Victorian flower language, foxgloves speak of insincerity. With their beautiful faces that smell so sweet, they call melodiously to the bees and hummingbirds—draw near; come closer. Plant them next to your front door and they'll serve as a beacon to fairies. Underneath their candy-colored exterior, however, lies the ability to stop your heart right in its tracks. Much like the Good Folk themselves, foxgloves are not just sugar-spun trifles giggling and dancing on the breeze without a drop of darkness at their core. They are what they are, just as fairies are what they are: intoxicatingly beautiful, with a black undercurrent of danger and completely alien to human minds and hearts.

From foxglove comes the medication digitalin, a cardiac drug used to treat heart failure or an irregular heartbeat. It picks up the heartbeat, whereas monkshood slows it down, the two acting as antidotes to one another. Do not ingest one if you've already ingested the other, however, because the results may not work out well for you.

Just as with so many of the other banes, all of this plant is toxic— from flowers and roots, to seeds and stems, to leaves and stalks. Death from ingestion is rare, mostly because of the plant's overwhelmingly bitter taste, but cases do exist, particularly in children younger than six years old. Early symptoms of poisoning include nausea, abdominal pain, delirium, severe headache, vomiting, diarrhea, hallucinations, and, as these increase in severity, irregular heartbeat, convulsions, and either bradycardia (slowed heart rate) or tachycardia (increased heart rate).

Never eat any parts of the foxglove plant, or inhale any smoke from burning it. Never drink decoctions or infusions made from it, or add it to any salves or ointments.

Beyond the Baneful

Now that we've walked some of the darkest rows in the garden, the sun has come back out from behind the clouds and is once again showing its face. All is not doom and gloom here among the green and growing, and not everything here can kill a body dead. Granted, any herb or plant is capable of causing sickness of varying levels of severity if it's mishandled, so even the gentle ones should be looked upon with deep respect.

Crack open any herbal tome and you will find a flurry of medicinal plants to learn about—catnip for relaxation, calendula for skin irritations, the leaves of feverfew chewed for headache, peppermint for digestive woes. Indeed, there are thousands of plant helpers out there to learn about and grow. The few we've listed below are ever-so-slightly outside of the scope of novice herbalists, and they have just enough bite that you must stay on your toes when interacting with them.

Mugwort (Artemisia vulgaris)

Mugwort—also known as dream weed, Old Uncle Henry, and St. John's plant (not to be confused with St. John's wort, mind you)—is the bringer of dreams. It comes from the extremely prolific *Artemisia* genus and is native to the most temperate parts of Europe, although it has spread far and wide throughout the globe. The caterpillars of some butterflies and moths belonging to the *Lepidoptera* family feed on its flowers and leaves. It grows about four to six feet tall and is a perennial, with its flowering point in midsummer to the beginning of autumn. Mugwort is extremely easy to grow, but it is recommended that you keep it and all its wandering roots in a large pot to avoid it traveling all over your garden or taking field trips to visit your neighbors' gardens as well. The gray-green leaves are quite feathery, and grinding them dry produces a delightful fluff. As a whole, mugwort grows in a rather bushy manner and quite likes full sun.

There are so many medicinal applications for mugwort that it can make your head swim. It's antifungal and antibacterial, as well as a stimulant. People brew its roots in a tea as a tonic, and use the rest of the plant to aid stomach and digestive woes. It's effective for treating women with irregular menstrual cycles and, with that action in mind, it should not be used while pregnant or attempting to conceive. It's best known for its use in dream work.

Drinking mugwort as a tea (careful, it's fairly bitter) or smoking dried mugwort before journeying is quite effective in opening the gates of dreaming and can lead you down paths you might never have found otherwise. As with anything, you should exercise moderation, as too much mugwort tea can lead to vomiting, nausea, and diarrhea. If you are sensitive to any of the plants and herbs in the *Asteraceae* family (daisies, chamomile, ragweed, calendula), you should avoid mugwort, as it will produce the same allergic reaction.

Wormwood (Artemisia absinthium)

O, wormwood! The bitterest of greens, the greenest of fairies, the verdant bearer of poetry and song. Wormwood is one of the main ingredients in absinthe, giving the drink a majority of its hue and taste, and its rumored ability to bring on madness. Deep within the bitter heart of wormwood lies the wildly maligned chemical compound known as thujone. Since the mid-19th century, thujone (and thus absinthe itself) has been accused of committing any number of villainous acts up to and including the destruction of the entire nation of France. In truth, thujone is just a simple chemical compound that may cause seizures and hallucinations if not used in moderation. As with any other chemical compound, the reckless use of thujone can make you very ill, very quickly.

That being said, wormwood is a uniquely beautiful herb. Its spiraling, feathery leaves are an ethereal greenish-gray on the surface and a ghostly white underneath. Generally a perennial, it can grow up to four feet tall and is boisterously naturalized across the United States and Canada. Its flowers are tiny, pale yellow, and tubular, and it spreads its seed upon the wind for pollination. While it prefers full sun and nitrogen-rich soil, wormwood will definitely grow under less-than-satisfactory conditions. No prude, our wormwood.

Medicinally speaking, wormwood has largely been used to treat indigestion and infection, and to stimulate hunger, but it is also used as an abortifacient and for the expulsion of worms, as well as for repelling external worms and fleas. Too much wormwood can cause nausea, vertigo, restlessness, delirium, and possibly even convulsions and seizures. Within witchcraft, it's used to call up spirits, bring down vengeance, and aid in protection.

Rue (Ruta graveolens)

Rue for remembrance, rue for repentance, rue against plague, and rue to repel witches. Its name is regret itself. Rue, also known as herb-of-grace, is native to the Balkan Peninsula, but has become naturalized all over the world. It has a woody stem and grows a bit large—generally about three feet tall. It has oval-shaped leaflets that are blue-green in color and, when it flowers, the clusters of small yellow blooms quickly turn to hard seedpods. It prefers full sun, but will grow in partial shade, and is an evergreen if grown in a warmer region.

Black swallowtail caterpillars will flock in droves to your rue and nip it away down to bare branches and clacking seed pods in a handful of days. Don't worry for the life of the rue, however; it will come back fully to green, and in less time than you might imagine. When you allow the plant to be trimmed down systematically once or twice a season like this, you contribute to the health of the environment (butterflies are important pollinators) and help the rue to grow back stronger than ever.

Rue is an herb for protection, both in medicine and witchcraft. It warded off plague and poison hundreds of years ago and still has its uses today in chasing off headaches (chew a leaf or two) and treating coughs and croup. Caution should be taken when handling any part of rue, as the leaves will cause phytophotodermatitis, a skin hyper-sensitivity to ultraviolet light that causes painful blisters to erupt on the skin wherever it was exposed to the sun. Always wear gloves and long sleeves when handling rue, even though some people are able to handle it barehanded with no effect.

Growing Your Practice

Your next step in gaining a deeper awareness of plants and herbs on a witch's level is simple in nature, but is still a lengthy (but very worthwhile) exercise. Pick a specific plant with which you would like to develop a closer connection. Even if you already care for an entire garden, choose just one. Ferret out every single piece of important information about the stewardship of this plant that you can find. Learn what it likes, how it will thrive, the folklore surrounding it, its medicinal and magickal uses, and any precautions necessary to its use. Learn them all. Learn them well. Then, purchase the equipment necessary for growing this plant—the appropriate potting medium, a suitably sized potting container, and any required tools or gloves. Only after you have everything in place and have acquired a solid foundation of knowledge, procure a live seedling of your chosen plant or its seed.

Then, just spend time with your plant. Cultivate the connection between you and this small life as you guide its growth. Spend time sitting in silent meditation with it; seek the green spirit within its leaves and stems and petals and roots. Every plant is a life; every plant has a spirit. What is your plant's like? Each one is as different as individual humans are.

This is an ongoing exercise and, technically, has no end. As you develop and maintain this relationship with your chosen plant, you can begin to expand your connection to another one—either one of the same variety or one of a different family. It doesn't matter; it only matters that you make another contact. Then reach out to another, and then another. And another. Keep doing it. Fill your life with green voices, each one unique to its own heart and each allowing you to view the world through more than just your two human eyes. You'll soon begin to find that your footsteps on this earth change when you know where you're treading. As witches, we should be acutely aware of the world around us, both seen and unseen.

SUGGESTED READING

Pharmako/Poeia, Pharmako/Dynamis, and Pharmako/Gnosis, by Dale Pendell.

Herbs and Things: A Compendium of Practical and Exotic Herb Lore, by Jeanne Rose.

Veneficium: Magic, Witchcraft, and the Poison Path, by Daniel Schulke.

Plants of the Gods: Their Sacred, Healing, and Hallucinogenic Powers, by Richard Evans Schultes.

The Witching Herbs: 13 Essential Plants and Herbs for Your Magical Garden, by Harold Roth.

CHAPTER 6

The Black Tree

T he Black Tree. The World Tree. The Tree of the Witches. That which unites Above and Below and all that falls between and outside. The Black Tree is our name for what is also called the hex sign, the hex star, or the witch's foot. Our use and spelling of Black Tree are derived from the Blacktree tradition and our deep appreciation for the blackthorn tree and its myriad associations with witchcraft and folklore. The blackthorn tree (*Prunus spinosa*) stands in duality with its savage thorns and delicate white flowers. The ultimate witch's tree, it is perpetually balanced between left hand and right. And it naturally represents the power that resides between.

The Black Tree symbol is comprised of three straight lines—a vertical line and two diagonal intersecting lines that form an X, making it look similar to a stretched-out asterisk (see Figure 16). While basic in appearance, this symbol reveals immense layers of wisdom and insight—if you know how to approach it properly.

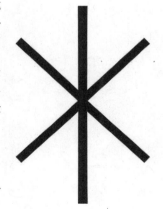

Figure 16. The Black Tree symbol.

The Witches' Hexagram

In our exploration of the Black Tree as a six-part model, and in light of our current understanding of witchcraft, we feel that the classic Witch's Pyramid requires an update. The Witch's Pyramid is a five-part system that grew from the original Four Powers of the Sphinx, as revealed by 19th-century French occultist Eliphas Levi. These original four powers are: *To Know, To Will, To Dare,* and *To Be Silent.* The Witch's Pyramid itself was created when Aleister Crowley added the fifth axiom, *To Go,* to the system. This turned the four powers into five, making it resemble a pyramid of which the original four powers established the base, with Crowley's new fifth axiom functioning as the apex. (Of *course* Crowley insists he be on top.) Since its inception almost a century ago, his pyramid-framed system has been the norm for many witchcraft traditions.

The Blacktree system builds off the Witch's Pyramid, adding a sixth axiom—*To Grow.* We feel this system, which we call the

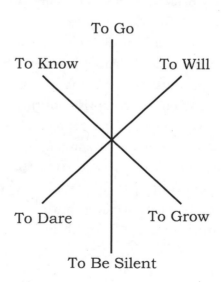

Figure 17. The Witches' Hexagram Star on the Black Tree.

Witch's Hexagram (see Figure 17), is more in line with the six paths of witchcraft (history and lore, magick, divination, herbalism, necromancy, and hedgewitchery). It also nicely rounds out the sequence of development in the system originally described by Levi and Crowley. Together, these axioms depict a natural progression that continues throughout a witch's lifetime, but it also reminds us of certain necessities as we continue along on our journey. While the axioms blend into one another as we work and develop, they also remain as constant reminders of what is valued, needed, and required throughout your life as a witch.

To Know

The first axiom of the Witch's Hexagram, to know, refers to general knowledge, as well as knowledge of the self, inside and out, physical and mental. This is an axiom of education, but also of awareness, maturity, honesty, respect, and honor. Knowledge is the vital means by which we can avoid carelessness in what we do; it also helps build awareness and allows us to be mindful of others. It governs our actions and gauges our responses to the different situations found in life.

This axiom also pertains to knowledge of the occult and magickal arts, and relates to all the things in which we may involve ourselves as witches. A huge part of a witch's path regards the acquisition of knowledge from the hidden realms and learning about the unknown itself. Conversing with spirits, performing acts of divination, and journeying to these other places are often accomplished through personal exploration, with the end goal usually being the acquisition of knowledge, esoteric or otherwise. Indeed, the old saying remains ever true: Knowledge is power—power over the self and power over others. What would a witch be without the gathering and application of power?

To Will

To gain knowledge, you must first have that spark of willingness to see beyond the simple awareness of the self and its mere existence. The second axiom of the Witch's Hexagram, to will, describes how we move through the world and how we exist within it. We will ourselves to be. Our actions are performed via willing them into form. Will implies individuality and responsibility. It is the desire and ability to reach out beyond the limits of our mind and flesh to engage with others and the world. Will carries us through all we do. When we fail to recognize this particular reality, we forfeit life itself.

Will also pertains to our ability to create and make magick happen. Ask artists what Will is like and they may describe an inner desire to reach out with limbs that do not bear form. Instead, they use clay or paint or pen to transfer their inner being onto an outer reality, to touch others in ways outside of tactile sensations, voice, love, or sexual union.

To Dare

As witches, we dare all the time. We know no other pastime, because to be a witch requires an immense amount of daring. It is one thing to know and to apply Will, but without the drive to dare, our endeavors may be short-lived and may not reach as far as we anticipate. To venture outside of both societal boundaries and our personal comfort levels requires daring and this requires no small amount of courage. In many ways, if your practice becomes too comfortable or routine, or too ordinary or blasé, it will lose its overall effectiveness, because it no longer sets your nerves afire with anticipation, excitement, concern, or fear.

Witchcraft should never be *wholesome*. Things and actions that are wholesome don't require us to risk anything—don't require us to dare. Lest you have any doubt about such matters, consider what becomes of wholesome things. They are taken for granted and later discarded and forgotten, or even viewed as one-dimensional or kitsch. Nothing that demands daring will ever be forgotten by those who dared. Nor should witchcraft ever be treated carelessly, taken for granted, or cast aside. If it can be, then it was never truly witchcraft to begin with.

To Grow

The fourth axiom, to grow, is our contribution to the Crooked Path. Growth is a by-product of knowledge, will, and daring. It is that which causes us to push our boundaries, move beyond our limits, and test our capacities across the spectrum of existence. Growth implies development, personal cultivation, and patience. But growth demands change and adaptation as well. In many situations in life, growth equals a healthy environment and ideal circumstances, while stagnation implies a lack of sustenance that can result in death, decay, or ennui. A firm foundation and well-tended soil are critical for any form of growth to occur, whether we are talking about plants or people. To grow as a witch means gaining independence and stability, which reflects upon our personal sovereignty. Growth is imperative to your path as a practitioner and thus, we feel, deserves its own axiom.

To Be Silent

Silence is power, because silence is an anchor. Silence is a grounding point; it is the taproot of the Black Tree itself. It is the one axiom upon which all the others are balanced. Silence, especially concerning the esoteric, implies secrecy—secrecy regarding any teachings and information entrusted to us by mentors and spirits, as well as in the workings that we do. For a variety of reasons, the journey of a witch is a personal one, and much of what it involves and offers is only for the individual witch to know or benefit from. We also work in silence for personal security and safety from those who may not be very understanding or tolerant.

Thankfully, in today's world, the prevalence of Wicca has made life far easier for many practitioners of the esoteric arts and, although we may not all be Wiccan, this does not mean we cannot benefit from the space that Wicca has made for all those who practice the Craft in whatever other manner or form. This veil of comfort should never negate the call for silence regarding what we do, however, as there will always be moments that make silence a witch's greatest ally. Learning how to determine which moments these are is an invaluable skill.

To Go

The sixth axiom, to go, is the culmination of the previous five. Through the union of these axioms, practitioners gain the ability to travel forth, to do, to act, and to manifest. It is a sign that the cosmos is open to the actions of individuals, removing all limitation and restraint from their magick. Without the other five axioms in their places, however, a witch's success is not so certain. In the Witch's Hexagram, there are five points to be mindful of to insure balance and success in your work. You must know, you must will, you must dare, you must grow, and you must be silent—so that you may then *go*.

EXERCISE: WITCH'S HEXAGRAM MEDITATION

How does the Witch's Hexagram function in your life? How do the opposite axioms reflect one another? How are they dependent? See what else you can discern from this arrangement.

Who Put the Hex in Hexagram?

The word "hex" typically pertains to spells and magick, although not exclusively. In our system, the word—and its many implications—sits at the core of the Black Tree itself. The word "hex" is not as commonly used today in English as it used to be, and it does have more than one meaning. Our understanding of it stems from two separate locations, Germany and Greece. In Germany, "hex" was used to refer to spells, curses, or other forms of bewitchment. In Greece, however, the word was also used in conjunction with geometry, specifically in the words *hexagram* and *hexagon*.

In magick, "hex" is an American English term derived from the Pennsylvania Dutch (German, *Deutsch*) word *hexe,* which means "to practice witchcraft." Outside its usage by the Pennsylvania Dutch, however, "hex" is most often used to refer to a curse or an act of baneful magick, thus giving it a deeper connection to the German language. In German, we find the same root in *hexen,* meaning "to hex," and in *hexe,* meaning "a witch." This understanding obviously guarantees the word's association with witches and witchcraft. Although this association is not commonly debated, it is nonetheless worth noting here.

Common
Hexagon

Common
Hexagram

Unicursal
Hexagram

Figure 18. Hexagrams.

When we consider shapes and chemical compounds, we find *hexa* used as a prefix to clarify six-sided or six-angled forms such as the hexagon and hexagram. It is also interesting, from an etymological perspective, that we find a connection between the words "six" and "sex" in Old English—"sex" denoting union, intercourse, and copulation. And it is worth noting that when six babies are birthed in one pregnancy, they are referred to as sextuplets rather than hextuplets, with the origin of the phrase being sextuple or "six-fold." So the terms "hex" and "six" and "sex" and "witch" are all bound up together with the idea of union. This relationship will become more apparent as we further layer these concepts and see how they pertain to the Black Tree, and, later, to the Witches' Sabbat.

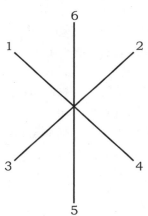

The Black Tree

	Six Paths of Witchcraft	Six Directions	Witch's Hexagram	Mechanics of Magick
1	History and Lore	North	To Know	Knowledge
2	Magick	East	To Will	Will
3	Divination	West	To Dare	Action
4	Herbalism	South	To Grow	Transcendence
5	Necromancy	Below	To Be Silent	Release
6	Hedgewitchery	Above	To Go	Manifestation

The apparent relationship between the number six and the term "hex," with all its associations with the practice of witchcraft, gives further credence to our notion that witchcraft is a six-fold path that aims at uniting the self, as touched upon in chapter 1. The six paths themselves can also be applied to the Black Tree in a way that portrays each path as a branch of the tree. This correlation reveals an interconnectedness that allows for additional correspondences and a deeper knowledge to be gleaned from their arrangement on the tree and in relationship to each other.

You can see here how some of the things discussed thus far may be applied to the Black Tree. A few of the ways we gain a deeper understanding of the paths involve acknowledging how we view the tree itself. For example, the paths of history and lore, magick, and hedgewitchery are paths of the Above (celestial), while the paths of divination, herbalism, and necromancy are paths of the Below (terrestrial). We also see that, while separate, these paths are all connected and are parts of the same whole. From a different interpretation of the tree diagram, the first four paths, in their association with the four cardinal directions, are of the earthly plane, while necromancy descends to the world below and hedgewitchery ascends to the world above. In a similar approach to the Witch's Hexagram, wherein we say that being silent anchors the tree, we can also conclude that the path of necromancy is the primary root of witchcraft as a practice, while the other four cardinal paths are supportive elements that all result in necromancy, which is naturally aligned with the art and practice of hedgewitchery.

EXERCISE: BLACK TREE CORRESPONDENCE MEDITATION

Consider the relationships between the various paths of witchcraft and their correspondences as they reside upon the Black Tree. What is the significance of paths that sit on the same line or opposite one another? How do the first four paths lead to the other two paths? How do they relate? How do they differ? Based on their arrangement on the tree, can the paths be grouped into other formations? If so, what can be learned from this?

Hex Stars and Hex Signs

Many of the mysteries involving the Black Tree are rooted in breaking down the image, finding how it relates to other symbols, or dissecting it in order to gain further insight into how to approach and understand it. Though this may seem superficial, the similarities that present themselves across different cultures are too distinct to ignore. Some of these will be touched upon in this chapter. One of the cultural uses we can examine appears in the hex signs of the Pennsylvania Dutch, who traditionally reside in central and southeastern Pennsylvania.

The beautiful hex signs decorating the barns and homes of the Pennsylvania Dutch are among the more noteworthy elements of the rural landscape of Pennsylvania, along with the Old World appearance of the culture existing there. These hex signs grew out of an earlier form of folk art called *Fraktur*, which mainly developed during the 19th century from the painting and decorating of barns. Fraktur is

Figure 19. Rosette of the Pennsylvania Dutch.

folk art and script associated with the ornamentation of household goods and documenting family history—births, deaths, baptisms, etc. The hex signs contain stylized animals and plants, alongside colorful geometric imagery. One of these images is the Tree of Life, which bears fruit and blessings. Another of the more common images is of a six-petaled star called a rosette, which is used for protection. The rosette is typically displayed within a circle or wheel, and is the result of six interlocking circles (see Figure 19). Variations of this image are also known as the Daisy Wheel, the Seed of Life, and the Flower of Artemis (due to its bee-like, honeycomb design), all of which are known for their protective properties as well.

Along with these associations, Figure 19 shows how the interlocking circles begin to resemble the image of the common hexagram in Figure 18, and are also reminiscent of the Nine Worlds of Germanic cosmology, making the center of the rosette the place where seven of the nine worlds intersect. The other two worlds in that cosmology (not represented by circles in Figure 19) would exist below and above the image of the circles shown, and the central circle would indicate Midgard, the natural or known world of humankind—a noteworthy parallel that will become more evident later in this chapter.

As further evidence of their mystical nature, hex signs are often directly associated with Pow-wow, also known as *Braucherei*, a folk magic tradition of the Pennsylvania Dutch that was described in John George Hohman's 1820 book *The Long Lost Friend*. Hohman's book, which has come to be seen as an American grimoire or spellbook, was once just as common as the Bible in many households. It contains folk remedies, recipes, and Christian-based charms designed to help rural farm folk in their daily life. An adept in this tradition is referred to as a *Braucher* or *Hexenmeister* ("sorcerer" or "witch master"). At one time, these practitioners were thought to be the only ones who could produce a proper hex sign, at least in the magickal sense.

The Black Tree as a Rune

Runes are ancient symbolic letters often used as a means of divination, magick, and writing. The original runic alphabet, the Elder Futhark, gave birth to variations as it was adapted over the centuries by other cultures. It is interesting that the Black Tree, as a symbol, can be built or recognized in some of the various runic systems, offering us a different glimpse into its significance and meaning. Along with the Eldar Futhark here, we will also touch upon the Anglo-Saxon and the Younger Futhark to see what they can reveal.

In the Elder Futhark, the Black Tree doesn't directly appear on its own, but is evident when the runes for "g" (*Gebo,* meaning "gift") and "i" (*Isaz,* meaning "ice") are combined, making what is referred to as a bindrune (see Figure 20). This bindrune thus means "gift of ice," creating a connotation similar to that of the *Hagal* rune of the Younger Futhark, which will be discussed later in this section.

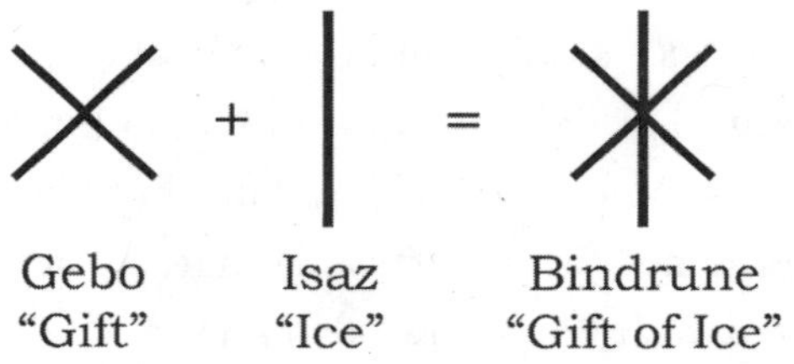

Gebo	Isaz	Bindrune
"Gift"	"Ice"	"Gift of Ice"

Figure 20. Bindrune meaning "gift of ice."

In some runic alphabets, the letter resembling the Black Tree appears in a manner similar to how we depict it in the Blacktree tradition, while in others, it may have a slight variation in its design, as shown in Figure 21. This variance depends on the specific depiction, as some versions of the runic alphabets differ from one another even when they are derived from the same culture. For example, depictions of the Black Tree found in some Anglo-Saxon runic alphabets vary in their appearance, as in the *Ger* (or *Gear*) rune, which takes several forms (see Figure 21).

Figure 21. Three variations of the rune *Ger*.

Some depictions of Ger will look exactly like the Black Tree, while other versions may appear in an alternate manner, as if the cross part of the symbol were flipped in on itself. Ger may mean "year," "summer," and even "harvest," depending on the source. These ideas allude to a type of calendar, a concept which we will explore later in the chapter when we discuss how the hex star relates to the year and seasons.

The other Anglo-Saxon rune in which the hex star can be recognized is the *Ior* (or *Iar*) rune, where, depending on the source, it typically means "eel" or "serpent." The curious tree-like appearance Ior often takes (as shown on the right in Figure 22) should also not go unnoticed.

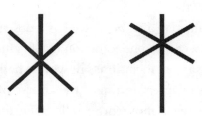

Figure 22. Two variations of the rune *Ior*.

Norse mythology features a great sea serpent named Jörmungandr who winds around Midgard (the Norse realm of the earth), holding its tail in its mouth. It is similar to the fabled Ouroboros—a symbol of regeneration, metamorphosis, and transformation. At the center of Midgard lies Yggdrasil, the great World Tree. Yggdrasil holds up the heavens and reaches down into the world below, connecting the nine worlds of Norse mythology, a concept mentioned earlier in reference to the hex star in the Pennsylvania Dutch tradition.

This idea of a serpent winding around the physical plane at the edge of the world is extremely significant to our understanding of the Black Tree. It sheds further light on the version of the *Ger* rune shown on the far right in Figure 21, which echoes the notion of a serpent winding around a tree when we consider its design and how it is physically written out (a vertical line and a circle). The runic variations of *Ger* and *Ior* were more than likely developed so as not to confuse the two letters in script. In retrospect, however, they do seem to have a tale all their own to tell.

In the Younger Futhark, we find that the Black Tree is identical to the rune *Hagal* ("hail"), which is related to the letter "h." The symbolic meaning of this rune is one of transformation and metamorphosis, as it relates to ice and hailstones that descend from above, melt, and sink into the ground below (reminiscent of the earlier bindrune meaning "gift of ice"), poetically uniting the sky, the land, and the world beneath. This notion of transformation also lies at the very core of the art and practice of thaumaturgy, or magick, as one of the six paths of witchcraft.

As hail, this rune may also be viewed as a destructive or unpleasant symbol, as the weather phenomenon itself is mostly unwelcome. Despite its unpleasant associations, however, hail brings an order of its own through its interruption of the course of daily life, giving us necessary pause and a moment to reflect. Further, the water that results from hail can be seen as beneficial to the world in the long run.

When we look at these three runic systems together, we see that they allude collectively to a union and the relationship existing between Above and Below—in other words, a union of opposites, a reconciliation of two or more different concepts to make something new. Moreover, they also allude to the cycle of the year and the ideas of metamorphosis and transformation, as union and transformation both relate clearly to witchcraft as a spiritual practice and a practice of sovereignty.

The Black Tree as a World Tree

Trees have generally served significant roles in a variety of religious traditions. The Tree of Life in the Garden of Eden, the Bodhi tree of Siddhartha Gautama the Buddha, the tale of Odin and his attainment of the runes, and the crucifixion of Jesus Christ all demonstrate the redemptive, insightful, and knowledge-giving qualities attributed to trees as silent stewards of the earth. The Tree of Life found in the Jewish Qabalah and the *Poteau-Mitan* ("pole in the center") found in Haitian Vodou are seen as representations of the *axis mundi*, as are symbols found in ancient Mesoamerican civilizations like the Mayan and Aztec, as well as in cultures found in Northern Asia and Siberia. The symbol of the Black Tree as a World Tree thus echoes an archetypal concept found throughout history and around the world.

We can recognize the Black Tree in the image of the Qabalistic Tree of Life, which also resembles Yggdrasil and its Nine Worlds (see Figure 23). Moreover, the Tree of Life has a particular cultural connection to the common hexagram in the Star of David from Judaic tradition (see Figure 18). Along with its six- or hex-pointed design, the Star of David is also made up of two triangles, one pointing up and the other down. In Western occultism, this arrangement of triangles also implies a union of the elements of Fire and Water, which, by tradition, are distinctly masculine and feminine. This then relates the Star of David directly to the ideas of sex, six, hex, and the union of Above with Below, in a way similar to the rune *Hagal* ("hail"), with its union and metamorphic qualities. In short, the Tree of Life is a map of creation or the manifestation of the will of Yahweh, which moved from the top sphere (Kether, the crown of creation) down to the bottom sphere (Malkuth, the earthly plane). However, the Tree of Life is a conceptually different World Tree in that it does not depict an Underworld. Its shape, design, and purpose are a map, and this difference is important for our discussion of the Black Tree.

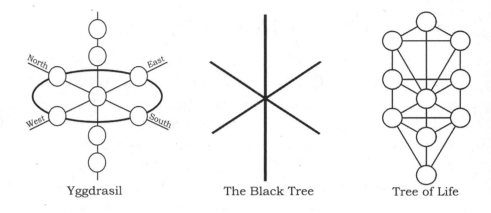

Figure 23. The Black Tree compared to Yggdrasil and the Tree of Life.

If we view the Black Tree as a three-dimensional image similar to Yggdrasil, its long vertical line unites Above with Below, while the other two intersecting lines create an X that indicates the four cardinal directions. Thus the Black Tree is also a map of the cosmos. In this interpretation, the Black Tree is emblematic of the witch's compass or the crossroads—a location where three roads part and three roads meet. One road runs east to west; one road heads north to south; one road connects Above and Below. This consistent notion of Above and Below alludes to a particular cosmology found in many traditions, but which the Black Tree itself also reveals. As with any tree, this one offers the opportunity to climb and explore, as the different worlds or planes can be visited or accessed through spiritual travel.

The Three Worlds

Related to our discussion of the World Tree is the cosmology of the three regions, or worlds of existence, that the tree encompasses—from its deepest roots up to its highest branches. These three worlds are often defined as the Upper World, the Middle World, and the

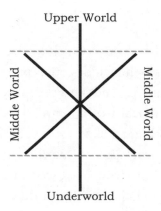

Figure 24. Division of the three worlds upon the Black Tree.

Underworld (see Figure 24). In some systems, these three worlds divide into additional regions, such as in Norse mythology, which contains a total of nine. This three-world motif can even be seen in most shamanic cultures, as well as in some of the major religions of the world, where the etheric notions of heaven and hell often encase a distinctly defined earthly plane. Though the specific details and concepts vary between these cultural cosmologies, the general three-world motif is still a common thread among them. This seems to imply a significant spiritual truth that underlies the makeup of the physical and spiritual realms of existence.

Upper World

The Upper World relates to Above, the celestial realms of existence that encompass the sky and the heavens in a literal sense. This world also includes the planets and stars, as well as ideas of divinity and those deities, spirits, and beings who dwell in and relate to the ascended planes of the cosmos. It also corresponds to our higher selves and can be viewed as a realm of light and wisdom, and a place of divine promise and spiritual ascension. In the Norse tradition, the Upper World was known as Asgard, the realm of the gods.

Middle World

The Middle World is the world in which we live and breathe. It relates to the earthly realm, which includes other people, the land, the landscape, trees, plants, animals, and the different spirits of the land, large and small. It is the physical world, with all its faults and glory, and relates to the ego and human experience. This is the world in which we begin and end our work. It is the world where the compass is laid and the crossroads sought; from here, we travel forth. From here, *we go*. In the Norse tradition, the Middle World was known as Midgard, the realm of humans, plants, and animals.

Underworld

The Underworld relates to Below, that which is in and of the soil, that which is deep down within the darkest caves of the earth. It also relates to the lower, or shadow, self; it deals with the hidden parts of ourselves. This world is also the realm of the ancestors and the dead—what we collectively refer to as the "Phantom Nations of the Dead," which we will talk more about in chapter 8. The Underworld is not a realm of punishment, as often described in some traditions, but rather a realm of both literal and figurative shadows and darkness that houses a variety of chthonic deities, spirits, and beings that vary wildly in temperament and friendliness. In the Norse tradition, the Underworld is called Hel, the realm of the dead.

The Three Worlds and the Black Tree

In relation to the Black Tree, the three worlds exist in a similar manner as found in the diagram of Yggdrasil shown in Figure 23. The intersecting lines are emblematic of the four cardinal directions and, thus, the earthly plane. The vertical line of the tree extends up into the Upper World and down to the Underworld. This knowledge also indicates that the arts of hedgewitchery and necromancy can reveal the means to access these upper and lower realms of the cosmos. Thus the Black Tree becomes a vehicle by which to travel through these three worlds and between them.

Seasonal Shifting

One of the interpretations given for the Anglo-Saxon *Ger* rune was "year." This is extremely interesting, given how revealing the Black Tree is in relation to the calendar of the year when it is combined with the three worlds.

When we look at the diagram of the Black Tree as a flat, six-spoked wheel and consider how it parallels the year, the extreme ends of the central vertical line mark the extreme ends of the year—meaning the solstices, the longest day and night of the year (see Figure 25). The equinoxes then fall at the halfway point between these two extremes,

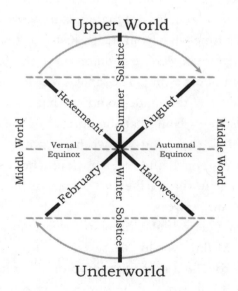

Figure 25. The cycle of the year and the three worlds according to the Black Tree.

bringing the perfect moment of balance, indicated by the intersecting lines of the tree. This arrangement then leaves the remaining four lines of the Black Tree at the cross-quarter days of the year, or the Greater Sabbats, as commonly acknowledged in Wicca.

Unlike many other witches, those in the Blacktree tradition do not follow the common eight-spoked Wheel of the Year. We recognize only Hexennacht and Halloween as significant parts of our calendar (see chapter 10). These mark crucial points in our year when the Upper World and Underworld affect the Middle World, resulting in a seasonal shift between these planes that occurs at two distinct three-month intervals. We then return to the Middle World for a period of three months, at the start of August and again at the start of February, until the next three-month cycle begins (see Figure 25).

This seasonal shift was revealed to us through our personal work and sheds an interesting light on those times of the year when we are not so fully within the Middle World. During the Underworld time of the year, we are more exposed to the effects of it and the inhabitants of that realm. It's not that we can access the Underworld only during this time—far from it. It's just that this world and its inhabitants are more accessible and present in our lives during that time, whether we like it or not. The same is true for the Upper World during its cycle. It is this understanding that leads us to refer to the Winter Solstice as being "at the bottom of the cauldron" and the Summer Solstice as being "between the horns." The cauldron is the cauldron of rebirth and regeneration, when the world is still and dormant. The horns are the two prongs of the stang that hold the light of the sun between.

These shifting periods also reveal the times of the year when we are fully in the Middle World. These are ideal times for reflection, relaxation, and touching base with loved ones before the next shift occurs. This shifting can also be observed in our lunar calendar, which we will discuss a little later.

In light of the material covered in this chapter, meditate and combine this knowledge with the image given at the beginning of chapter 2. What else can you learn about the year or the tools involved from this pairing? How does this idea of seasonal shifting between the worlds relate to your experience and your location?

The Queen of Heaven and the Queen of Hell

In contrast to the Witch Lord, whom we met in chapter 1, there is also the Witch Queen. In the chant *The Witch's Rune*, Doreen Valiente describes her as simultaneously the Queen of Heaven and the Queen of Hell, denoting a complex nature that isn't entirely explained in many traditions. Many witches prefer to just write her off as a mother figure or simply as "the Goddess." This kind of simplistic description severely undermines her value and significance, however. She is not just the moon; she is also the sun. She is the deep earth and the starry heavens. She is all the spaces between. As such, she relates directly to the Black Tree and to the three worlds.

The Witch Queen rules the world above and the world below. She is decidedly *not* a goddess, just as the Witch Lord is not a god. She is a gatekeeper to the other realms. She is a mystery who has revealed herself in different ways in different cultures throughout time. She brings the light and the darkness that ebb and flow with the year. She is not of the Middle World, as that is realm of the Witch Lord—the Uniter of Paths and the Uniter of Worlds. The Witch Queen is an enigma. It is nearly impossible to define or depict her, although we

Figure 26. The Witch Queen.

BESOM, STANG, AND SWORD

have tried to give you an image that conveys something of her nature in Figure 26. Only through personal work, contemplation, and reflection can you fathom some of her mysteries. The most direct way to understand her, however, is to speak with her yourself.

MEETING THE WITCH QUEEN

The following ritual helps to get you in touch with the Witch Queen, to come face to face with her. Perform this rite on the night of a dark moon. You will not necessarily be traveling to the Underworld, but you will be approaching its gateway, so you will need your stang and a suitable incense—something like a good protective and purifying blend made from equal parts of lavender, mugwort, rosemary, and thyme. Wearing protective jewelry is never a bad idea, but we also recommend carrying a piece of labradorite, as it has protective properties and assists in traveling.

To ground and center yourself for this ritual, stand or sit and clear your mind. Breathe deeply and calmly, making longer than normal inhalations and exhalations. As you inhale, draw in peace and calm. Think about the moment. As you exhale, let go of stress and any worrisome thoughts. Feel your body relaxing.

As you relax your body, work your way up from your feet, all the way up to your head. As you exhale, release any tension from your body. Continue breathing, relaxing, and clearing your mind until you feel ready to proceed with the rite.

First, lay a compass. Light your incense and, if you like, mark the quarters in any manner you choose, delineating the space as described in chapter 2. Depending on the work you are performing, you can make some variations in this process, but, for this particular rite, you'll be dealing with Underworld energy and will want to lay the compass counterclockwise. Hold your stang in your right hand to accomplish this task, but, when you have delineated the space, don't anchor the stang or perform the Compass Chant. Instead, proceed to the Crossroads Rite given in chapter 1. After you say, *I call upon thee to beseech thy power,* you are ready to raise the stang.

You raise the stang to unite the worlds and alert them to your work. Placing your stang into the ground allows it to connect with Below and creates a vertical component that stretches into Above—just like a tree with its roots in the soil and its branches reaching for the sky. In this rite, you will be traveling to the gate of the Underworld, so you will need a way to access the realms below. Raising the stang allows this to happen.

Stand in the center of your working space and face south. Hold your stang before you as if you were about to plunge it into the earth at the center of the space. Before you anchor it, call the Witch Lord using the following incantation:

> *Witch Lord, with this stang, I unite the worlds,*
> *So that I may travel beyond the veil.*
> *Around, about, above, and below.*
> *As I desire—it is so!*

End the incantation just as your stang is stuck into the ground—or, if you are working indoors, into your stang holder. This moment also completes raising the stang as a ritual component.

Begin walking counterclockwise around the space, keeping your stang in the center. This precise, circular movement helps to induce an alpha state for trance. Feel yourself walking down to the Underworld, knowing that, with each pass, you descend deeper and deeper. Chant the following:

Around, about, and down I go.
To meet the Queen at the gate below.

Keep walking until you perceive a shift in atmosphere. Go around once more, then stop in the west. Face the west and say:

Queen of the Witches!
I have come to meet with you at the gate of the Underworld.
The Witch Lord vouches for me, as he brought me here.
I seek knowledge of you and the world below.
Visit with me upon this night and show me what I seek.

At this moment, sit or lie down and the Witch Queen will make herself known to you in some manner. Dwell in silence for as long as needed. Interact with her. Ask her questions. Tell her your thoughts.

When the time comes, thank the Witch Queen for meeting with you here at the gate. Depart and return to the Middle World by walking as you did before, but moving clockwise around the space. With each circumambulation, know that you are leaving the Underworld, climbing higher and higher. When you feel that you have reached the Middle World, take hold of your stang and say:

Thank you, Witch Lord, for seeing me there and back.

Remove your stang and conclude the rite by knocking three times upon the ground with the butt of the stang and state:

This rite is done.

A Point of Note

During our exploration of the mysteries of the Black Tree, we referenced a variety of cultures, symbols, and concepts in our quest to deepen our understanding of it. The diverse relationships it contains reveal a multilayered blend of associations and insights that offer their own teachings when analyzed. The noticeable similarities between different cultures throughout this chapter were not used to validate the significance of any one tradition or the mysteries offered by the Black Tree itself. Instead, they are given to demonstrate the synchronicities at play in human history and how these and other elements can serve to distinguish and define one another, despite their disparate origins or evolution. As with any puzzle, the missing piece will always be defined by those that surround it.

SUGGESTED READING

The Way of the Shaman, by Michael Harner.

Magical Alphabets: The Secrets and Significance of Ancient Scripts—Including Runes, Greek, Ogham, Hebrew, and Alchemical Alphabets, by Nigel Pennick.

Runelore: A Handbook of Esoteric Runology, by Edred Thorsson.

CHAPTER 7

The Hidden Landscape

Woven into the dark underbrush of the land, an enigmatic presence lurks just beneath the face of the local landscape. It remains hidden, existing quietly in spaces where it is often overlooked by those who spend their daily lives ignorant of its presence. It is still so close—a breath away at any given time. It creeps around the edges of everything and—by the grace of our animistic observance of nature—we as witches can recognize the scope and depth of this presence in the world around us. This understanding draws back the caul that lies across the hidden landscape, uncovering the bowered shady places where spirits dwell. This shrouded reality, this hidden landscape, dwells at the foundation of witchcraft itself. For us, as witches, the land is one of the most important resources we have.

If the land is sick, we are sick. The land supports us, literally and figuratively. We walk and stand on it; we interact with it in a variety of ways. It provides us with necessary shelter, air, and food; it sustains a certain quality of life. It's also the home to a community of spirits and even has its own consciousness that we can utilize in our craft. As witches who work with both herbs and spirits, it behooves us to look to our local landscape as a vital component of a deep, thriving practice—not just for how it undergirds our magick, but also out of pure respect. We should never want to upset the "locals" with what we do, especially when entering their domains.

The Genius Loci

The phrase *genius loci* is a Latin term meaning "spirit of the place." It was originally used by the ancient Romans to describe the protective spirit of an area. Conceptually, the genius loci has two faces: the local spirits of the land, and the actual consciousness of the land—its personality and presence. In any environment, you feel its distinctive quality. It's unmistakable—a flutter in the gut coming up through your own roots. A park, forest, grove, town, or city—enter any of these and you will automatically know if the land there welcomes you with a friendly warmth, or if it is repulsed and angry at your intrusion.

You can interact with the genius loci of an area, just as you can with any spirit. You can call to it and feed it, and petition it for magick, influence, and aid. Thus, the feeding and leaving of offerings to the land are an extremely important part of building and developing your relationship with it.

In chapter 2, you learned how to acquire your Token of the Land. Another way to further align and unite yourself with the land is to leave a small and intimate offering on the soil where you live. Go to an area you feel particularly attracted to and straight-out ask if that place is agreeable to establishing a connection with you. Once you receive permission, leave a few drops of your blood or hair, nail clippings, or urine at the base of a nearby tree to help imbed you into the local landscape. These bodily artifacts will feed the various flora and fauna, intertwining you and your body even more intimately with the land. This union not only grounds you and roots you into the earth; it also unites you with the sky through the growth and natural expression of the tree you selected. By default, this offering also instantly puts to ground any ill will or magick directed toward you, which is always an added benefit.

Connecting with the Land

After centuries buried on a particular parcel of land, the dead who have been laid to rest there become a part of the landscape, cleaving to the earth itself. A connection is forged. This inescapable action merges the ancestors and our very bloodlines with the regional genius loci, creating a heritage tied directly to the land—an ancestral bond to the soil itself. This in no way ignores the horrors visited upon any people indigenous to a particular land by those who came after. There is no brushing aside such atrocities and they must be met and recognized with fully open eyes. We must always recognize those first peoples and be mindful not to appropriate their sacred customs or intrude in their places. Here, we only mean to acknowledge the ancestral connection to the land that naturally develops over time because of those who have lived and died there.

Home is home and the soil of your home is vital—especially soil from places where your blood relatives are buried. If you relocate away from an ancestral place, fill a jar with its earth and keep it in a safe place. Once you have settled in a new area, take a small amount from the jar and mix it with the soil of your new home. This helps to establish a stronger connection with a new place and helps avoid any of the normal disconnectedness to which you can so easily fall prey when on unfamiliar ground.

EXERCISE: SENSING THE SPIRIT OF PLACE

Wander to a variety of places nearby—a local landscape, a forest, an unused wing of a hospital, an abandoned building, or a historic prison. Choose a wide selection of different places. Notice how your perception changes from area to area. Some places may feel warm, welcoming, light, accepting, or friendly. Others may feel threatening, cold, stressful, tense, heavy, or uneasy. In shifting from exposure to exposure, you will begin to find it easier to sense how each spot is in the world, how it exists. In doing so, you will also become more accustomed to varying your own reactions—shielding against negative energy, extending your hands in gracious acceptance of a welcome, pouring out positive light, or knowing when best to exit graciously. You'll know how to react properly once you have a good handle on where you are.

Living Spirits

An animistic worldview essentially holds that everything has a soul or divine spark within it. It doesn't recognize all life as being interconnected on a spiritual level (as in a pantheistic worldview); instead, it views everything as individual emanations of life that are separate in spirit as well. Some friendly, some ornery. Some bearing good will and some with sharp teeth. This recognition then leads into the notion that, if everything has a soul or spark within, everything may also possess a certain level of awareness, depending on the type of creature, plant, insect, element, or mineral considered.

For as many different types of life as there are in this world, there are corresponding spirits. Some entities have a consciousness more relatable to humans than others. After all, the sentience of a house cat is far easier for a human to understand than that of a spider. Be assured, however, that relating to *any* non-human presence will be wildly different purely by virtue of how differently our brains work. We humans have a tendency to anthropormorphize everything around us, despite the fact that the way we process information is quite unlike the way other creatures do—even the higher primates. This tendency, however, underpins our belief that, if a thing has a consciousness, it can be spoken to, interacted with, or perhaps even befriended.

Tree Spirits

Whether you live near the towering redwoods of northern California or on the outskirts of the Pine Barrens in southern New Jersey, the majestic power and presence of tree spirits is something to behold. Like Tolkien's ponderous Ents, trees are blessed with age and steadfastness. They stand sentry over the land, slow to the point of unchanging. The knowledge and wisdom of trees are as strong and as deep as their wandering roots. Sit quietly with a tree for long enough and, if it likes you, it will open up. You may find that some trees don't actually prefer the company of humans; thankfully, however, many do. Just as there are all types of humans with many different personality types and attitudes, this world also contains all manner of trees with all sorts of natures.

Trees can be great allies. They offer shade and protection to those who live near them. Sometimes, they even provide food. And they can grant even more benefits to seasoned witches who are in tune enough with their presence to sit and speak to them. Conversing with trees, or sitting underneath them, or touching them establishes a bodily connection that helps develop a healthy relationship with them. If you're fortunate enough to work ritual outdoors, incorporating a tree into your work can be extremely rewarding. After all, what more wonderful way to unite the land and sky than by working under a tree?

Plant Spirits

The small, green voices. Plant spirits can be young and fresh, or wizened with age. They can be flowers, herbs, moss, or ferns—anything from the green world—and they will each have their own story to tell. Plants are extremely aware of their environment; they react to light, as well as to sounds and our emotions. It pays to treat them with respect, kindness, consideration, and love. Witches who garden often form strong relationships with their plants. In doing so, they deepen their knowledge and experience of these green lives with each passing season. Depending on where you live in the world, your access to and experience with different plants will differ tremendously.

In areas with changeable climates and perennial plants that sleep through each winter and rise anew in spring, the plant spirits grow old together. With the passage of time, as with any aging entity, they gather their own wisdom—the kind gained only from watching short days turn into long years. Annuals in these areas are rather interesting as well, as they die completely each winter. In the time before they die, they drop their seeds to the earth or send them soaring on the breeze. Their memories string together on an ancestral line, carrying instinctive knowledge from those who came before. In climes that do not vary all that much—areas in which the local plant life does not die back in winter—the plant spirits have other types of knowledge and will be even more familiar with the humans living in their environment.

Fungi Spirits

While fungi are not classified as plants (they're in a separate kingdom designation), their spirits are similar to plant spirits, with a few small, but key, differences. Fungi do not perform photosynthesis or generate their own nutrition as plants do. With their mycelium, they interact via mycorrhizal networks—underground connections created by the fungi themselves to transfer nutrients and water. These networks are dependent on a variety of factors—soil condition, availability of resources, and seasonal changes. Using these networks, the fungi share nutrients with each other and also act as the support system for what has been nicknamed "the Internet for plants." This network allows trees and plants growing near it to utilize these connections in much the same manner—for instance, ousting interlopers by spreading toxins to run them off.

All of these qualities make fungi spirits especially helpful for building relationships. As carriers of information and conduits for energy transfer, fungi spirits are perfect allies for witches in pursuit of knowledge or communion with the land. Acknowledge your local fungi spirits; greet them with fanfare when they follow the rains that call them into being. Most important, exercise all manner of caution when dealing with them and be completely mindful of their nature. Do not pick mushrooms unless they have been identified by a mycology expert and, if you do harvest any fungi, do it responsibly and in a sustainable manner. This will go far to ensure that the fungi spirits look favorably upon you.

Insect Spirits

Insect spirits are probably one of the most alien types of spirits that exist within the living realm. Their thoughts and voices are wholly unlike humans and can sometimes be quite difficult to parse, particularly when they are in a swarm. However, insect spirits can present us with a unique perspective on plants and the earth—one that merits close attention. As predators and pollinators, insects are as varied and complex as any other living species—and perhaps even more so, as they outnumber us 200 million to one.

From household spiders to praying mantids, beetles to ants, mosquitos, crickets, and fireflies, the assortment of insect species reveals the diversity inherent in your local land. Insects can range from intimidatingly large—especially when found in your bathtub at night— to adorably tiny, gliding on air currents or burrowing deep into the rich soil. The lives of insects know no bounds. No matter where you are, there is undoubtedly an insect somewhere surprisingly close to you and you will never know it. Insects are simply everywhere, inescapable. Their spirits click and clatter on the level of individual species, but they are also all interconnected with the overarching, collective consciousness of all insect spirit forms—The Many.

Animal Spirits

Household animal companions are great. However, when we discuss animal spirits, we are most assuredly not referring to the pets we love and care for—although they have their own connections to the spirit world, in their own fashion. We are also not referring to the traditional witch's familiar. Instead, we refer here to animals in the wild or, at least, those animals who are more exposed to and in touch with the local landscape than the average pet is.

Animals who have only experienced an indoor environment know nothing else and are cut off almost completely from the land upon which they live. Likewise, the level of insight they possess may only reflect the scope of their life experiences as a whole and not much more. Our house cats have never touched a blade of grass in their lives and the world they see through our windows probably doesn't look much different to them from the one we see on television programs. This is why we do not consider pets to be familiar spirits in the traditional sense. They are far too domesticated and have usually been acquired through practical and mundane means—not as a gift from the devil or the Queen of Elphame, as is traditionally believed.

Some pets, however, are much more deeply aligned with their wild instincts than others and can revert with breathtaking speed to their feral nature if driven to do so. Cats in particular are quite adept at shoving aside their innate predatory drives in favor of regular food, affection, and a warm place to sleep. But just watch them rip apart a catnip mouse or see how they stalk some hapless bug that has the bad luck to wander into their territory. They are still tiny predators at heart, with fangs and claws and a taste for hunting. Even so, a cat (or any other domesticated pet) should still not serve as the link between witch and animal spirit, no matter how strong the heart connection between the pet and the witch may be. Spirits can potentially be involved in some quite nasty work, and it isn't fair to our pets to involve them in such things unwittingly.

To work with animal spirits, we must engage with them and experience them along with the rest of the natural world. It is their specific connection with that world—that wild flame—that serves us as witches. The squirrels of the land and the crows of the air can become lenses through which we view and experience the regional landscape. In exchange for this partnership, they help us reinvest ourselves in the land on a deeper level and connect with those who live upon it in new and transcendent ways.

EXERCISE: CONTACTING THE LIVING SPIRITS

Politeness is the key to making contact with the spirits of the land. A sincere greeting opens many doors in the everyday world; the spirit world is no different. Go to an area close to your home that either supports a wide variety of wildlife or is home to a particular life-form with which you want to connect. Even if you live in an urban environment, there is still an enormous amount of animal and insect life scurrying about unnoticed just under your nose. Don't assume that a forest is the only place you can contact the spirits of the land.

There are also many different plants living and thriving in urban environments; they are not difficult to find. Locating trees in a city may prove a little more challenging, but any public park will most likely suit your needs. Find a safe and comfortable place to sit, one where you can stay for some time without intrusion. Sit and stay quiet, either near your intended plant or tree, or watching for any animals or insects that begin to go about their regular business once they feel you're not a threat. Observe the movement of the animals or insects. What are they doing? How do they look? How do they sound? If you're there for plants or trees, watch them for their own movements; follow their patterns. Breathe slowly and deeply to relax your body, clear your mind, and allow your awareness to fall into a semi-trance.

Eventually, your attention will shrink to a pinpoint. Try to catch the eye or notice of the life you are studying, then maintain that contact. When you feel as if you have been sufficiently noticed that you are not just another feature of the landscape, send out your awareness to your target—a small feeler of *hello*. An animal or insect may immediately react with fright and flee, but the barest beginnings of a connection have now been established. Return to this area as often as you can to repeat this exercise until you feel comfortable with the connection you have established with a particular animal or plant. Always remember to leave an offering for these spirits—some neutral consumable (water is always a safe bet) or something small and shiny that can be buried with little disturbance to the land.

Once you feel you have a solid connection to these specific spirits, try to make contact with others of the same species, but in a different location. Again, always be polite, never force an interaction, and immediately leave if you sense any aggression or panic.

Land Wights

Land wights present themselves under an enormous variety of guises. They are neither plant nor tree, animal nor insect. They are not wholly of the spirit world, nor of the middle realms where humans dwell. Some align with the Good Neighbors or the Other Crowd, but they are not completely of that realm either. They are intrinsically of the land and outside of the land at the same time. They are not the spirit *of* a tree, but may be the spirit living *in* a tree. They are large, they are small; they are friendly, they are fierce. They can converse on human levels or completely simplify their communication into bursts of instinct and waves of emotions. Communication occurs entirely on their terms. They are everywhere, at all times. When you catch their notice, you may see them flicker at the edges of your perception, dancing just out of your sight.

The best way to see land wights is by not looking directly at them. If you feel as if one is close to you or is attempting to get your attention, establish an idea of where in your vicinity they may be, *then look away*. Try to see them from your peripheral vision, from the corners of your eyes. Stand or sit very still and see if they approach; make note of their appearance and demeanor. Greet them quietly and, if they are amenable, stay in their company for a short time to see what you can pick up from them. Eventually, you will learn what your particular land wights are fond of and, if you leave them offerings, they will think more kindly of you. Never lose the awareness that they are not human, however, no matter how human their shape may be at the moment. Remember that their intellectual processes are radically different from our own.

Wights are also found in homes and other types of dwellings; every structure has its own resident spirits. Sometimes they are guardians of the home and anyone who lives there; sometimes they lived on the land on which the building stands. All of them have their own protocol for how they want to cohabit with humans. The Russians know them as the *domovoi*, the Norse as the *húsvættir*. The English have the *hob*, and Scandinavians have the *tomte*. It is all the same general concept—spirits living within a structure as keepers of the household. They despise slovenly people and grow quite irritated at those who take no pride in their surroundings. Neglectful people often find their sleep disturbed and their belongings either broken or stolen. Nastier wights may even cause accidents or directly drive the offenders out with violence.

In our home, we keep our wights happy with regular tidying and strong black tea. Whenever we break something made of glass, we place the shards into a jar designated for their enjoyment, as following the unpredictable edges of something broken provides them with random entertainment. Other wights may prefer different offerings, and anyone wanting to connect with them must take their own steps to learn their habits, their preferences, and what angers them.

Local Living

Witches have always been thought of as living on the outskirts of society, forced into contact with their neighbors only when someone wanted something of them. Stepping out of that time-honored outsider status can be uncomfortable and difficult—particularly for those of a more introspective and solitary bent. Many witches find that plants, insects, and animals are easier to interact with than humans and prefer their company above all else. However, in this modern age, we strongly recommend that witches maintain at least an occasional presence in their local communities—if for no other reason than to know what is going on around them. This not only gives you a necessary awareness of the local climates (figurative and literal); it also brings you closer to the land and its spirits.

Tapping into the spirits of a region by attending local community events like festivals, carnivals, and parades is a great way to stay connected to the local landscape. Strong energies are generated at these events, energies that feed into the heart of the land itself. Participating in these gatherings makes witches into direct conduits for these energies and possibly allows them to direct these forces into different areas as needed. Local landmarks, human-made or natural, are also places that tend to gather quite a bit of spirit energy to them, evolving in a natural progression into an area that feels as if it has a life all its own.

Eating locally, buying from local farmers, eating at family-owned restaurants that also support local agriculture are all ways you can attune yourself with the spirit of where you live, fully engage with it, and even give something back. For example, New Jersey has a robust wine industry, so any wine we drink—for social, ritual, or magickal purposes—is usually from a local winery. This helps the local industry, and we are also drinking the blood of the land when we drink local wine. This practice, having a heavy symbolism all its own, also makes the local region a part of our very flesh and blood.

The eating and partaking of food grown on local farms—or better yet, your own home garden—is another great way to engage with the local landscape and to unite with the soil itself. Tending a garden gets your hands into the dirt, which can be extremely beneficial and therapeutic on numerous levels, and it causes you to interact with plants and their individual spirits. Gardening shows other people, animals, and spirits something of your character as a person and witch, making them more likely to work with you, help you, and accept you more readily as a fellow inhabitant of the land.

Jogging, hiking, biking, camping, hunting, fishing, and foraging in your area are all wonderful recreational ways to immerse yourself in the land. When you incorporate trance work into these activities and get into the habit of leaving offerings, you ensure that the local spirits will be less disturbed by your presence. Playing, coaching, or watching an outdoor sport may, unfortunately, actually work against you as a witch, because almost all outdoor sports require the excavation of land—with golf being the worst offender—in order to create a manufactured environment in which to play. This isn't to say that spirits can't be found on a golf course or a baseball field, because spirits will inhabit any area or dwelling that suits them. They just may not be all that friendly due to the disrupted landscape and may pick on you or your teammates out of anger. So, if you are involved in an outdoor sport, leave an offering or bring a gift to the land every once in a while. It may go a long way toward smoothing over these feelings of animosity.

All the ways we engage with the land are reflected in our successes and failures as witches. If we are mindful of those interactions, we can attempt to steer them to the mutual benefit of both our own interests and those of the landscape. Even if you live in an area without much in the way of a local community (community-at-large, not specifically a Pagan or witchcraft community), there are definitely still ways you can engage with others and with the land. It may be more of a challenge and you may need to get a bit creative in how you define things like "landscape," "community," and "local," but witches are nothing if not skilled at solving conundrums by ignoring common constraints.

Local Lore

A cultural element that is often overlooked is the understanding and observance of folklore, whether local or ancestral. It's easy to do, particularly as a lot of folklore is immersed in archaic thoughts and stories that may not resonate with the modern mind. Consider, however, the possibility that folklore is actually a direct manifestation of the genius loci—indeed, perhaps its very voice.

A place's folklore is a direct expression of the spirits of the land and of the people who interact with it on a regular basis. A prime example of this is the story of Herne the Hunter. Great Herne, the leader of the Wild Hunt, haunts Windsor Forest and Great Park in the English county of Berkshire. One of the earliest sources of this tale comes from William Shakespeare's play *The Merry Wives of Windsor* (1597). Here, Herne is described as "a spirit" and "a keeper in Windsor forest." Moreover, the tale bears strong similarities to other stories, like that of Odin, who also led a Wild Hunt, or Cernunnos, another horned figure from folklore. There are also some who believe that Herne derives from an actual historical personage—Richard Horne—who lived during the time of Henry VIII. The who, where, why, and when of this story are not what's important, however. As witches, we must always cast an eye to our histories, collective and personal, while staying grounded in the present.

The story of Herne persists to this day throughout this particular forest in Berkshire. Not only has the spirit clung to the collective consciousness, it has also been elevated to divine status over the centuries, resulting in a deity who has made a comfortable home in modern Pagan paths like Wicca and Druidry. And if this can happen in England, why is it that so many of us seem to overlook our own local monsters and spirits who fulfill similar roles? Are they not worthy of recognition or magickal elevation?

Regional spirits should perhaps hold more relevance and value to us as witches than spirits who exist in far-off lands or in unfamiliar cultures. Working with and elevating our local spirits only makes sense. If this appears a bit daft, look at it this way. When performing a household task like vacuuming, it's always more practical to use the nearest electrical outlet rather than one from the other side of your home or down the street. The strongest energy source is generally the one closest and most accessible to you. Working with magick and spirits is no different.

The Jersey Devil

The story of Herne led us to look for the spirits in our own backyard. We live in southern New Jersey, a stone's throw away from the Pine Barrens, a protected pineland forest reserve that covers 1.1 million acres. These dense woods, remote and largely uninhabited in many areas, are home to the Jersey Devil—our state monster, the Great Dragon of the Pines. The stories of the Jersey Devil can be considered comparable to those of Herne in that they are both horned entities and each haunts a forest. Moreover, both are associated with blood-curdling shrieks bursting from deep within the woods, causing a moment of pure terror to those unlucky enough to cross their paths. These obvious parallels led us to start viewing the Jersey Devil as our own primary land spirit, given where we live.

Figure 27. The Jersey Devil.

The folklore surrounding the birth of the Jersey Devil only adds to his role and significance in our work. Most legends of the spirit start in 1735 with a woman named Leeds who was pregnant with her thirteenth child and exhausted. The child's human father was a drunkard, but some claim the actual father was the devil himself. According to the legend, Old Mother Leeds was a witch—a startling accusation, particularly because this occurred only forty years after the Salem witch trials.

On the night Mother Leeds went into labor, a hellish storm descended, rumbling and ominous, across the land. A perfect night for a visit from the devil. Mother Leeds labored long, bone-weary and in great pain. With every ragged breath, she dwelt with dread on the idea of yet another mouth to feed, finding it almost too much to bear. Lightning flashed and the wind howled, and she sobbed in powerless frustration. She just wanted it all to end—the endless laboring pregnancy, the thankless child-rearing, the absent drunk of a husband. All of it! Into the wailing storm she screamed, cursing the coming child and calling him a child of woe. With a final panting push, she declared: "May this one be a devil!" And then the child was born.

Her baby appeared normal at first, all pink and perfect, but then, after a moment's breath, he began to change. He shrieked like a struck bell, as his fingers grew into claws. He sprouted bat-like wings from his back and his chubby baby legs twisted horrifically into those of a hairy goat. A serpentine tail burst forth from his backside, foul and whipping, and his all-too-briefly cherubic features morphed into the head of a gaunt horse with the sly face of a dog (see Figure 27). Before any of the attending women in the room could react, this devil, borne of Old Mother Leeds, flew up the chimney and into the storm, where it circled the village and then soared out into the pines.

Since that fateful night, sightings of the creature regularly occur throughout the mid-Atlantic region. One of the more notable was in 1820 when Joseph Bonaparte, former King of Spain and brother to Napoleon, was hunting on his estate in Bordentown, New Jersey. Twenty years later, another incident involved the heavy loss of livestock across a wide area. Strange tracks were found at those scenes, and monstrous sounds were heard by many the night before. The most famous period of sightings occurred during a week in January of 1909, when the creature was witnessed by thousands of people because of its exploits throughout the entire region. Since then, sightings and experiences continue to occur, with the most recent happening in Galloway Township in 2015, when the creature was allegedly spotted at a golf course before it took to the air. The photos that circulated online afterward were blurry and strange.

We have incorporated some elements of the tale of the Jersey Devil into our own practice. We view him as our primary land spirit—a manifestation of the genius loci in our area. We call to him when we raise our stang, alongside the Witch Lord. In a similar fashion, we view Old Mother Leeds, a reputed witch, as a primary ancestor spirit, in some ways akin to the Witch Queen herself. This relationship presents the interesting notion of the primary ancestor giving birth to the primary land spirit.

As thirteen is the traditional number of members in a witch's coven, and the Jersey Devil was said to be the thirteenth child of Mother Leeds, we view him as the thirteenth member of our coven. This also suggests that we are the children of Old Mother Leeds and we commit to having no more than twelve flesh-and-blood members in any given coven. It also suggests that, on a spiritual level, the Jersey Devil is, in fact, our brother.

Find Your Own Path

Not all regional folklore may fit easily into your practice and you should never try to force its incorporation, just as you should never try to manufacture a myth where none is present. You may live in an area that has local spirits with whom you don't feel comfortable aligning yourself. Or you may live in an area with unknown lore. This is where you need to exercise your natural ingenuity and find your own spirits. Forge your own folktales through your engagement with the land. Not all stories are already known to us; seek them out for yourself. Spirits similar to the Jersey Devil include:

- The Alkali Lake Monster (Nebraska)

- Angeline Tubbs, the Witch of Saratoga (New York)

- Bake-danuki, the tanuki spirit (Japan)

- Congolese giant spider (Congo region, Africa)
- The Enfield Monster (Illinois)
- The Goatman (Maryland)
- The Loveland Frog (Ohio)
- Mngwa (Tanzania)
- Moehau (New Zealand)
- The Monkey Man of New Delhi (India)
- Mothman (Virginia)
- Nandi Bear (Republic of Kenya, Africa)
- Old Nabbie (Maine)
- The Snallygaster (Maryland)

SUGGESTED READING

The Eldritch World, by Nigel Pennick.
Demons and Spirits of the Land: Ancestral Lore and Practices, by Claude Lecouteux.
The Tradition of Household Spirits, by Claude Lecouteux.
Secret Commonwealth of Elves, Fauns, and Fairies, by Robert Kirk.
The Fairy Faith in Celtic Countries, by Evans-Wentz.

Necromancy

The great irony of this past century's witchcraft revival is that the majority of its practitioners often overlook one of the most pivotal practices that was ever associated with witchcraft—the art and practice of necromancy. The good news is that a handful of authors (see recommended reading for this chapter) who fall under the umbrella of Western esotericism have introduced, tackled, or touched upon this very core aspect of what it means to practice witchcraft. The bad news is that the practice has been mostly ignored by a surprising number of modern witchcraft traditions. This may be due to the controversial nature of necromancy, or it may be due to a lack of understanding regarding what necromancy actually is.

Admittedly, necromancy is certainly not for the faint of heart—afterall, it is "death divination" or "the art of divining via the dead" or "divination by means of a dead body." Indeed, it may very well be the ultimate endeavor for those reaching outside their personal comfort zones and is sure to challenge what most would-be witches know and love about themselves and the world.

When we look into the history and lore surrounding necromancy, we can easily see that witchcraft has had a continuous love affair with the death-defying art. Hekate, the Greek goddess of witchcraft, besides being associated with the crossroads, wild places, liminal spaces, and the moon, is also connected to ghosts, infernal spirits, and necromancy. *Pharsalia* (*The Civil War*), a first-century Roman epic poem by Lucan, tells of the Thessalian witch Erichtho who relished the rampant death and bloodshed of battlefields, from which she could harvest the bodies, limbs, and spirits of the recent dead for her army of shades. The Old Testament (Samuel I 28:3–25) tells us of the Witch of Endor who, despite being banished for her ability to traffic with ghosts and spirits, is sought by King Saul to perform an act of necromancy. As an example of its Old World relevance, in the *Poetic Edda*, the Norse god Odin performs an act of necromancy when he conjures a dead seer to learn the fate of his deceased son, Baldr.

Necromancy can be observed in a variety of European cultures. It was even taught alongside other forms of divination in medieval Spanish schools located in Cordova, Toledo, Seville, and Salamanca, where classes were purportedly held deep in the dark caverns wandering beneath the cemeteries and mausoleums of the city. Because of its often gruesome nature and heretical tendencies (as over time, raising the dead became viewed as an act appropriate to God and no other), necromancy became demonized—literally—by its association with the summoning of demons. Those committing acts of necromancy were thought to be raising up actual demons rather than the deceased spirits of individuals and ancient teachers, in the same way that fairy lore was given horns and a forked tail.

Not only was necromancy roundly condemned by the Catholic Church, but in Jacobean England, an expansion of Queen Elizabeth's original statute from 1563 (the Witchcraft Act of 1604, instituted by King James I) completely outlawed it by directly denouncing the use of a corpse for sorcerous purposes. The cultural diabolization of necromancy eventually led to it being relabeled as "nigromancy" (black divination), which eventually was simplified to "black magick" or the "black arts." This transformed perceptions of the art, darkening it and equating it with the devil. This ensured that anyone who claimed the practice as their own would be ostracized.

Even by modern standards, some forms of necromancy are considered detestable—for instance, when animals are sacrificed to utilize their blood as an offering to the dead. This practice is thought to attract and even fuel the spirits of the dead, who come to drink the life-bearing fluids that instilled them with recognition and sometimes speech. In *Greek and Roman Necromancy*, Daniel Ogden describes how animals—and in some instances, small children—were dispatched for necromantic purposes or ritually killed in order to read their entrails.

In his *The Fourth Book of Occult Philosophy*, Heinrich Cornelius Agrippa claims that, to summon a spirit, "new blood" or "a relic of the body" is needed, along with other ingredients, recalling a necromantic rite performed by Odysseus in Homer's *Odyssey*. In the story, Odysseus digs a pit and pours into it three separate libations—one a mixture of milk and honey, one of sweet wine, and one of water. These offerings are then topped with an offering of barley. After praying to the dead, Odysseus sacrifices a black goat with a bronze sword and uses the goat's blood to fill the pit. The presence of the blood draws the ghosts of the dead near to partake of the offering, giving Odysseus the opportunity to command the proper spirit to come forth through the authority instilled in him by his sword.

Necromantic Theory

Why would someone want to summon the dead for help or insight? The theory behind necromancy and working with the dead is based in the fact that, since the dead are no longer bound to the physical plane, they have a deeper understanding and awareness of life and the cosmos. In a similar way, the pool of ancestors stretching from time immemorial also provides us with a unique advantage in recollecting past lore and practices; it is valuable to maintain connections with them for this very reason alone.

Necromancy takes a variety of forms, with alleged bodily resurrection standing only as the most dramatic. The necromantic arts also include ancestor work, working within dreams, summoning shades, spirit communication, and combining any of these practices with other forms of divination, magick, or spell work. It was also not uncommon in the past for cadaver parts to be utilized for magickal purposes. The most popular of these rites, the Hand of Glory, featured a hand that was severed from the body of an executed felon as it hung from the gallows. The hand was preserved using a combination of herbs and dog-day summer sunlight, then fitted with a candle created from the fat of the same hanged felon. Once lit, this grusome relic would cause all in its presence (other than the candle-bearer) to become motionless and was even said to have the power to open any locked door.

The idea behind using the dead in such particular magickal practices is that a person's bodily remains are thought to contain remnants of their talents and accomplishments. The body of a warrior was thus seen as an ideal source of fortitude, strength, and courage, while an artist's corpse could house tremendous levels of skill, inspiration, and creativity. These characteristics were also thought to extend to the deceased's final resting place, making it a key resource in the execution of magickal endeavors. The popular grave of Marie Laveau in New Orleans is a perfect example of a grave being used in such a manner. Laveau's grave is visited by hundreds of devotees every year to pay their respects.

The Ancestors

The most important thing to keep in mind when working with the dead is that they are people. Granted, they have moved on and no longer live among us; but they should still always be treated as people, not as foreign entities or something to be feared. *People.* Treat them as you would any other person, and only get hostile toward them if their actions warrant it. Like all people, they have their good and bad sides, good and bad days. They have their own flaws and hang-ups, much like everyone else. Be polite and follow the proper protocol for each situation you encounter.

In general, the ancestors are those individuals who have made a significant mark on human history, the world, and life as we individually (and sometimes collectively) know it. They are not necessarily your own blood kin, but instead are a collective of minds and hearts that have existed over the centuries. They include those who reached the peak of human accomplishment and endeavor, as well as the wastrel dregs of society. The more benevolent ancestors have a vested interest in your success, and in humanity's success as a whole. As practitioners, they are our touchstone and our home base. They are the house in which we live. They offer us their support and shelter; they will provide for us when able and intervene when asked.

When we discuss the ancestors, we classify them into groups—as Homer did when, in *The Odyssey*, he called them "the Phantom Nations of the Dead." This allows us to acknowledge and distinguish them collectively. The passage of time has yielded us many ancestral allies, so grouping them into categories is quite helpful. You may never need to contact some of the following ancestral groups, but they are there because they are a reflection of life and the people we encounter in the world. These Phantom Nations include the Mighty Dead, the Beloved Dead, the Honored Dead, the Forgotten Dead, the Dishonored Dead, the Untimely Dead, the Nameless Dead, and the Hidden Company.

Mighty Dead

These are the shades of people whose accomplishments in life have greatly benefited humanity and, as a result, earned them a place of vast respect in human history—whether or not they are recognized universally. Their impact is more important than our recognition of them. The Mighty Dead are not limited to those who gained fame or fortune, as death is the greatest equalizer. They know their own and there is always a deep resonance through a community when someone meant to stand with them passes.

You can petition the Mighty Dead for power, strength, inspiration, transformation, and similar needs. Offer them beer, mead, liquor, cooked or cured meats, and savory foods.

Beloved Dead

These are the loved ones lost through the perils of life and time who were viewed as family, whether through blood, marriage, or another bond. These dead are keenly mourned by those left behind with broken hearts.

Seek their assistance when you need support, guidance, love, nurturing, good health, opportunity, grief, or emotional support. Your offerings to them should be strongly personal and take into account their individual tastes, but may also include flowers, wine, candy, desserts, honey, rose quartz, heartfelt poems, and other tokens of love and acknowledgment.

Honored Dead

These are the heroes who sacrificed themselves for others, either through the loss of their own lives or simply through their commitment and dedication to improve the lives of others. We hold them in high regard because of their noble actions in life.

The Honored Dead are generally useful for resolving conflict, opening doors, miracles, blessings, and the need for good fortune. You can offer them roses, lilies, scotch, whisky, cigars, tobacco, or incense made of frankincense and myrrh. Selfless acts such as volunteering or giving blood are also appropriate offerings for them.

Forgotten Dead

What is remembered lives. In an effort to maintain that belief, we acknowledge the deceased—both family and unknown—who are the victims of time and forgotten because those committed to remembering them have also passed on. The responsibility to keep them on our altars and keep their memories alive falls to us.

Ask the Forgotten Dead for help with perseverance, memory, duty, clearing the air, and removing obstacles. Offerings to them include lighting a candle in their honor, cemetery soil (not from a grave), old photographs of unknown people, chocolate, small shiny antique items, unleavened bread, and red grapes.

Dishonored Dead

Not all the dead are fondly missed. The Dishonored Dead are those whose actions in life resulted in a death marred by their deeds. Some Dishonored Dead find redemption in death by receiving forgiveness from the living, but this may not always be the case. Many are still quite nasty, so they are good for sentry work. Set them in a place that needs a fearsome guardian.

You can petition the Dishonored Dead for help with acts of vengeance, cursing, torment, and other acts that may stain your own heart. Offer them dead insects, shiny coins, cheap gin, broken glass, unshelled peanuts, roots, or dirt from the grave of a criminal or an individual of known questionable moral character.

Untimely Dead

The Untimely Dead are those who died before their time, robbed of life by sudden illness, tragic accident, or murder. These individuals frequently have unfulfilled goals and are seeking retribution or to help someone in need. They are cut off by the natural barrier between life and death and may seek help from the living so they can finally move on. You can work with them in a general manner, but if a specific deceased is more suited for a particular task, then petition that spirit directly so that both parties can find some sense of resolution.

You can also ask the Untimely Dead for their assistance with acts of vindication, retribution, recovery, redemption, justice, dispelling gossip or rumors, and other related needs. Offerings to them include vegetables, pure water, barely ripened fruit, airy cakes, and other light desserts.

Nameless Dead

Those who died without an identity and without the ability of ever recovering it through either research or records are known as the Nameless Dead. Their anonymity results in a deep separation between them and the living world, as names are critical for communication and acknowledgment. These dead are distinctly different from the Forgotten Dead, who, at one time, could be named and acknowledged by the living. To be entirely without a name, however, is to be *not known*, and this is only a breath away from never having existed at all. In our acknowledgment of these deceased, we give them back their presence in the universe.

The Nameless Dead should be approached only in matters of grave importance, as petitioning them and giving them offerings is a great responsibility. Seek them out for assistance in lost causes and last resorts, when all else has failed. To work with them, you must first make direct connection with one of their number by journeying to the land of the dead through either meditation, trance, or a near-death experience. (We most assuredly do not recommend intentionally pursuing NDEs for this purpose.) Once you establish contact, ask the spirit's name. Depending on how long the individual has been deceased or how tenuous their attachment to this world has become, you may only receive a breath or two, a few murmured syllables, or even less. Once you have a name, however, you will be able to make an offering.

Offerings for the Nameless Dead should be something you have constructed with your own hands—a poppet in their likeness, a spirit bottle, a story or poem about them, anything in which their name may settle and live on. If you are not even remotely gifted in the creative arts and find yourself casting about for an offering, a small sign decorated with the person's name will even work. After you have created and named your project, you must then release it out into the world. Give it away to someone or sell it; it doesn't matter. As long as the deceased's name is somehow intrinsically attached to the item and is passed into someone else's hands, the offering will be complete. The Nameless now stands Named.

The Hidden Company

If you have developed your ability to scry and have been doing some of the rituals explained in this book, you may have occasionally noticed shapes dwelling in the depths of the candle-lit darkness—shades assembling about your compass space, watching quietly and perhaps even engaging with you in your practice. Who can blame them? If you are succeeding at your work, some spirits are going to get nosey. It can't be helped; a good ritual is a beacon for local spirit activity. These otherworld observers are known as the Hidden Company—a concept that comes from the Clan of Tubal Cain—and are believed to be the very ancestors of witchcraft itself. When they gather on the outskirts of your work, they may just be curious about what's going on and simply wish to watch. They can also provide aid and remain involved in your daily craft. Their presence is a blessing to any witch's practice.

Petition the Hidden Company for aid in protection—for yourself or your coven, from another coven or individual witch, for magickal aid, or for any other assistance regarding witchcraft. Offer them strong spirits (whisky, vodka, gin, etc.), handcrafted witch's tools, flying ointment, or fresh herbs.

Feeding and Petitioning the Ancestors

Working with the ancestors doesn't necessarily mean you're forced to deal with a deceased relative with whom you battled in life. This work allows you to interact with people from throughout the history of humanity, as well as with more personal friends and loved ones. If there are those you don't want to include in this company, just remove them from the lineup. Keep in mind, however, that ancestor work can also help heal the familial soul and work out lingering grievances, if that is what you seek.

To begin ancestral contact, you must first set up an ancestor altar as discussed in chapter 2. Follow up by making offerings to the deceased in the form of food and drink. Generally, any food or drink that feels appropriate will do, but known favorites are ideal. These offerings should be changed on a regular basis to avoid attracting unwanted vermin. Dry items fare better than wet and liquids like water, juice, or alcohol. Old offerings can be disposed of outside or thrown in the garbage.

You can petition the ancestors for service at any time, and doing so can also act as an extension of your daily or weekly altar visitations. Simply provide them with the appropriate offerings and explain your situation. Their response may come to you as a sensation of agreement or as a desire for more payment beyond your offering. Breaking out the good scotch may sometimes be in order. However, if you are unable to give them what they request, tell them. They will inform you of acceptable substitutions.

A DAILY ANCESTOR RITE

Communing with the ancestors regularly is vital for witches who want to deepen their craft. One way to do this is with the following basic ritual. The practice is best done in the early morning or evening, as these periods exist on the boundaries of day and night. If you want to be particular about the time, sunset is ideal, as this time of day relates to the west, where the ancestors dwell. Sunrise, or the early morning, will also work, as these are quiet and solitary times that hover on the border of dreaming and sleep.

Go before your ancestor altar with your favorite drink in hand. Light any altar candles. Present a small amount of drink or food as your offering. Light a piece of palo santo wood (or another incense) and give the altar area a quick dose of the sweet fragrance. Then knock three times upon the altar and say:

Hail to the ancestors, the Phantom Nations of the Dead,
Those who have gone before, and those who have yet to be.

At this point, just talk to them. Tell them what's on your mind or if there is something troubling you. Tell them about recent problems, blessings, failures, or successes. Tell them what you are thankful for. Tell them what you regret. Tell them what you plan to do later that day or the next. Ask them for favor in what you are seeking. Ask them for guidance. The point of this rite is to start a dialog with them, to connect.

The responses you receive may manifest in random thoughts and feelings as you speak, or even come to you later in the day or as you sleep. This period of dialog can also be combined with meditation, contemplation, or divination, or in leaving a message for them in the message box described in chapter 2. Your message can be anything from a note of gratitude to a request for their attention in a particular matter. It doesn't much matter what you do as you sit before them; it's just important to start a relationship and then dialog with them on a regular basis. To conclude the rite, simply express your thanks and knock three times on the altar. Extinguish any candles you lit and you're done.

TAPPING THE BONE

This concept was first introduced to us by the late, and very much missed, Peter Paddon (1964–2014) in his *A Grimoire for Modern Cunningfolk*. In his book, Paddon discusses tapping into the ancestral memory contained in your own blood to retrieve lost lore. This method can also be used to obtain answers about the present or past, whether your questions are related to family or to life in general.

As a living relation, your direct connection to the past through your genetic heritage can be used to retrieve lost information or lore through meditation and trance work. Some of the information found in chapter 6 about the Black Tree was obtained in this manner, using a deep trance while seated before our home ancestor altar. Sitting there with the ancestors, it was as if a floodgate burst open and visions and insight poured out. The feeling was so strong that the visions kept coming even an hour later. Some came as imagery in the mind's eye; some came more as a sense of understanding, like a series of revelations. No matter how important books and research are, they hold no promise of success, no notion of infallibility. So whenever you find yourself flummoxed or at odds as to where to turn next, performing this rite can provide great results.

You can use this act as the main working of a larger ritual, or you can incorporate it into your daily practice. Be warned, however. This rite potentially has some heavy residual effects, including involuntary trance or a spacey lack of mental clarity that can linger for a few hours. Be sure to eat or do something mentally engaging when you are done, before returning to your normal life. Having a scribe or digital voice recorder can help document anything you may say during the rite, as well as any anomalous voices that may come through.

After having called to the ancestors using the Daily Ancestor Rite above, sit cross-legged facing your ancestor altar and say:

I seek conference with my ancestors, of blood and beloved,
For insight and clarity, so mote it be.

Pick up the skull from the altar and hold it in your lap so that you're both facing in the same direction, cradling it with your hands. Be sure to keep your hands in constant contact with the skull during the entire rite to maintain connection. In this posture, you are mimicking a skull and crossbones—aligning yourself with the ancestors and associating the ancestral current with your reproductive center.

Once in position, close your eyes and begin to rock slowly forward and backward to induce an alpha trance. This kind of movement helps to throw off your equilibrium and you should feel as if you're floating in water. When you feel ready, clearly say aloud the question you wish to answer. Dwell on this question; hold it in your mind as you continue to rock, with your eyes remaining closed. Answers may come to you in the form of imagery, emotions or physical sensations, sounds, tastes, etc. You may find that the pace of your rocking intensifies during this portion of the rite. If you are working with a partner, be sure to voice any revelations aloud for documentation. Continue in this manner until you feel as if you have the answers you sought. This rite can last for ten minutes or longer, depending on the situation.

When you are ready to break the connection, thank the ancestors for their insight, then begin to slow the pace of your rocking and gradually regain your sense of balance. Perhaps not unsurprisingly, it isn't easy to regain normal consciousness after rocking back and forth with your eyes closed for a long period of time. Give yourself enough opportunity to come back safely and, once you've found your sense of equilibrium, sit and breathe for a few minutes with your eyes still shut. Once all functions have returned to normal, open your eyes. Place the skull back on the hearthstone and conclude the rite by expressing your thanks and knocking three times on the altar. Extinguish any candles you lit.

The Dead Art of Corpse Divination

The most definitive practice associated with necromancy is the infamous art of allegedly raising a body from the dead. After all, the term "necromancy," which comes from the Greek word *nekros,* meaning "corpse," literally means "corpse divination." Though there are tales of such accomplishments, there is, as one might expect, little actual evidence to support them. The story of Jesus raising Lazarus from the dead in the book of John contains very little drama. Indeed, his performance might even be considered lackluster next to the elaborate and gory necromantic ceremony contained in Aleister Crowley's novel *Moonchild,* which results in one character being possessed by the evoked spirit. Arguably, the most cited depiction of necromancy is found in the previously mentioned poem by Lucan, *The Civil War.*

Lucan wrote of the disheveled witch Erichtho, the Witch of Thessalia, who was sought by Sextus Pompeius for her renowned necromantic skills in order to learn his destiny. Reluctant at first to oblige his request, she was quickly persuaded by his knowledge of her exalted reputation. After being thoroughly praised by Sextus, Erichtho set out to retrieve a suitable body from a local battlefield—one recently deceased and still in possession of firm flesh and lungs untouched by any wound. Having found the perfect candidate, she dragged the body of the soldier to her cave by the neck to perform the rite. There, she called upon an assortment of deities to grant her request to summon the soldier's spirit from the Underworld to answer her questions. Upon the spirit's appearance, she filled his body with reheated blood and a list of other rank ingredients, including the froth of rabid dogs, marrow from a snake-fed stag, the entrails of a lynx, dragons' eyes, and other even more gruesome components.

In hatred for his former body, the soldier refused to re-enter it, claiming that his living corpse would be unnatural and thus impervious to death, trapping him in it forever. This was not a future the soldier cared to accept. Erichtho grew irritated and scourged the soldier's body until he submitted to her demands. The body awoke and he answered her questions, but only in exchange for the promise of permanent rest—the destruction of his body on a funeral pyre, insuring he couldn't be summoned again, to which she agreed.

Erichtho is depicted by Lucan as a foul and filthy creature, one to be feared and avoided at all cost. She lived among the dead and had a taste for harvesting battlefields for corpses and body parts. Her necromantic exploits were either inspired by known practices of the time or would serve as templates for later acts, as the poem contained some of the other tropes often associated with this practice—alignment with the dead, wearing their clothes, not bathing for a period of time prior to the act, self-ostracization from society, not thinking about or engaging in sex (or any life-affirming activity), living in a tomb, eating putrid and rotting food, etc. The idea behind this type of physical and mental preparation is that, if you seek to bring the dead back to life, then you must live as the living dead—an excellent example of sympathetic magick.

On some level, it is reasonable to suspect that necromancy never took a literal form, despite the exaggerations found in fiction. History does bear out the existence of the art, however. We know definitively that necromancy was taught and performed by many people centuries ago. But what form did it actually take?

Many argue against the notion of literally raising a body from the dead, because it sounds completely beyond nature. You'd be hard-pressed, after all, to find a ritual similar to Erichtho's laid out plain in a grimoire. *The Grimorium Verum* offers only methods to rejuvenate someone who is near death, while *The Eighth Book of Moses* contains a short and simple incantation to raise a body. In *Forbidden Rites* by Richard Kieckhefer, a related procedure is discussed that causes a living person to appear deceased or a deceased person to appear as if they were alive. *The Lesser Key of Solomon* contains at least one spirit (#54, Murmur) who can help specifically in necromantic spirit-summoning, but says nothing about resurrecting corpses.

You could argue that all material pertaining to such a magickal procedure has simply been lost over the centuries. However, grimoires tend to be quite incestuous, sharing a lot of the same rites and spells. If such a ritual ever existed, it would almost certainly still be found in some manner. Yet, despite the lack of evidence or ritual documentation, we must wonder. Did necromancy ever actually involve a corpse? And is there perhaps something to the notion of the speaking dead?

In the process of decomposition, the body slowly breaks down. Gases are released through any available orifices (mouth, nasal passages, anus, etc.) and, prior to the development and institution of embalming practices, these expelling gases created audible inflections that could be interpreted as (or mistaken for) actual speech. In the same way that anomalous messages are heard in digital recordings, it's entirely plausible that corpse divination was actually the interpretation of the sounds emerging from an actively decaying corpse. This would explain why Erichtho needed a fresh corpse with firm lungs untouched by a wound, as damaged lungs would inhibit the corpse's ability to produce vocalizations. Her scourging of the corpse would also have caused any lingering gases to bubble up through the throat, thus providing her with the answers she sought. Despite its origin in fiction, it may be that the story of Erichtho and some of what she did was based on actual divination techniques known at the time, but now lost.

All this rationalization, however, neglects the other primary aspect of necromancy—summoning the spirits of the dead, or *sciomancy* (shade divination). In conjunction with spirit contact, some Roman necromantic practices often included dream work in which practitioners commanded spirits to meet with them in their dreams so they could speak to one another. A similar approach might involve journeying, using deep meditation in a ritual environment. Even scrying, combined with this type of evocation, could achieve potent results.

NECROMANTIC SLEEP RITUAL

The following rite was inspired by a Roman necromantic practice in combination with a similar rite taken from the *Grimorium Verum*. Because dreams are a different reality unto themselves, one in which we journey Above and Below on a regular basis, they make a wonderful liminal space in which to interact with the dead.

To summon and converse with a spirit of the dead, you will need:

- Your sovereignty cord

- Unlined paper

- A black pen

- An incense burner

- An incense blend (equal parts of wormwood and sandalwood)

- A wearable sachet (containing equal parts of lavender, mugwort, and valerian root)

- A dream diary (optional, but strongly encouraged)

- The aid of your familiar (see chapter 9)

To accomplish this work, you will be using the following three sigils, which were expressly given to us by the ancestors:

| Communication Sigil | Summoning Sigil | Protection Sigil |

Figure 28. Necromantic sleep sigils.

While wearing your sovereignty cord, light your incense. Carefully walk the smoking incense in its burner about the space where you will be sleeping and then place it in a safe location for the duration of the rite—somewhere where it cannot be knocked over or disturbed.

Sitting in your bed, create the parchment of summoning. Using your pen and paper, draw out the triangle as shown in Figure 29, with the pictured sigils and full name of the spirit you want to contact. While looking at the name, recite the incantation.

Figure 29. Necromantic sleep parchment.

I summon you, (state the spirit's name),
Whose name is written upon this parchment,
To come forth from the land of the dead
And meet with me in my dreams upon this night,
Until the rising of the morning sun or sooner,
For safe conversation and peaceful engagement
To tell me (reason for summoning) during this night of slumber.
So, shall it be!

Place the paper underneath your pillow. While wearing the sachet, lie down in a supine position with your hands placed palms down on either side of your solar plexus. The sachet should lie over your heart so you can smell the herbs contained within. Take several moments to inhale their fragrance and feel their effect take hold.

Once you are comfortable and in position, summon your familiar to act as a spirit guardian throughout the rite. As you drift to sleep, fix the idea of your desired encounter in your mind. If you prefer, visualize yourself sitting at a table or relaxing on a couch, waiting for the intended spirit to join you.

When you wake from your encounter, if you have a dream diary, quickly write down as much information as you can before your memory fades. Be sure to thank your familiar for its help and thank the spirit for its council. If your session went especially well, you can leave additional offerings on your ancestor altar as a further display of gratitude.

NECROMANTIC SPIRIT SUMMONING

This rite should take place close to the dark of the moon and on a Saturday night—ideally when they fall together. Saturday—literally, "Saturn's Day"—is an ideal time for necromantic rites, given Saturn's common association with necromancy itself. Wear your sovereignty cord and set up your working space as described in chapter 2, using your besom, stang, sword, and your ancestor altar. Instead of setting up the sacrificial altar, however, place your Token of the Land there because you will have no need for a surface or table in the northeast during this rite. In the center of your space, set up your crystal ball tripod (see chapter 4) with candles surrounding it to define an equilateral triangle. Within the triangle, place the sigils used in the Necromantic Sleep Ritual given above. You will be working with spirits, and this arrangement will contain their activity.

For this rite, you will also need:

- A lighter or matches

- A bell

- Locally produced red wine or juice

- A loaf of locally baked bread

- Salt water

- Incense charcoal

- Incense tongs (to safely light your incense)

- An incense blend (equal parts of mugwort, wormwood, and dried rose petals)

To begin, ring your bell three times in each direction, beginning in the east and moving counterclockwise, to alert the spirits and clear the space. Light your charcoal and add a liberal amount of incense— enough to last for the next several minutes. Lay a fortified compass (see chapter 2), but skip the Compass Chant and the Crossroads Rite and move directly into raising your stang (see chapter 6), placing the stang in the south. Once you have raised the stang, descend into the Underworld. You will sense the shift in the air as you march counterclockwise. Chant the following:

Around, about, and down we go
To the Underworld so dark below.

Chant and walk around the space as many times as needed to produce the desired shift in atmosphere. When you feel the moment coming, adjust your pace so that you end in the west before the ancestor altar, to call upon the dead.

CALLING THE ANCESTORS (OPENING THE WEST GATE)

This is a special rite that was inspired by the late Peter Paddon. In it, you use your own breath to bring the ritual skull to life and enable it to function as a vessel for the dead. If you are successful, the skull itself may take on a new appearance and you may even see eyes form in its sockets as it observes the rite from the ancestor altar in the west.

To enact the ritual, knock three times upon the surface of the altar and say:

> *Witch Queen—Queen of Heaven. Queen of Hell.*
> *Please grant us access to your kingdoms as we*
> *Go about our rite on this dark moon.*
> *Allow those who have passed before*
> *To return through the veil,*
> *So that we may converse with them.*

Pick up the skull and take a deep energized breath, with the intent of summoning the dead. Exhale that breath into the mouth of the skull. As you exhale, fill your breath with the intention of breathing life into the skull. Do this three times and then say:

> *Hail to the ancestors! The phantom nations of the dead,*
> *Those who have gone before, and those who have yet to be.*

Please be present for this rite upon this dark moon.
And reveal to us all that we desire to know.
Hail and join us in peace.

Exhale one last energized breath into the skull, then place it back on the hearthstone. If you are working with a particular ancestor, make any suitable offerings, then open the West Gate by drawing an invoking west pentagram above the ancestor altar. You don't have to speak with a specific spirit, as the ancestors in general are often willing to help regardless. If you are interested in speaking with someone in particular, call that person forth at this time. If not, then simply state:

The ancestors have arrived!

Now make your offerings of wine and bread to the ancestors by placing them on the altar. We suggest locally prepared wine and bread, as they are a testimony to the land, but feel free to make any appropriate substitutions as you see fit.

To begin formal communication, sit in the east and face the tripod and the west. Add more incense to the charcoal as needed and allow a relaxed gaze to fall on your crystal ball. Observe how the rising incense smoke creates a morphing visual effect within the heart of the crystal. Allow yourself to slip into an alpha state and then ask your questions. Answers may come as a combination of visual elements from the smoke, as sounds, or as mental images. The important thing is to observe and be present for whatever information may come your way.

When you're ready to conclude the session, make your way to the west and thank the ancestors for their cooperation. Kiss your fingertips and touch them to the skull. Thank the Witch Queen and draw a banishing west pentagram above the altar. Then walk clockwise around the area to leave the Underworld and return to the Middle World. When you've arrived home, thank the Witch Lord and lower the stang. Finally, walk around to the north, pick up your besom, and sweep the space in a counterclockwise direction. When you are finished, knock three times on the floor with the end of your besom and say aloud:

This rite is done!

SUGGESTED READING

Communing with the Ancestors: Your Spirit Guides, Bloodline Allies, and the Cycle of Reincarnation, by Raven Grimassi.
Communing with the Spirits: The Magical Practice of Necromancy, by Martin Coleman.
The Return of the Dead, by Claude Lecouteux.
Greek and Roman Necromancy, by Daniel Ogden.
The Mighty Dead: Communing with the Ancestors of Witchcraft, by Christopher Penczak.

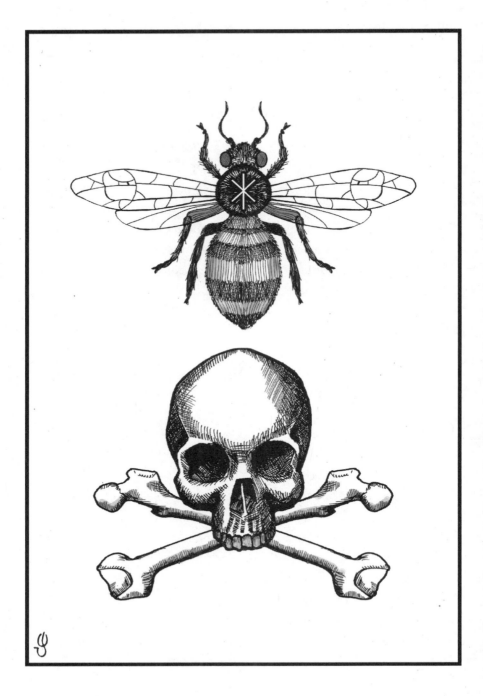

CHAPTER 9

Hedgewitchery

There are worlds beyond these, it is known, and witches have long traveled between them. Alongside each world lies another space entirely—an area that is neither here nor there, a boundary line, a demarcation zone that indicates which area is which. How else would we know where one place ends and another begins? There has to be a border; there will always be a border.

A *haeg*, or "hedge," is a fence, a delineation, and fences are boundary markers. They tell you "this place is here" and "that place is there." The words *haegtessa* and *haegtesse*, roughly translated as "hedge-rider" or "hedge-crosser," come from Saxon and Old English. In modern English, the word is "hedgewitch." To hedgewitches, going to or traveling across these in-between places means nothing more than moving from one room to another—from parlor to kitchen, or bedroom to hall. We have the map to do so and we hold the keys. With these words, with these ideas, witches fly.

Hedgewitches are folk healers, spirit healers. They generally have a strong knowledge of plants, particularly those that help them attain altered states of consciousness for trance and journey work. Along with spellcraft, herbalism, divination, and necromancy, witches require a solid base in hedgewitchery. Without it, we are blind in our travels and deaf to our spirits. Hedgewitchery has a shamanistic quality to it that is wholly separate from herbalism. That is what gives hedge-witches their ability to travel and make contact with entities beyond their normal ken.

Journeying to other worlds to visit with fairies, trolls, demons, the ancestors, and other spirits, either in dreams or using trance states, was not uncommon during the Early Modern Period in England. Owen Davies, in his book *Popular Magic*, tells us it was by such ventures that knowledge, power, and even healing modalities were gained by witches for use in the waking world. This practice is found in many cultures, throughout many eras, and still exists to this day in the hearts of hedgewitches.

We journey for insight and wisdom, to connect with spirits, or to find our familiars. We explore, we chart our passage, and we learn from our experiences. Finding our ways to these worlds and back isn't easy, as nothing we witches do is really so simple, but there are a variety of ways to get there and home again.

Trance States for Hedgewitchery

There are particular people who seem to go through their lives in the Middle World, half in and half out of full connection with reality. Some places just naturally have thin borders and possess areas where the veil between worlds isn't quite as substantial as it should be. Some people are the same. For those who straddle the boundaries, it is almost as if a perpetually thin veil follows them wherever they go. They live within a constant or easily accessed trance; it is a blessing and a curse.

In chapter 3, we talked about brain waves and trance states, and how they relate to each other, but because we were discussing magick at the time, we only focused on one state—alpha. The other states of consciousness (delta, theta, and gamma) offer an additional advantage to the other paths and practices of witchcraft and each serves a distinct purpose. Delta and theta states are easily the best suited for all things associated with hedge crossing—for example, treading the mill, soul flight, shapeshifting, and some forms of spirit communication. Gamma is good for acts of creativity, divine inspiration, epiphany, prophecy, and visions. Although we offer these general suggestions here, the various trance states and their successful application will be different for everyone. It is up to each individual witch to determine which states and methods are best for their practice and goals.

Delta State (0–3 Hz)

Delta is the state of deep sleep without dreaming—an endless black canvas of nothingness that the human brain brushes against during its nightly slow dive into the deep end. It is a liminal space nested between consciousness, the subconscious, and the unconscious. It's the darkest trance you can fall into, occurring just before REM sleep. In delta, you no longer have conscious awareness of the physical world around you.

Delta is ideal for healing both physical illness and injury, and emotional, mental, and psychic blights. Studies of this state indicate that, when the delta state is interrupted or when not enough time is spent in it, anxiety, depression, and all manner of other issues can take hold, digging their claws in and making a person mildly snappish at best and horribly unbalanced at worst. Maintaining a long enough period in delta allows your brain and body to rebuild themselves anew. It's necessary on a regular basis, simply for healthy living, but it is also extremely helpful for witches who find themselves in need of serious care.

EXERCISE: SHIFTING INTO DELTA

Triggering a delta state on your own can be tricky, but practitioners of yoga nidra (a state of yogic sleep) induce it via systematic relaxation. The key is to relax your body slowly enough that your awareness doesn't cling to external stimuli. Steadily bring your consciousness down to a pinpoint and, after each exhalation, let the waves of relaxation close over you. At first, you will fight against it, struggling violently to maintain connection to sight and smell and hearing and touch, but this state is a place of comfort and healing, not drowning. Fix that perception in your mind and hold it there as you slip beneath the water.

Theta State (4–7 Hz)

In the theta state, we walk in twilight, sometimes with one foot on one side or the other of consciousness. This is the dreaming gate of ivory and horn, in which we sit just on the boundary of sleep and waking. While in this state, we are ripe for entering possession or aspecting, ready to stand aside for a divine voice. It's debatable whether we remain in theta while in the throes of full-on possession. In some paths, like Haitian Vodou, when you are ridden by a *lwa*, some think that the core personality and awareness of the spirit carrier are no longer there—which actually sounds more like a delta state. In other magickal traditions, aspecting a god or goddess is more like merging divine consciousness with human consciousness. The two speak as one, rather than one moving aside. With possession and aspecting in mind, theta is a good place if you are seeking outside assistance in your magick, or if the task at hand requires disconnection of personal awareness, but with slight tethering to lead you home again.

EXERCISE: SHIFTING INTO THETA

Moving into a theta state is extremely easy, but takes a learned lack of awareness. The theta state is one step deeper than alpha, but not as deep as delta. You must immerse yourself into an action and then let your mind wander as your body runs on muscle memory and autopilot. You can easily find yourself stepping sideways into theta while doing routine tasks like washing dishes or driving home from work. Suddenly, fifteen minutes have passed and your awareness has simply dwindled away on the clouds. Fiber arts like knitting or crocheting are also quite suited to bringing on a theta state, provided your skill is fluid enough. Within a ritual context, you can lose yourself in rocking back and forth while seated, or by tracing spirals on a Troy or Mazy stone—any action that allows your mind to drift off will work.

Gamma State (32–100 Hz)

Gamma waves are the fastest of all the frequencies, and therein lies the flow of our highest cognition, our peak concentration, our *awen* (divine inspiration). Gamma is where your brain goes when it's "in the zone," wallowing deep in a creative project. This is an entirely different experience from the wandering mind we experience when performing actions by rote within theta. Gamma is pure creation. You're happier in gamma—calmer and at peace, more likely to feel compassion. Your focus is enhanced, but not in a way that lets it drill down into a singular point of clarity. In gamma, the experience is more of pure expansion. Focus, in gamma, has flung its arms out wide to take in as much of the whole world as it can at once. It wants it all. Moreover, your brain processes and recalls incredible amounts of information while in gamma, making it an ideal state for retrieving ancestral memories or making connections with the land itself.

EXERCISE: SHIFTING INTO GAMMA

Delivering yourself into gamma doesn't specifically require artistic talent, but it does require creative action in and of itself. You must immerse yourself in a creative act of personal expression, whether by your own artistic nature or by following the direction of another. Drawing, writing poetry, playing music, singing, and even dancing can all serve as suitable vehicles. Not everyone possesses the talent to sculpt marble images true to life, or paint oil portraits that capture light in such a way as to make grown adults weep. But we all hold the ability to express ourselves in some form and that is the essence of gamma.

Trance Inducers

It can prove vastly difficult to shift your consciousness out of alpha or beta and into another level of trance purely by force of will. Our brains are built to flow without deliberate direction, so suddenly diverting your thought stream is an act your awareness may struggle against. Fortunately, there are any number of induction methods that can help facilitate this flow.

How we each choose to reach trance is immensely personal and its success ties directly into the individual witch's personality. The way each person's brain loses itself and becomes fully able to let go of its physical surroundings and conscious awareness depends on an internal knack. It's also entirely possible that one method may be completely useless for you, and it may take a little experimenting with several methods to nail down the one that works best for you. Some may find that they have a wide selection of induction methods at hand; others may find that only one or two methods work sufficiently well for them.

Physical Methods for Inducing Trance

You may find that allowing physical sensations to wash over you in wave after wave of tactile input sends you directly into your desired altered state. Using sex as the essential pivot for trance is a time-honored and well-practiced tradition, as is the infliction of pain. All the normal cautions should apply here. Don't throw away self-responsibility and caution in the name of achieving a perfect trance.

Physical methods can take hundreds, if not thousands, of other forms as well. Some involve a change in breathing patterns, either to increase oxygen or deny it, both of which can change your consciousness. Other types of physical methods include rocking until you lose your equilibrium and ecstatic dancing in which you lose yourself in committed muscle movements using repetitive actions as a focal point. This can lead your awareness away as easily as the Pied Piper led the rats and children out of Hamelin. Combining this method with other ritual actions, like Treading the Mill (see below), can be surprisingly satisfying.

EXERCISE: TREADING THE MILL

This technique was used and popularized by Robert Cochrane in his own coven and the various traditions of witchcraft that followed.

Walking in a circle in combination with the described posture can create a trance state by inhibiting blood flow to the brain by turning your neck.

With your stang raised in the center of your working area, begin walking counterclockwise around it. Close your right eye and lift your left arm so that it is parallel to the floor. Turn your head to the left to look over your shoulder at the stang, while pointing your left index finger at the center of the space. Circle the stang while focusing on it intently. You may find it helpful to perform a chant, or perhaps a particular song, while doing this in order to keep rhythm. Some traditions add "the lame step" in their practice, either to symbolize that they are walking between worlds or to give honor to their tradition's own divine mysteries. The lame step also adds a structured and rhythmic quality to the pace of the movement.

Treading the Mill is generally looked on as a method of ritual trance-induced spirit evocation and conversation. It is a way in which a witch or coven of witches can travel to the Underworld, but can also be used to travel to the Upper World by simply changing your chant and direction. Others insist that it was only a way for Cochrane to teach his debatably oblique mysteries. At its core, however, it does induce trance and can be used for that purpose or combined with a variety of other intents.

Herbal Methods for Inducing Trance

There are three types of herbal preparations that aid in trance induction: incense, smoking blends, and tea. All three methods are rather simple to prepare and very effective, but may not always smell appealing or taste very nice. We try to keep all the senses in mind when making blends, so that working with them isn't entirely unpleasant, but this type of work isn't meant to taste like rock candy or smell like flowers. Most burning flowers smell quite odious, making them ideal for darker forms of magick.

All of the following blends may be used in conjunction with one another, depending on the work performed. There are no baneful herbs in any of these blends; however, all of them should still be used with caution.

None of the blends listed here are safe for women who are currently pregnant, in any gestational state, or trying to conceive.

INCENSE BLENDS

The use of homemade incense blends requires a proper burning container, preferably filled with sand, and a lit incense charcoal. You can get incense charcoal at a metaphysical store or, if you have a local smoke shop that carries hookahs and other smoking implements, they may also sell it. Incense charcoal is very different from the charcoal used in a barbecue or grill, and the two are definitely not interchangeable. Incense charcoals are generally round disks or rectangles of tightly compressed charcoal that are sold in small boxes or foil wrappers. Barbeque briquettes are more pillow-shaped, are quite a bit larger than incense charcoals, and are sold in big bags at hardware stores specifically for barbecuing or grilling. They are not for indoor use at all.

The following incense blends involve working with dried plant material and essential oils. If you use one portion of dried and ground plant material, then all other dry components should also be ground to avoid any lighter bits sifting to the bottom. A coarse grind is fine and powdering it is unnecessary, but your product needs to be consistent.

When using a combination of plants and oils, the basic ratio is one drop of oil to one teaspoon of plant material. Mix your herbs together first, then add the oils and stir thoroughly to ensure an even distribution.

Crossing the Hedge

1 part mugwort (*Artemisia vulgaris*)

2 parts white sage (*Salvia apiana*)

1 part star anise (*Illicium verum*)

Conversing with the Dead

Frankincense (oil)

Myrrh (oil)

1 part dittany of Crete (*Origanum dictamnus*)

2 parts patchouli (*Pogostemon cablin*)

1 part marigold (*Tagetes erecta*)

Protection

1 part rue (*Ruta graveolens*)

Dragon's blood (oil)

2 parts hyssop (*Hyssopus officinalis*)

2 parts lemon verbena (*Aloysia citrodora*)

TEA BLENDS

Brewing and drinking tea to alter your consciousness is an ancient and eternal practice. When done mindfully, the act is sacred unto itself. The entire process is a performance of patience. You heat the water almost to boiling then pour it over herbs, which steep for what seems like the longest of times, but is actually only about three to five minutes. Then you cool the mixture and drink it. Even the amount of time it takes to experience the effects of your brew can seem like forever, but you'll be where you're going before you know it and the whole experience will end in what feels like a blink.

Both tea blends given below will make far more than one serving, so you may either share them with a partner or save what remains for later. For one serving of tea, use one teaspoon of the tea blend for each eight ounces of heated water. Be sure to filter the brewed herbs out and discard them before drinking. A coffee filter is good for this. You don't want to be picking bits of wet plants from your tongue and teeth in the middle of journeying.

Dreaming

1 tsp mugwort (*Artemisia vulgaris*)

1 tsp valerian (*Valeriana officinalis*)

2 tsp catnip (*Nepeta cataria*)

1 tsp clary sage (*Salvia sclarea*)

½ tsp rose hips

2 tsp peppermint (*Mentha x piperita L*)

Seeking Visions

½ tsp wormwood (*Artemisia absinthium*)

1 tsp mugwort (*Artemisia vulgaris*)

1 tbsp lemon balm (*Melissa officinalis*)

SMOKING BLENDS

To smoke an herb is literally to bring it into your body and combine it with your own breath and spirit. By inhaling the spirit of a plant, you grant it permission to live briefly within your blood and bones, beneath your skin, and in your lungs and heart. It's a possession of sorts, these measured inhalations, and they can quickly open doors behind your eyes. It can be easy to lose your way. Be slow to burn and pause as often as you need.

If you live in an area where cannabis is legal, it makes a helpful addition to both of these blends. Just be sure not to add so much that its effects completely take over and leave you in a giggling stupor, desperate for a burrito. *Indica* strains, or preferably an *indica*-leaning hybrid, are best, as they have more sedative qualities than a *sativa*.

A spice grinder can be used to achieve a good consistency. To use either blend, smoke ¼ teaspoon in your favorite smoking apparatus.

Contacting the Ancestors

1 part skullcap (*Scutellaria lateriflora*)

2 parts mugwort (*Artemisia vulgaris*)

2 parts clary sage (*Salvia sclarea*)

½ part lavender (*Lavandula angustifolia*)

Calling Spirits

1 part damiana (*Tunera diffusa*)

1 part passionflower (*Passiflora incarnate*)

2 parts vervain (*Verbena officinalis*)

2 parts mallow (*Malva sylvestris*)

The Poison Path

As discussed in chapter 5, a witch's garden contains a great variety of extraordinarily powerful and dangerous plant allies. From time immemorial, witches have held a reputation as poisoners. One could argue that the long-held common mistrust of witches stems directly from their knowledge of plants and herbs. The average person prefers to keep as far away from the fragile line between death and life as possible. So they are loathe to look upon the faces of those who not only tread this line quite willingly, but also have the ability to inflict pain and suffering on others with what they know. As with all of the other witchcraft paths, working with poisons is not a comfortable place for innocent passersby to be. They look sidewise at those on the Poison Path and view them with fear and trepidation, as if poisons were something virulent and contagious, something whose effects can be transmitted through direct sight alone.

At the core of the Poison Path is a working knowledge of *entheogens*—any substance with psychoactive properties used to induce a spiritual experience. The word itself, which comes from the Greek, translates as "generating the divine within." In essence, entheogens are simply drugs that may assist your spiritual endeavors. In *Veneficium: Magic, Witchcraft, and the Poison Path*, Daniel Schulke puts forth several categories of drugs—sacred, libertine, efficient, and philosophical. Poison lies outside of these categories; it sits beyond the singular act of taking drugs just to get high or commune with the nine billion names of God. It stands as a representative of magickal power itself and indicates the teetering point on which witches must always stand to achieve their goals. This fulcrum is the heart of witchcraft, the very soul of the Crooked Path itself.

Poisoners don't seek to harm or kill their perceived enemies through Borgia-inspired machinations or surreptitious draughts of death-dealing potions. Instead, they seek congress with spirits and aspire to mystical knowledge. Traveling the Poison Path is how they accomplish this. In *Veneficium*, Schulke describes the formula of Gnostic Poisoning—a spectrum that shows healing at one end and harming at the other, with divine madness at the very center. This road between benefic and malefic clearly illustrates the way of the poisoner. It shows us where we need to fly.

It must be noted, quite loudly and at great length, that this is not a prescription for any witch to start quaffing huge amounts of nightshades in an effort to see the face of God. Working with entheogens, with poisons, is not something you should ever undertake lightly, no matter how benign the plants you are using may seem. We strongly recommend that witches who wish to embark on the Poison Path spend several years growing the plants themselves before they ever try to ingest one in any fashion. Growing plants on your own forges a connection with them, creating bonds between you and your plant allies—bonds that strengthen as time goes on.

Those walking the Poison Path (or any other type of magickal road, for that matter) must never rest on their laurels, thinking they hold all the available knowledge on their chosen subject. Therein lie only arrogance and distraction, both of which can prove disastrous to witches who (willfully or not) fail to enter into each working with virgin eyes, with humility and discernment, to avoid falling prey to hubris.

Soul Flight

Behind all of this talk of trance states and brain waves lies one immense purpose—soul flight. Soul flight, or astral projection as some call it, is the act of detaching your spirit and sending it out from your body into the world—whether this world or any beyond. It is the crux of all hedge crossing; without soul flight, witches cannot journey.

The trick to successful soul flight lies in simple visualizations often associated with daily or regular ritual experience. For example, visualizations directly employed in such rituals as the Lesser Banishing Ritual of the Pentagram, the Middle Pillar, or the Star Ruby (all similar rites) involve seeing symbols in the air and visualizing the circulation of energy in the form of Light. Without the ability to form a full-blown visualization, however, these rituals all fall apart rather quickly. With this in mind, witches should seek to bring their visualization skills to optimal levels. The stronger your visualizing, the more *real* your experience becomes. The more immersed you are, the stronger your magick.

EXERCISE: ATTAINING SOUL FLIGHT—PART 1

Envision an apple. Bring your point of focus to the experience of touching, holding, and eating the apple and how it relates to the five senses. How does it feel? Is its skin slick to the touch or slightly rough? Does it have heft in your hand? How does it sound when you tap it with your finger? Finally, when you have all of the apple aspects fixed in your brain, bite into it. How does it feel to sink your teeth into its flesh, down to its heart? What does it taste like? Does it go down easy or put up a fight when you swallow? Are you still hungry after eating it? Try to feel the nutrients from the apple spreading throughout your body.

EXERCISE: ATTAINING SOUL FLIGHT—PART 2

Now get outside your head. Sit comfortably in a room where you will be undisturbed. Pick an object in that room and feel it with your mind in the same way you did the apple. If the object is not of the edible sort, don't eat it, but go through steps similar to those you used with the apple. Examine the object from all angles and avenues. When you've explored it thoroughly, envision another version of yourself sitting face to face before you. This other you is your astral self. If you have to, close your physical eyes. When you are ready, move your consciousness to your astral self and begin observing the room from the perspective of this other you. Try to be completely within your astral body, experiencing the world from where it sits. Look at the room and your physical body seated before you. What sits behind the physical you? How does the room look? Examine all of these things.

EXERCISE: ATTAINING SOUL FLIGHT—PART 3

After you feel comfortable enough in this other you, stand up and walk around, without noticing what your actual physical body is experiencing. Allow all your awareness and senses to be present to what your astral body is experiencing. Once you have gotten a firm grasp on inducing this at will, there are no limitations to what your experiences may hold for you.

With this level of focus fully attained, you can begin to explore the rest of the world and the cosmos. You can create an astral temple or memory palace and even do full works of ritual and magick. You can visit beings and speak with them; you can embark on journeys, like traveling the Sephiroth on the Tree of Life or moving throughout the three worlds of the World Tree. So many avenues are open once you've achieved soul flight with proper understanding.

Shapeshifting

In the context of witchcraft, shapeshifting is the act of magickally transforming a piece of your spirit into a beast and sending it forth. It does not involve literally transforming yourself into the shape of an animal. In some cultures, this spirit is called a *fetch*. In the practice below, this spirit leaves your body to embark on a variety of journeys across our world, as well as the Upper World and the Underworld—not to mention worlds beyond.

You may sometimes hear shapeshifting connected to astral projection or called skin-slipping. A theta-level trance is ideal for shapeshifting through mimicry, while a delta trance is optimal for shapeshifting through trance.

EXERCISE: SHAPESHIFTING THROUGH MIMICRY

There are a few methods for shapeshifting. Some involve taking psychoactive substances to alter your consciousness. You can costume yourself as your chosen animal to further convince yourself of the change. You can even go as far as to crawl about on all fours, or bonelessly slither about, or howl, or hiss. Disguising yourself in this way brings your brain more into the moment. If you are able to overcome the nagging pressures of self-consciousness and an underlying sense of silliness, you'll find this a successful enough method.

EXERCISE: SHAPESHIFTING THROUGH TRANCE

Another way to go about shapeshifting—one dependent upon strong visualization and a thoroughly developed ability for soul flight—is to bring yourself deep into trance with the pure intention of either hitching a ride under an animal's skin or transmuting your spirit into the shape of an animal and traveling thus. Your spirit, either hidden deep in the whorls of a beast's heart or existing in the shape of another, can then go anywhere it pleases—into the forest for a run, down to the Underworld to converse with the dead, or out into the Upper World for any number of divine pursuits. Any of these methods are effective. It just depends on how you want to go and what you want to achieve.

Familiar Spirits

Hedges aren't only borders that delineate one area from another and specify lines of demarcation; they are also homes. Within any hedge there exists a wide variety of life—animals and insects and plants that are separate from the hedge itself. The places between worlds, the hedges we cross as witches, are much the same. They contain a multitude of spirits and other life-forms with which we can connect.

The concept of the familiar is one of the aspects from the history of witchcraft that has been co-opted by many modern practitioners, either to further enhance their ownership of a black cat or some other suitably spooky pet, or to give them some sort of "witch cred" that validates their witchy lifestyle. These individuals tend to be the same ones who do little research into their craft beyond the initial exposure they received and appear to be in it only for notoriety among the slightly more mundane people around them. Beyond that sort, there are those who believe familiars are merely pets with whom they hold an extraordinary bond. While neither of these ways of thought are generally harmful in and of themselves, this is not what familiars actually are.

The idea of the familiar started sometime during the 14th century, when it was believed they were sent to witches by the devil himself for their use in magick—treasured gifts received upon initiation, a gesture of appreciation for joining the team, so to speak. Familiars were spirit helpers who lived with witches and followed them around, giving them advice and helping them perform their magick. Some confusion arose about witches and their familiars when the idea of shapeshifting was thrown into the mix, causing witches to be thought of as actually becoming the familiar itself. It was also commonly believed that, if you killed the familiar, you destroyed the witch as well—an efficient way of getting rid of witches for those foolish enough to try, at least until they realized they'd murdered the beloved cat of the village cut-wife and now she's *pissed*.

According to Emma Wilby in *Cunning Folk and Familiar Spirits*, familiars were "commonly employed to use their magickal powers to help cunning folk in their attempt to discover the whereabouts of lost goods, identify criminals, and divine the future." At the time, cunning folk were mostly looked upon as beneficial to have around and were largely not treated the same as witches, although they were really just two sides of the same coin—something that individual cunning folk would sadly find when Inquisitors rolled into their village. Familiars were believed to have been given to witches by some power beyond, usually fairies, and were looked on as the source of their abilities. They were seen as a cherished gift whose entire purpose was to assist. Prior to the official demonization of witchcraft later enacted by the Witchcraft Act of 1542 under Henry VIII (repealed in 1547, but then returned under a new bill in 1563), these trusty spirit helpers were sometimes thought to be trolls, dwarves, elves, fairies, or other fantastic or mythical beings. Andro Man, a Scottish cunning man from Aberdeenshire who went under trial in 1598, claimed to have a familiar by the name of Christsonday, who served the queen of the fairies and held all the power of God.

In Puritan America, familiars were never even remotely considered as gifts. Instead, they served as hard proof that accused witches had sold themselves to the devil and were seen as the rewards for such diabolical covenants. In this environment, familiars were more demonic and their purpose was to hurt those against whom they were directed. They fed on the blood of witches through "witch's teats," unnatural protrusions on witches' bodies. This concept wasn't unique to America and the Puritan witch craze, however. Accused witches on both continents were stripped naked by their accusers and searched for any possible mole, birthmark, or fleabite that could be declared as a teat and thus evidence of malefice.

In modern witchcraft, proper familiars are generally considered to be incorporeal, without a specific form or body. They do not normally feed on blood from witches' bodies and are not proof that individuals have sold their souls to the devil. They are seen rather as helpmeet spirits, sometimes with specific purposes and time frames in mind. While the familiars that Wilby spoke of were primarily visual experiences, these modern familiars interact with their witches during journey work, or in hedge crossings, meditations, and trance work. Individual witches may envision their familiars with a specific shape or body, as it is easier to work with an entity you are able to understand or identify. It's not necessary, however.

Just as with the historical familiar spirits of yore, familiars today can fulfill any number of tasks. Generally, they act as protectors or guardians of a particular place dear to their witches. They may also be employed to watch over the body of a witch during acts of soul flight, or leaned on for power transfer in spell work. Or they may be spirits with whom a witch has become companionable through frequency of contact. Just as with corporeal personalities, the more you engage favorably with someone, the more they will enjoy your company purely for the sake of your company. Familiars are like friends to their witches—like family. The relationship between them is more one of a balanced give and take than one of servitude.

As spirits of service and companionship, familiars can be obtained in several different ways. Some believe every witch has a familiar—a lid to every pot—and that they only need to make contact with this already present spirit. Other familiars are found much like any other friend might be—through interaction with your surroundings. Still, you can find and begin working with familiars by intentionally petitioning one for its service. All of these ways are valid. No single one is better than another. It only depends on how you wish to go about this.

FINDING YOUR FAMILIAR

To discover your personal familiar, you will need to perform a working. Put on any protective jewelry you feel is necessary. (Wearing your sovereignty cord is also recommended.) Perform the Crossroads Rite (see chapter 1) on the night of a waxing moon, using your blackthorn cane to establish a liminal space. Sit or lie in the center of that space while burning an incense made from equal parts wormwood and angelica. This facilitates spirit contact and encourages visions. Sit with the incense for a few moments, allowing it to work its effect on you, and then say:

> *Familiar spirit of my soul,*
> *Please make your presence known.*
> *Familiar spirit of my head*
> *From birth, through life, till I am dead*
> *Familiar spirit of my flesh,*
> *Show yourself at my request.*

Close your eyes and wait to see if your familiar makes itself known. If it does, try to engage it in conversation. Learn about it. Ask its name. Get a feel for its personality. How can you call upon it from here on out? Take this opportunity to become familiar with your familiar.

PETITIONING A FAMILIAR

As mentioned before, sometimes you may want to call upon a specific familiar for a particular task.

For this ritual, you will need:

- A small bowl or glass of milk
- A cauldron that contains an ounce of Florida Water
- Loose incense (equal parts wormwood, angelica, and meadowsweet)
- An appropriate vessel for burning the incense
- A piece of incense charcoal
- A white candle
- A 4-inch square of unlined paper
- A black pen
- A red pen

On the full moon, place the milk on the windowsill, being sure to catch the moon's glow in its surface if it is visible. Set up your incense, candle, and cauldron on a surface suitable for the working. With your candle lit and the incense burning, say aloud the following incantation and use your black pen to draw the familiar-summoning sigil shown in Figure 30 on your piece of paper:

Figure 30. Familiar-summoning sigil.

By the light of the moon, I offer up food
To request the service of a familiar spirit
For one lunar cycle from now
To fulfill a need and a job be done.

Over the sigil, write in red ink what you wish the spirit to do. Roll up the parchment tightly and light it on fire using the candle. Quickly and carefully, toss the burning paper into your cauldron, into which you have already poured the Florida Water. Be careful; the solution should ignite immediately, bearing a blue flame that licks the cauldron's inner walls. The flames should be manageable, but keep them away from anything flammable. Concentrate on the flames until they go out, then say:

The deal is made, the spirit has come
To seek to do the deed prescribed.
Upon the sill, you shall be fed
For your efforts, fresh milk and bread
On a daily basis, until again,
The moon grows full and bright.
Til that time you shall be known,
As (name the familiar).
As I will it, it shall be so!

From this day forward, until the next full moon, be sure to keep your familiar fed as agreed. You can communicate with it either aloud or through scrying, dreams, or some other method. When the next full moon comes, simply honor the committed contract and stop feeding the spirit. If you need more time to complete your original task, you can always re-petition it.

A Brief Dose of Reality

A smart witch will take caution when practicing soul flight or shape-shifting, as dangers always exist. Don't take yourself so deep that you lose your way home—don't forget you are actually human, standing upright in skin, fangless, clawless, wingless. Also, be sure not to go too far in your trance and become stuck there—for instance, in a coma or unconsciousness, or in an overdose of entheogens. If your spirit becomes untethered and loses its finite connection to your body, whether by physical reaction to substances or magickal attack in other realms, it can definitely be a threat to your well-being.

To avoid peril, be smart in your practice. Set up tethers that your spirit can find to help it quickly bring itself home. Tie one of your limbs to something physical in the Middle World, or carry protective sigils and talismans with you. In her excellent essay on shapeshifting, herbalist Sarah Anne Lawless recommends having a return incantation as a possible precaution.[3] She specifically mentions Isobel Gowdie's chant:

Hare, hare, God send thee care.
I am in a hare's likeness now,
But I shall be in a woman's likeness even now.

Of course, it's always best if you can come up with one of your own.

It's also important to understand that entheogens and psychoactive substances are only *assistants* within your work as a whole—particularly in hedge crossing, where they are used the most. They should never be taken in such doses as to be considered reckless or with such frequency that they become a crutch. Think critically and go into any rite or action with eyes fully open. Our sovereign nature as witches

---

3   Sarah A. Lawless, "On Shapeshifting," *sarahannelawless.com*, April 14, 2010.

isn't just about waving the banner of freedom; it's also intrinsically tied into the concept of wild survival. That which survives is smart. *That's how it survives.*

SUGGESTED READING

Cunning Folk and Familiar Spirits: Shamanistic Visionary Traditions in Early Modern British Witchcraft and Magic, by Emma Wilby.

Witches, Werewolves, and Fairies: Shapeshifters and Astral Doubles in the Middle Ages, by Claude Lecouteux.

Witchcraft and the Shamanic Journey: Pagan Folkways from the Burning Times, by Kenneth Johnson.

To Fly by Night: The Craft of the Hedgewitch, edited by Veronica Cummer.

Animal-Speak: The Spiritual and Magical Powers of Creatures Great and Small, by Ted Andrews.

CHAPTER 10

The Witches' Sabbat

One of the most alluring concepts found in the folklore surrounding witchcraft is the Witches' Sabbat. Steeped in mystery and controversy, this event has survived well into the 21st century by way of the modern witchcraft movement, and fascination with it shows no signs of stopping. Although the sabbats found in some forms of today's witchcraft tend to be a bit more sanitized and involve far less heresy, blood, and orgiastic sex, the inner flames of the Witches' Sabbat still clearly burn in the hearts and minds of those who convene in darkest night to practice their craft. After all, the sabbat is where we witches gather to be among our own. It's where we call the dead down to dance among the spirits, where we seek knowledge and wisdom not found anywhere else on earth. Witches are the ones who dare to walk in this fire, with the sky and stars spinning wild overhead. The song of the sabbat is ever in our bones.

What's in a Name?

The origin of the word *sabbat* is often just as controversial as the historical veracity of the gathering itself, with scholars divided on both. Italian scholar Carlo Ginzburg, in his 1989 book *Ecstasies:*

Deciphering the Witches' Sabbath, argues a connection to the Sabbath, as in Saturday, the Jewish day of rest and observance. He presents a direct correlation between the anti-witch hysteria and the anti-Semitism that persisted in areas of Europe throughout the Early Modern Period. Early 20th-century scholar Dr. Margaret Murray dismissed this notion a half century earlier in her iconic book *The Witch-Cult in Western Europe*. In her book, Murray suggests that the word "Sabbath" itself is possibly derived from the Old French word *s'esbattre*, meaning "to frolic" or "to amuse oneself." Other experts, like Montague Summers in his *History of Witchcraft and Demonology*, cite a relationship to the Phrygian deity Sabazios—specifically, his connection to Dionysus, as noted by the Greeks. This Dionysian connection is especially noteworthy, as author and historian Jeffrey B. Russell states, because the Bacchanalia, the Roman version of a Dionysian cult gathering, was actually a prototype for the famed Witches' Sabbat. These Roman gatherings bear a distinct similarity to the lecherous aspects and appetites of the Witches' Sabbat, in particular those involving drunken revelry, ecstatic dance, veneration of spirits, and good old-fashioned sexual escapades with strangers and friends.

In our practice, we agree with Ginzburg on the origins and use of the word "sabbat" in conjunction with the Jewish day of rest. This Saturday connection becomes even more significant when we consider *The Key of Solomon the King*, as it dictates that Saturn-day is the best day for acts of necromancy. Moreover, sabbat lore itself developed during a similar period in which Jewish people were persecuted by the local authorities and the Catholic Church. The start of the witch trials in Spain during the 14th century coincided with the advent of the Inquisition and the return of the Black Plague, a horror that both Jewish people and suspected witches were thought to have had a hand in creating.

Jewish people accused of crimes (usually the crime of just being Jewish, it should be noted) were fairly easy to recognize and their communities were easily located. The elusive witches, however, with their secret gatherings and supposed allegiance to the devil, represented a far more intimidating and mysterious threat. Anyone could be a witch, hiding in plain sight. It is possible, therefore, that sabbat lore was born alongside this campaign of fear and paranoia so that the lurid tales could be used to incriminate those accused of witchcraft with charges more definitive than just the nebulous "cavorting with the devil."

The Historical Sabbat

During the Early Modern Period, the notion of the Witches' Sabbat (and witches in general) stood as the epitome of human fear and scandal among everyday citizens. By its very nature and its ties to sin and heresy, witchcraft represented the height of all transgressions; it was the worst accusation that could be made. Throughout human history, pointing a righteous finger at a portion of the population for whatever self-serving reason was not out of the ordinary, and we see these actions deeply ingrained in society even today. In retrospect, we can see the concern over witchcraft, which existed outside of normal conventions and appeared to be almost untouchable, as an early "tinfoil-hat" theory promulgated to stir up and unite the mindless masses against a vague and ambiguous threat.

The idea of a devilish communal gathering gave Inquisitors an opportunity to indict other supposed witches, undesirables, and outcasts by association. The trials even proved to be useful arenas in which corruption, land theft, and revenge for infidelity could all be played out with little or no risk to accusers. Indeed, it was almost impossible to stand against an accusation of witchcraft and be declared innocent. The trials themselves developed into a booming industry throughout Europe, with a brief and violent appearance in Salem, Massachusetts, in 1692. The reality of the Witches' Sabbat continues to be a mystery in more than one sense, even in the 21st century.

Was the Witches' Sabbat a real and in-person event? Or was it a type of communal shamanic experience accessed through dreams and soul flight? These questions continue to be debated among experts.

Murray—who, for better or worse, plays a heavy role in the modern witchcraft movement—felt that sabbats were indeed actual events. Ginzburg, meanwhile, related them to acts of astral projection, of soul flight. This theory was heavily endorsed by other scholars like Emma Wilby and Éva Pócs, as well as modern practitioners who follow the path of Andrew Chumbley. The strange irony in discussing the lore and reality of the Witches' Sabbat is that, as an actual event, it probably never existed in any specific or literal sense as physically flying to a location to have congress with the devil and other revelers. Instead, it more likely represented just the demonization of prevailing folk celebrations. Indeed, the main problem when considering if the Witches' Sabbat was an actual event or a shamanic journey is that, historically speaking, we can find practices suggesting both.

Accounts of events (which could easily have been demonized by Inquisitors) as well as episodes of shamanic soul flight can be found throughout Europe. Dionysian gatherings, the hilltop celebrations on Bald Mountain or Brocken peak for Hexennacht, and other similar cultural gatherings may all have contributed heavily to sabbat lore with their fire festivals, their dancing and chanting, their drinking and feasting, and their sexual excesses. Certain witch trial confessions, like that of Jeanette Clerc in 1539, implied the use of entheogenic ointments and substances to aid in soul flight, and this is not dissimilar to methodologies used in shamanic journeying.

Emma Wilby also points out that there are undeniable similarities between journeying to the sabbat and visiting a fairy revel, as explained in some Scottish witch trial records. Wilby writes in particular of Isobel Gowdie, whose confessions sometimes blurred the lines between whether she feasted with the devil or the fairies—an interesting notion when one takes into account how often fairies were broadly connected with the devil. Fairies had once been viewed very differently by the common population, with an established (albeit sometimes uneasy) relationship between human and fairy, but that eventually underwent a definitive and literal demonization.

This transformation was due largely to the regents and churches of the time making sweeping pronouncements against any perceived devilry—for instance in the Scottish Witchcraft Act of 1563 promulgated by the parliament of Mary, Queen of Scots, or in treatises like *Daemonologie,* written in 1597 by Mary's son, James. And that's just in Isobel Gowdie's home country of Scotland alone. Beyond Scotland, philosopher Thomas Hobbes wrote in *Leviathan* (1651) that fairies served Beelzebub, whom he calls "prince of demons." English Parliamentarian Reginald Scot implied, in his 1584 work *The Discovery of Witchcraft,* that the devil encouraged belief in false spirits (fairies) in an effort to have humans expose themselves to Satan and turn away from God's grace.

So it appears that Gowdie's confusion may have hinted at a larger truth—that fairy revels and Witches' Sabbats do, in fact, contain many of the same elements. Accounts of both show wild dancing, feasting, copious drink or other inebriants, animalistic sex, and the reverent worship of those plainly against God—the devil or the King and Queen of Fairy. Given Gowdie's status as an illiterate farmwoman, we can probably assume that she was never in possession of any finger-pointing diatribes decrying fairy beliefs. However, she was raised in a culture heavily influenced by them, with one foot still firmly rooted in the old traditions.

Elements of the Sabbat

Historical accounts and descriptions of the Witches' Sabbat often contain similar elements and/or themes that can enhance our practice as witches. While the following may not be relevant for everyone, the various components given here should be considered—even if they seem superfluous—as they provide us with insight and a usable framework.

The Masked Procession

Masked ritual processions often led by a Queen or King were just as common in past celebrations as they are now for holidays and parades. Donning a new face or temporary social status enables attendees to transcend reality and play out different ritual roles, but also allows them to release from their common selves and engage with the spirit of the nightly gathering.

The ritual Queens and Kings embodied divine or sacred roles of spiritual authority and significance. And, while animal masks can assist in shapeshifting, the masks of ghosts, spirits, and demons also helped practitioners survive the evenings when those beings were more prevalent on the earthly plane. In her confession and description of the sabbat, Isobel Gowdie spoke of attendees arriving and leaving in animal form. Was she referring to the practice of shapeshifting or just the wearing of masks? Or, as we so frequently find on the Crooked Path, is the answer both? Does someone wearing a rabbit mask not only take on the appearance of a rabbit and assume its qualities, but also actually become a rabbit on some level?

The procession itself also serves as a shamanistic journey to another plane of existence for the duration of the night's celebrations. Revelers literally move from one plane to another, in all senses of the word. In their movement, they change and take their bodies and spirits to another place.

Sacrifice

Sacrifice is often viewed as a dirty word in modern witchcraft circles and communities. For our ancestors, however, sacrifice was a means of personal responsibility and survival. In the context of the historical Witches' Sabbat, sacrifice often alludes to the ritual killing of an animal (as given in some older grimoires) or of a human baby in order to use the child's fat to make unguents. This alleged practice resulted in witches being accused of stealing the babies of townsfolk and villagers for use in grim ointments, and eating the remainder of their tender bodies once the fat had been extracted for their purposes.

While we are certainly not making a claim that the ritual killing of children was an actual practice, it was certainly something of concern for Inquisitors and was a frequent charge in many witch trials, particularly in areas where children had recently disappeared. Despite the fact that these children could have gone missing for any number of reasons not related to witchcraft, these accusations served as another bit of propaganda put forth to horrify and heighten the distaste and disgust for any act of witchery among the masses. The spurious charges were then used to justify the torture and execution of those under suspicion or deemed guilty. Older woodcut images of witches cavorting with the devil often include people handing over babies to him for some nefarious purpose—whether as an offering, a blessing, a payment, or an after-sabbat snack.

Conceptually, the notion of sacrifice is about submitting to loss in an effort to fulfill a higher purpose. We give up something dear for the sake of attaining something better. The idea of sacrifice thus plays alongside the notion of sovereignty, which sits at the very core of any magickal practice. Self-governance and control sit within the shadow of sacrifice and the decisions we knowingly make. Another way of looking at sacrifice is to see it as an act of metamorphosis. To sacrifice something—from the Latin *sacra* (sacred things) and *facere* (to do or perform)—is literally to "make something sacred." The act itself transforms the object of sacrifice from something mundane into something holy and divine; offering it to deities or spirits completes this ascension.

Initiation

Buried at the core of modern witchcraft dwells the concept and controversy of initiation, which, by its very nature, is a transformative act of rebirth and new beginnings. Initiation, the formal process of being brought into a practice by another, is an act many believe to be necessary in order to become a witch. This view of initiation, however, begs the question of who initiated the first witch. Some traditions look to different gods or goddesses, the King or Queen of Elphame, Aradia, or Tubal Cain for the answer. However, the history and lore of the Witches' Sabbat maintains instead that witches are initiated by the devil himself—an act that often includes some of the reconfirmation aspects of the Black Mass.

According to Isobel Gowdie, aspects of a witch's initiation typically involved signing the devil's black book, being marked by him (usually by being bitten), being baptized by the devil with the blood of that wound, and being given a new name. All these actions represent deep transgressions against everything considered good and godly by societal norms. Stepping outside of the cultural bubble is considered empowering within any initiation and can be seen as an actual act of freedom—setting aside previously confining chains to embark on a new life. That's what an initiation is meant to do at its heart—change your life, open your eyes to a new world of perception. This is the main purpose and drive of all initiations.

Initiations—whether into a tribe, gang, lodge, fraternity, or sorority—are often accompanied by an ordeal that initiates undergo either before or after the initiation itself occurs. The ordeals given in historical accounts of witchcraft include the renunciation of a formerly held religious belief, participation in the initiatory process itself, or other acts like copulating with the devil. The ordeal challenges initiates, giving them an opportunity to show their worth and their desire for the benefits about to be conferred on them. Such participation says: "I want to be part of this so much that I am willing to go through this horrible thing, all just to prove how much I want this and how worthy I am of this notice." It is a close cousin to sacrifice.

In the ritual at the end of chapter 1, the ordeal prescribed is the performance of the ritual itself. On the surface, journeying into the outdoors to experience and perform the ritual without knowing what may happen seems like such a small step, but it is not, particularly if you go at it completely alone. Many people in this modern age have no concept of what it feels like to enter the wilderness alone, especially those more accustomed to suburban or urban environments. The wilderness is a very frightening place to dwell in for an extended period of time for the *uninitiated*.

The Black Mass

The Black Mass, along with the blatant acts of heresy associated with it, can easily be regarded as a performance of personal liberation from religious authority and persecution. It represents a complete regaining of self and a spitting in the face of spiritual oppression and the threat of eternal damnation. Arguably, taking part in a Black Mass is an initiation act all its own.

It's safe to say that the fascination and hysteria regarding witches during the height of the witch trials, combined with a fear of anti-Christian backlash, caused the (mis)understandings and (mis)information about them to snowball into an incestuous knowledge loop that drew in the various "experts" of the day. This resulted in a list of alleged heretical acts that were a reflection of what an anti-Christian ceremony might be. Inquisitors viewed the Black Mass as the ultimate act of heresy against the Church. Alleged Mass-related activities included kissing the devil's anus, stomping on the cross, desecrating the host, renouncing Christ or the sacrament of baptism, killing and eating babies, and sex with animals, other people, or the devil himself. Indeed, the Black Mass included nearly every horrendous act a depraved soul could muster up.

The Mass provided an added opportunity for witches to prove continued allegiance to the devil by listing all the evil acts they had committed since the last gathering—resulting in an inventory of worthy villainy served up for their master's approval. This is a strange reversal of Catholic confession, when you think about it. Witnesses to the sabbat, and to the Horned Lord himself, might easily have been observing just a masked participant playing the role of the devil or fulfilling some kind of role as the ritual King for the night. One origin myth of Herne the Hunter involved him wearing the head of the deer who killed him in order to resurrect his body. It's all completely plausible. In some modern practices and traditions, a similar type of mask or helmet is often worn that would certainly appear quite frightening to any outsider when viewed from afar during a midnight stroll.

Ecstatic Dance

Within the revelry of the Witches' Sabbat lies a key ritual component that can be found in tribal and shamanic practices all around the world—ecstatic dance. Combined with a blazing campfire and proper music, ecstatic dance is an unbridled form of dance meant to be trance-inducing and meditative, because it does not require strict mental focus or thought. While typical meditation is about calming the body and mind to achieve a particular state of awareness, ecstatic dance takes the opposite route by over-exciting the mind and body to achieve a point of stillness, calm, and release within a sea of chaos—like the eye of a tornado. This technique is about letting go completely. Participants often lose sense of themselves as they merge clear minds and bodies with the music played. Masks depicting animals or spirits can be worn to encourage this loss of identity, thus helping participants to let go and facilitating a mental and spiritual transformation. When these dances are performed at night, the flickering ambient light from a campfire naturally alters participants' perceptions.

Visions and possession can occur during sessions of ecstatic dance, as chemicals in the brain are released and combine with any entheogens in use. Long periods of dance cause the release of serotonin, epinephrine, and dopamine in the brain—all of which elevate the dancer's mood. The additional release of endorphins contributes to a sense of euphoria, along with an increased tolerance for pain. The ability to ignore pain completely, and apparently bear no physical impact from it, is an effect often observed in Vodou ceremonies as signs of possession manifest themselves in ritual participants and those ridden by their *lwa* are whipped to greater frenzy.

The wearing of loose—or little to no—clothing can help dancers achieve completely uninhibited freedom of movement. However, constant movement from long periods of dance can result in dehydration without dancers even realizing it. Be sure to hydrate properly both before and after engaging in ecstatic dance to avoid this.

Feasting

Isobel Gowdie spoke of feasting at the Witches' Sabbat in her confessions, in conjunction with visiting the King and Queen of Elphame. It makes sense, since the sabbat was often thought of as a celebration or gathering, almost like an office party for the associates of hell. However, with the sabbat feasting, there never seemed to be any concern of being trapped there, as one risks when visiting the fairies. Sabbat feasting may also have involved the consumption of entheogenic substances to help with journeying, and so may have served a ritual function, rather than just a purely celebratory one.

From a practical perspective, the consumption of food is a very grounding act that can be employed at the end of a rite. The inebriating effects of alcohol can also be quelled by food, and eating quickly lessens the trance state resulting from ritual fasting or dancing on an empty stomach, something needed to come back to the Middle World and leave the fantastical behind. Even further, breaking bread with others shows respect and mutual acceptance, and the shared experience of eating a delicious meal with others lies at the very core of community and our humanity. Food is primal.

Maleficia

While harmful magick to cast injury and misfortune upon others (*maleficia*) was known to be performed at the Witches' Sabbat, spirits and the magick they produced could be either harmful or beneficial. Their maleficia was not always indicative of the performers' base nature. Demon or fairy folk were both petitioned to perform acts of healing as well as cruelty. Isobel Gowdie and Italian witch Maria Panzona[4] both confessed to learning about healing modalities from the devil—a statement we can take as evidence of the dual purpose and usefulness of witchcraft and the resounding "grayness" of it, despite attempts to view all magick as either entirely black or entirely white.

The Witches' Sabbat thus appears to have been an opportunity for great learning—a sort of "convention" for the general performance of magick. Acknowledging that maleficia was one of its aspects may simply have reflected the common viewpoint of witches and witchcraft in the days of Gowdie and Panzona. Remember, however, that the idea that the practice of magick was diabolical by its very nature and indicative of transgression shows a true lack of understanding of the deeper role and significance that magick can play in the world.

Sexual Frenzy

Communal sex, in conjunction with feasting and revelry, is something that persists in modern society. Bar and club scenes may not erupt into a wild sexual frenzy after a few hours of sloppy drinking and licentious dancing, but participants do often travel home together at the end of the night to engage in further intimate shenanigans. These "rituals" may reflect a modern version of a Dionysian cult gathering, minus the sacrifice and infused instead with fried food, light beer, and bad haircuts. Arguably, the DJs, wait staff, and bartenders are unknowing servants to the god of wine and debauchery himself. What energy these ribald evenings must generate!

Of course, many discussions about sex during the sabbat involved carnal relations with anyone and anything. Little stood in the way of revelers and their pursuit of animalistic pleasure. Such tales are either demonstrative of the uninhibited manifesting frenzy, or they may just have been an entertaining way to freak out Inquisitors by telling

---

4   Carlo Ginzburg, *The Night Battles: Witchcraft and Agrarian Cults in the Sixteenth and Seventeenth Centuries*, Johns Hopkins University Press, 1983, pp. 100–101.

them exactly what they wanted to hear in the first place. Consider, however, that if shapeshifting, mask wearing, and animal mimicry were practiced at the sabbat, "sex with animals" takes on a different connotation entirely and may not pertain to actual bestiality.

In a Dionysian sense, the sexual frenzy described at sabbats was all a part of the ecstatic worship and drunken madness exhibited by those in attendance and played a central role in the success of the ceremonies. The racheting up of this frenzied power, fueled by wine and song and orgies, resulted in an all-night affair that throbbed and pulsated and shrieked until the cock crowed at dawn.

The Sabbat and Modern Witchcraft

As societies change, the common folk are often the last to transition into new ways of thinking and living. Indeed, it is futile to expect old and beloved traditions to fade out or accommodate burgeoning cultural ideals or religions. Change will eventually occur, as change is an inevitable and inescapable force—but at a snail's pace. As Christianity grew and became the norm in Europe, older ways of thinking and relating to the world became less acceptable and more threatening. This resulted in the condemnation, and even whole-cloth eradication, of existing folk traditions that preserved earlier religious and spiritual practices. The mention of magick or spirit helpers and the possession of any unusual books or paraphernalia came to be seen as an existential threat by those who sought to replace the old ways. It was often this fear and concern that caused passages of the Christian Bible to be incorporated into incantations and ancient grimoires to make them heavily favor the power of the Christian God.

Ritualized agricultural celebrations of all types were common in the countryside, both before and after Christianity swept over the land. People lived and died based on the success of the harvest, so completely eradicating these festivals from the hearts and minds of those who lived close to the land was nigh-on impossible. Back-country areas were more removed from the Church's eye, so it was common for celebrations that took place in these rural areas to be less influenced by both regent law and Christian doctrine. Thus these observances resembled the traditional Witches' Sabbat more than others and were of particular concern to those who feared the older ways.

In modern witchcraft and Neo-Paganism, sabbats relate largely to the yearly course of the sun. A series of eight holy days, derived from the harvest cycles and often collectively referred to as the Wheel of the Year, are generally observed by a large majority of modern witches and/or Pagans. The modern Wheel of the Year is cobbled together from a variety of different Pagan sources, deriving mostly from Celtic and Germanic traditions and their yearly points of celebration. These holidays center around the solstices, equinoxes, and cross-quarter days—the days midway between equinox and solstice—and have an agricultural significance relevant to the cultures from which they came.

As a coven, path, and tradition, Blacktree specifically does not follow this system and holds no particular reverence for an agrarian calendar of holy days that (we feel) has little or no personal significance to our lives. We may connect deeply with the land and work with its spirits in our witchcraft, even to the point of stewarding our own green places, but we are by no means farmers. There is simply nothing for us in the focus on the rise and fall of the crops as it relates to mythical birth/life/death observations. We most assuredly recognize our extreme privilege in this regard, however. To acknowledge the separation of our importance and impact in the food-supply chain is not a boastful statement by any means, nor is it an especially pleasant one. Acknowledging our distance from these cycles indicates a sacrifice of control and a willingness to acknowledge our smallness in the grand scheme of things. We may live alongside nature and revere it; we acknowledge its power and give it true honor and dues. But nature does not need us and will thrive when we are gone.

Personal connections to the harvest aside, at the very core of our witchcraft is the idea that regionality is inherently important to every witch's practice. Within Blacktree, witches seek to forge connections with the land on which they currently live and with its local spirits. With our roots sunk deep into a particular area and its specific environment, we may not align well (or at all, depending on hemisphere) with the traditional Neo-Pagan Wheel of the Year. We also understand that, since witchcraft is a practice rather than an actual religion, not all those who may come to Blacktree are necessarily Pagan in their deity work—if, indeed, they work with any deities at all.

The moon, however, is eternal. All witches see the face of the moon, no matter their path or tradition. We therefore go into far more detail in the next chapter when discussing the lunar year and how it can be used to mark the passage of time—not as a grand high sabbat, mind you, but with specific work and ritual observances we feel are more suited to our lives, both on a regional and magickal basis. The two sabbats recognized in Blacktree are another matter entirely.

Hexennacht and Halloween

Without a doubt, the two most significant nights of the year in Europe have historically been May Eve and November Eve. Both are known by many names, depending on region or cultural affiliation. Within the Blacktree tradition, we refer to them as Hexennacht and Halloween. We observe these nights as our only two sabbats to mark the seasonal shifting of the year. Their place on the calendar denotes the ebb and flow of the year, similar to the waxing and waning of the moon and the rise and descent of the Upper and Lower Worlds into the Middle World for alternating three-month periods.

Hexennacht, which means "Witches' Night," was traditionally observed on the evening of April 30th. These observances banished winter and frightened away any witches close by who might be flying to the sabbat for their own celebrations on that night. Hexennacht also marks the start of summer. In times past, only two seasons of the year were recognized—summer and winter—in contrast to the four seasons we recognize today. This is why the summer solstice is also referred to as Midsummer. Hexennacht has its ancestral roots in Germany's Harz Mountains on the highest peak, known as the Brocken, and similar gatherings and observances can be found throughout Europe. Hexennacht is still celebrated in various forms today, with bonfires, masks and costumes, loud music, heavy drinking, and dancing. Then and now, bonfires warm the land, symbolically bringing light and life back to a region while vanquishing the frigid darkness of winter.

For many, Midsummer is a fertile time of the year and celebrations surrounding this night embrace that concept. Some call it Walpurgisnacht or Beltane or May Day, and the days of observance may shift minutely, but the general celebration remains the same. It is a grand day of festivity and rejoicing, an ode to vanquishing the dark and looking forward to a green and glorious future. It is a time for joyous feasting and the encouragement of growth, a time for lovers and life.

In Blacktree, however, we see Hexennacht as a night when witches fly to their own gatherings and revels. On this night, we also acknowledge and honor our genius loci and other land spirits. For us, Hexennacht is literally a night of witches; it says so right in the name. On this night, we howl at the moon, wild in our power and in love with our very nature as witches. We connect deeply with the land and spirits around us. On Hexennacht, we call the Witch Lord; we fly to his side. This is the Witch Father's night of power. Hexennacht (or any of its equivalents) is not typically part of the cultural holidays we have grown up with, and we hold no personal ties to its celebrations or observances. Instead, this night speaks to us from within our blood as witches and our relationship to the land and the spirits therein.

Sitting opposite Hexennacht on the calendar is All Hallows' Eve—Halloween, as it is called today. Halloween is traditionally observed on the evening of October 31st. Like Hexennacht, it is a fire festival, but one that marks the start of winter and our crossover into the Underworld. The Gaelic name for the holiday—the name by which a large majority of modern Pagans call it—is Samhain, a word generally understood to mean "summer's end." This is why the cross-quarter night of winter solstice is also known as Midwinter. In older observances, Samhain marked the end of the harvest and was a time when livestock were slaughtered for the coming winter months. Just as on Hexennacht, and because everyone loves a good pyre, bonfires were lit for their protective powers and it was seen as a time when the boundaries between this world and others were particularly thin. Thus the spirits of the dead were thought to come home and walk among us on this night, and offerings were left out for them, as well as general invitations to feasts in their honor. Guising and mumming were common in many areas and people costumed themselves to go from home to home with song and verse in exchange for food.

With the introduction (and indoctrination) of Christianity and its common observance of All Hallows' Day, a day to honor the saints and remember the dead, the customs of this seasonal shift began to merge and morph into a wholly new creature—Halloween. A perfect con-glomeration of Christian and Pagan beliefs, this night sang a familiar song to those living in the countryside and hills. The dead rose from their graves on Halloween night, but instead of being welcomed with honor and open arms, they were feared and guarded against. Despite the early settling and colonization of the Americas, Halloween did not make a significant appearance there until at least the mid-19th century, when a large influx of Irish and Scottish immigrants brought their customs of Halloween, which quickly took hold and became popular. This celebration is widely seen today as a primarily secular holiday that is most common in North America.

As a witchcraft tradition founded in North America, Blacktree looks at the more modern viewpoint of Halloween when we observe this night. Our celebration of this night is distinctly derived from the North American culture in which we grew up and the perspective of its associated holiday, rather than the Celtic Samhain. We realize how backward this may sound to the pedantic, as Halloween itself is derived from the Celtic holiday, but our practice is regionally based and, as Americans, we naturally employ an American perspective in our practice. On Halloween, we call the Witch Queen to honor and engage with the Phantom Nations of the Dead.

We venerate our ancestors at all points of the year and constantly invite them into our homes and lives, so this isn't necessarily about the dead. We further believe in crossing the boundaries between this world and others whenever we please, so this also isn't a time of the year particularly special to us by virtue of its thinner veil—although it doesn't pass without note. Instead, we see this as the time of year when people can show their true faces, the time of the year when the masks actually come *off*. Everyone has a face on the inside that they hide from the rest of the world. Whether these faces portray who they actually are or who they wish to be does not matter. What matters is that these faces are there within us.

Halloween is the time for us, for witches, to connect with our inner selves and to embrace them with love and acceptance. This inner face, your shadow self, should always be acknowledged and accepted; indeed, you risk poisoning your entire being by ignoring it. As witches, we walk all paths—both dark and light. Preference for one over another causes imbalance, and in imbalance lies a sickening chaos that can quickly grow out of control.

JOURNEY TO THE SABBAT

Now let's look at the shamanic form the sabbat can take. Andrew Chumbley wrote extensively on his belief in a hypnagogic sabbat and how witches ritually prepared themselves and flew to revels under the influence of sleep and dreams. In his book *Azoetia*, he lays out a sequence of steps to help you reach a hypnagogic state—a state similar to, if not identical with, a delta-level trance. Chumbley describes the true meeting place of the Witches' Sabbat as the crossroads where waking, sleeping, and mundane dreaming meet.

If you were to participate in this type of sabbat, it would be via a ritual act of deep trance and self-induced soul flight similar to lucid dreaming, a state that develops from combining over-stimulation of the senses with sheer bodily exhaustion. This is achieved through the consumption of one or more entheogenic substances, ecstatic dancing, and sexual intercourse, the effects of which are intensified by a period of sacrifice involving offerings, abstinence, and fasting prior to the rite itself.

We each journey to the sabbat for our own reasons, whether it's to seek congress with the Witch Lord or Witch Queen, to visit the spirits, or just to have a good time. Though the next ritual may seem grandiose, try following the steps given to attend the great gathering.

To journey to the sabbat, you will need:

- Locally produced red wine, bread, and a bottle of water

- Your besom, stang, sword, token, sovereignty cord, and some protective jewelry

- Incense charcoal, tongs, and an incense blend (we suggest equal parts of damiana, mugwort, blue lotus, and white sage)

- Salt water

- A source of music for dancing (a drummer can also be a helpful lookout)

- Your entheogen(s) of choice based on your previous use, experience, and preference

Prepare your body and mind by meditating on the upcoming event and making offerings to the land and ancestors. Be sure to abstain from heavy food, alcohol, psychoactive substances (continue the use of any necessary prescriptions), and sexual intercourse for two or more days prior to the rite.

On the night of the journey, safely prepare a bonfire in a location that will permit privacy and space to dance around it. Place your Token of the Land in the northeast point of the space. Wear your Cord of Sovereignty and any protective jewelry you may own.

Lay the compass (see chapter 2), fortify the space, and follow this up with either the Compass Chant or a chant of your own making. In the southern point of your space, raise the stang (see chapter 6) and call the Witch Lord. In the northeast point of your space, make an offering of wine and bread to the spirits. Partake of the wine, but not the bread. Be sure to save enough bread for after your journey. Apply or consume any entheogens you may be using.

Pursue whatever method of overstimulation and exhaustion you planned. Be careful not to become dehydrated from all the activity and the heat of the fire. Dance clockwise on Hexennacht and counterclockwise on Halloween.

Once you are thoroughly exhausted, lie down comfortably, close your eyes, and commence your journey. Upon your return, eat the remaining bread, drink your water, and rejoice.

To close the space, thank the spirits, lower your stang, put out the fire, and clean up the space with your besom.

The Many Roads

Dreams and the experiences they offer are as valuable as any other method and should not be discounted simply because they are dreams or enabled by an entheogenic substance. The dream world is simply another layer of the world we inhabit. The experiences and interactions we have while attending the sabbat serve to deepen our practice and our understanding of who we are and what our roles are in our greater journey.

There are indeed many roads a witch can travel to attend the sabbat. The paths are laid out before us, although most are hidden from general perception. Given how few actually dare to tread them, even among witches, these paths may not be all that clear and may hold an inordinate amount of peril and distraction along the way. To properly open your eyes is to find the way to the sabbat. True seeing is what will lay bare the way, and this is only the beginning of your work and journey as a witch.

SUGGESTED READING

Ecstasies: Deciphering the Witches' Sabbath, by Carlo Ginzburg.
The Night Battles: Witchcraft and Agrarian Cults in the Sixteenth and Seventeenth Centuries, by Carlo Ginzburg.
Hands of Apostasy: Essays on Traditional Witchcraft, edited by Michael Howard and Daniel Schulke.
Between the Living and the Dead: A Perspective on Witches and Seers in the Early Modern Age, by Éva Pócs.

CHAPTER 11

The Lunar Year

In beauty and beheld in starlight, the moon shines in sheer grandeur over the sleeping sky—an enamoring mystery suspended in utter darkness. The ancients knew not of its whereabouts as it waxed and waned, migrating across the evening landscape of velvet night. It is from the moon that we have terms like "lunatic" and "lunacy," both derived from the Latin *luna*, which acknowledges the moon's arguable impact on the mental state of humans and animals alike. Although we'd be hard-pressed to locate any supportive scientific evidence of these phenomena, the lore surrounding the full moon is imbedded deep within our subconscious. It is a continued presence in our lives and stands as living kin to the only other celestial being with such control over us all—the sun.

Magick and the Lunar Phases

As witches, we seem to have a natural affinity for the moon. After all, it is the closest of the celestial bodies. Moreover, the moon has its own inherent ebb and flow that mirror and influence the normal push and pull of life as during its monthly course, the moon causes the tides to rise and fall. The power, presence, and influence of the moon are imminent and we can channel these qualities by working certain forms of magick at the proper times. In Blacktree, we are generally not concerned with the rigmarole of magickal timing found in high magickal systems or texts like *The Key of Solomon the King,* where the planets, zodiac, days of the week, and time of day all become just as important as the color and occult integrity of the clothing worn. We are witches and if the moon is right, then so are we. If our magick works, then no one can say anything about it—including King Solomon.

One of the most common problems faced by newer magickal practitioners is deciphering how to go about defining their magickal intent. Neophytes are often caught up in timing games because what they want may not necessarily coincide with the phase of the moon. Perhaps the moon is waning and you want to draw something into your life that is more aligned with a waxing moon. In Blacktree, we believe that there is no need to wait for the moon to be in the correct phase; just perform the opposite action. If you want to draw something toward you during a waning moon, then banish the opposite of what you want, which by default will cause the opposing element to be drawn to you. For example, you find yourself in need of a job. During the counter-moon phase, simply banish the lack of having a job or the condition of being unemployed. It is not always as clear-cut as this, but reversing your intent is a useful trick for dealing with this kind of situation and still keeping your magick in line with the phases of the moon.

Moon Phases

Our moon has a mutable spirit as capricious as quicksilver. As the days and nights flow from one to the next, her face changes. The moon's full luminosity, her entire glory, is a remarkable sight as she gleams pearl gray and white, hanging heavy in the night sky. The full moon is a woman in love, one with an open heart. Sometimes, however, she turns away. Or is it toward us? In profile, from either side, we cannot hold her in our hands and we are lost in a perpetual state of anxious anticipation, wondering and wandering. On other nights, the moon is gone completely from our eyes. Yet, somehow, she is still there and a sweet madness lies behind her obsidian veil.

Waxing Moon (Waxing Crescent, First Quarter, Waxing Gibbous)

The waxing moon is growing fat with promise and now is the perfect time to draw things toward you. This is an opportune time to perform magick dealing with beginnings, fostering, increasing, growth, and cultivation. Start at the top of the curve, just as the moon is entering the waxing phase, and put into motion a magickal working that extends throughout the period. As the moon gets closer to fullness, so shall your spell.

Full Moon

The peak of the moon's power and the culmination of its waxing phase. Magick dealing with the waxing of the moon is best performed around this time, when possible. Here, the moon's face is entirely illuminated by the sun and faces us. There are no shadows, as the sun's full power shines on her face. It is a time of magickal harvesting, ideal for reaping the benefits of the seeds painstakingly cultivated during the waxing moon.

Waning Moon (Waning Gibbous, Third Quarter, Waning Crescent)

The moon withers thin and turns away. This is when the light of the moon is decreasing bit by bit. As such, this is the optimal time to remove or banish undesirables. Magick dealing with cleansing and concluding will also be successful at this juncture. If you want something to waste away to nothing, beginning your working at the time of a waning moon will bolster the power of your intent and will.

Dark Moon

This is the moment of endings. It is the time when the shrinking face of the once brilliant moon has disappeared from the night sky. It seems to have winked from existence. This is the vanishing time, and this is the essence of the magick you should work in this period. The dark moon is the pivotal point of the waning phase—a time of finalization, endings, and banishing. She is a dark sister to the full moon and her perfect alignment with the sun and earth. Here, the moon, although still aligned with her cousins with her face illuminated by the sun, now stands with her back to us and all is blackness.

Working Outside

For a variety of reasons, the outdoors is probably the best environment for witches' work. Unfortunately, however, this may not always be possible for you—if ever and at all—depending on where you live. For some of us, working outside is never an option and you may find that the layouts we give are clearly more aligned with an indoor environment. As a working coven, we appreciate having a choice of options and a variety of methods in our practice to encourage spontaneity in our approach to ritual and witchcraft. For the sake of those who are able to work outside, we suggest coming up with a condensed work space setup that you can utilize. We say this because lugging ritual materials can be exhausting, and breaking everything down at the end of a working performed outdoors to be transported back home is often just impossible when you are still starry-eyed and in ritual headspace.

The value of a flexible setup, or the ability to pare things down, lies in its ability to instill a sense of spontaneity, as well as in combatting the notion that there can only ever be one way to work. We cannot stress enough that, in your practice, you should work in a manner that is reflective of the work being done and not in a manner that has come to be expected simply because it's always been done that way.

The ideal outdoor setup combines all three of the altars we have described (ancestor, genius loci, and sacrificial) into one arrangement. Since this traveling setup is somewhat reminiscent of Robert Cochrane's minimal and spontaneous ritual style, anchor the stang in the northeast. On the ground before it, place a black cloth to define an altar surface upon which you can place any additional items you may need—the skull and hearthstone for the ancestors, salt, water, the Token of the Land for the genius loci, a drinking horn or other vessel, wine, bread, etc. Because you are outside, there is no need for an offering bowl. Any offerings can go right onto the ground or into a small central campfire, if you build one.

You may need to replace the sword with a small ritual knife, since we don't recommend lugging one's coven sword around in public. You may need a candle for extra light, and you can make a temporary besom from a fallen branch with leaves still attached if someone forgot the besom—again. This reduced setup makes travel and working outdoors easy and practical, without sacrificing any symbolism. Of course, you can still set up a full ritual space outdoors if you feel so inclined and have the place to do it.

The Lunar Calendar

The Blacktree tradition does not follow the standard Neo-Pagan Wheel of the Year. The Wheel's holy days derive from cultures heavily influenced by agriculture (usually named for Anglo-Saxon or Celtic customs) and we do not currently live in an agricultural society. Thus we do not find that it meshes well with our practice and we have developed something that resonates with us.

One factor that we considered in this endeavor is that our world is always changing, and the present shifting of climates is undeniable. Some seasonal characteristics are now slowly morphing into others—not just hot and cold, as some suggest. This is a subtle shift that is not always immediately obvious, but it is happening nonetheless. With this in mind, and in the absence of true agrarian living, it seems counter-productive to follow a calendar that has little connection to our present lives.

The moon, however? The moon is different. Its passage is eternal and without fail. No matter what may come, the moon still rises and sets—endlessly. It will always face us and turn away.

Various cultures have different "traditional" terms for full moons. Some, like those called "Native American Full Moons," actually contain elements from unrelated cultures and ignore the racism implicit in lumping together different tribes and traditions into one general category. Further, giving different culturally based names to specific full moons only dates back to around 1706, when the Oxford English Dictionary referred to the "hunter's moon." Before that, there were few indications that there were names for each monthly moon. That said, the practice of naming each full moon in a way that reflects the surrounding environment remains a valuable tool, especially when combined with lessons or practices that exist in relation to the standing moon at the time. It may hold little historical legitimacy, but it seems to work. So why not?

In Blacktree, we have defined our own lunar calendar using this bastard idea and have also taken instruction from the land on which we currently live. The Mid-Atlantic region of the United States contains certain weather patterns and flora and fauna that are tied to specific times of the year. We named our full moons with this in mind, as well as our corresponding dark moons. As everyone learns at some point (whether the easy way or the hard way), life is decidedly not consistent. What happens in one month may not occur precisely at the same time or in the same way the following year. This makes any calendar inherently subject to adaptation and change, and you should feel free to create your own, based on your own specific environment.

A note: There are four months that do not ever change for Black-tree, as they are dedicated to four of the six spirits of the paths of witchcraft and remain as eternal and constant as the moon itself. The Crow Moon is dedicated to history and lore; the Serpent Moon is dedicated to magick; the Hare Moon is dedicated to herbalism; the Toad Moon is dedicted to divination.

January—Dreaming Moon

Days are long and gray in the month of January; the sky precariously shivers, ever on the edge of snow, rimed with frost and ice. Green and growing things are but a weak memory, half a world away. Will the sun ever return? It certainly feels as if it never will. But we still hold a fragile hope for resurrection close to our hearts—the only fire to warm ourselves against as the nights stretch out, endless and bleak. That tiny spark of life may be kept alive only with flurries of daily practice and internal activity. This is the perfect month for busy hands and drifting minds, personal reflection and mindful crafting.

During the full Dreaming Moon, apply yourself to general meditation and any workings designed to hold out hope for better times. Prosperity spells are also good for this period, to sweeten the coming months.

During the dark Dreaming Moon, focus on oneiromancy. Sew a mugwort-and-lavender sachet and keep it beneath your pillow; record your dreams. Anoint pulse points with a flying ointment, close your eyes, and take on the skin of a rabbit to race across the silent snow. Just as during the full Dreaming Moon, keeping fingers nimble drives away despair. Twist together a fragrant besom or construct a spirit bottle. Sew an altar cloth or draw sigils. Make incense, candles, and soap.

February—Winter Moon

Sit by your fires and spin your yarn, says Death from behind the wet and frigid face of February. A blank, bone grin sits just below the skin, waiting, rising slowly and methodically from the depths. Shudder and shiver against a sudden chill kiss of nothingness—skeletal fingers lightly brushing the tender nape of an unknowing neck. Whose Death is this? How long will it wait? Is it on the doorstep now?

The isolation of the Winter Moon naturally allows for this cold contemplation of our own mortality. Pull Death's face up to the surface; dive deep into the shadows. However, as one door closes, another is slated to open. You know this. We all know this. Beneath the impermanence of the grave lies a small seed of rebirth, waiting for the next cycle to begin, on the very precipice of chance and choice and paths to be taken. That moment after the intake of breath—of anticipation, of total potentiality—is the very essence of the Crossroads itself.

Spend the full Winter Moon in the arms of Death, burning necromantic incense for the names of the ancestors and meditating on the eventual and inescapable nature of fleeting life.

Spend the dark Winter Moon banishing bad influences in your life. What holds you back from living mindfully and in the moment? This is the story that Death carries to you. Let it go. Let it go.

March—Crow Moon

In March, the world is slowly waking from a long, wet sleep and begins to stretch its fingers and arms and legs and toes. Unkindnesses, parliaments, murders, and mobs all take to the sky and blacken the air with their wings, carrying messages and telling tales. Count every crow you come across, using this old rhyme:

One for sorrow,
Two for mirth,
Three for a wedding,
Four for a birth.
Five for silver,
Six for gold,
Seven for a secret never to be told.

Eight for heaven,
Nine for hell,
And ten is ten for the devil's own sell.

The full Crow Moon is the time to send and receive messages, the time to study your history and lore. Write a letter you could never send—words you've slept on all winter long. Burn it beneath the full moon and scatter the ashes where crows congregate. Read your histories; study the lore of your path. Take this information to your heart and commit it to memory.

During the dark Crow Moon, drink tea brewed from coltsfoot, skullcap, mugwort, and wormwood, and slide beneath the feathers of your favorite corvid. Is there a story unspoken or a tiding you need to receive? Now is the time it will be heard. Tell the crows and they will bring you back thoughts and memories.

April—Garden Moon

Is there a garden under your care? Under the watchful eye of April, it is just beginning to unravel pale roots beneath the earth, long dormant and brushing against the edge of the soil waiting to burst forth. April is the time of the year when we look to new beginnings, to awakenings, to the renewal of bonds left shaky by the close confines of winter. This is the Garden Moon, where everything perches waiting between the edges of death and life.

During the full Garden Moon, cleanse your space thoroughly and reset your wards. If you feel the need to lay extra protections, create a witch bottle. Practice grounding and centering; strengthen the shields that protect your tender blood and bones. Keep up your defenses.

The dark Garden Moon is a time for readiness, a time for the study of offensive maneuvers, as a truly competent witch should be able to hex as well as heal. Plants are not the only things that grow and live and thrive in the garden, after all. There are armies of insects that awaken under this moon as well, girding themselves for the coming battles for territory, food, and procreation. Listen to the beetles pounding their war drums; see moths fluttering ragged banners of fealty in the night sky. The worms are turning the soil as they begin to tunnel into enemy territory. What can you learn from this?

May—Horned Moon

He comes—the Lord of Beasts, the keeper of the green and growing. He comes—the horned one, our brother in the Blacktree tribe. He comes—guardian of the hidden landscape, the Witch Lord. In the delirium and joy of May's annual rebirth, the Witch Lord moves through the sunlit forest, the life of the land. Beneath his breast beats the heart of all the wild things; in the wake of his stride, the land awakens green and glorious from winter's pall.

During the full Horned Moon, go deep into the woods—as far from civilization as you are able. Burn juniper, sage, cedar, and pine over a smoldering fire. Lay your compass and raise your stang. Call the Witch Lord to come forth from the trees and greet you on this night to converse, commune, and dance. If the full moon lies close to Hexennacht, his power will line the edges of everything. You will feel him all around you, everywhere.

For three nights of the dark Horned Moon, one before and one after its height, leave offerings of fresh milk at the base of the oldest tree you can find.

June—Serpent Moon

With forky tongues, serpents awaken under the warmth of June and creep out from their slumber to mate, to feed, to hunt. They shed their skins, wriggling out from the redundant, casting away everything about themselves that is old, that no longer works as it should. Serpents are continually reborn, constantly changing; yet they remain ever the same. We can learn a lot of wisdom from snakes, if we only listen. They are not only subject to endless death and rebirth; they are also the very embodiment of deliverance. If you harass a serpent, if you chase it back to its home and continue to torment it, poke and prod it, it will strike and deliver a sharp, swift jolt of venom for your trouble. For some, this venom is a death-bringer and cringing agony is sure to follow. For others, it opens their eyes and lays bare the path.

How clear is your path? Is it time for you to shed your skin? Perhaps under the full Serpent Moon you will finally be able to discard the obsolete, all of the unnecessary baggage you've been clinging to for far too long. Where is your magick? Slide forward into the coming day with a new skin.

When the dark Serpent Moon makes its way around to your house, perform magick that encourages visions.

July—Firefly Moon

There is a tiny light hovering in the darkness. And then another. And another. And another. They flicker in and out of existence. Now you see them. And now you don't. Fireflies come in and out of your life as they please, with nary a fare-thee-well. They burn fiercely against the night, illuminative bursts of light on a blank black canvas. Lamp-holders. Light-bearers. Some say they are the ancestors, blinking in and out and around us as we move through life—guiding us, if only we can still hear their voices.

The full Firefly Moon is a time to examine and refresh your connections to the ancestors. Clean off your altars; offer up their absolute special favorites; then ask your questions and seek their guidance. Whenever you find everything all odds and ends, whether with yourself or someone else, or if you are unsure of which way to turn while wrestling with a potential problem, go first to your ancestors for help and support. Every night during this month, bring a portion of your evening meal to your ancestor altar and sit with your ancestors for a moment while they feast. Or visit them at dusk when the fireflies begin to blink. Burn dittany of Crete and copal.

During the dark Firefly Moon, close your eyes and look within for your personal tether to the Mighty Dead. Pin prick their names into bay leaves on the first night of the dark moon. Then, on the last night, burn the leaves along with a necromantic incense of cedar, wormwood, and mullein.

August—Cricket Moon

Sultry August nights swell indolent with cricket song. They herald the deepest nights of summer; they sing for love. Interwoven in their voices lie sweet hymns to the season's beating heart. Crickets the world over portend luck and signal rain and windfalls, so this is always an opportune time for magick of good fortune or petitions for financial gain.

For the full Cricket Moon, brew a tea of valerian and cat mint—not enough to sleep, just enough to set your head to spinning. If the moon is bright, stand bathed in its glow and drink the tea slowly, savoring how it smells. This time of the year is simply inundated with heady perfumes, fragrances wafting from every straining blossom—night-blooming daturas, climbing jasmine, pink and perfect evening primrose, all the vespertines. Their scent rises to the Upper World, an offering to the very heavens from the land itself, escorted by the crickets' tiny songs. This is when you can journey to touch fingertips to the divine.

When the dark Cricket Moon comes, apply your favorite flying ointment and send your spirit out into the night to sing with the crickets.

September—Hare Moon

In September, hares gaze at the moon. Spring is long gone and any jackrabbit frenzy is past. Now the moon is all they have; the moon is all they see. In the night sky, the great Queen Cassiopeia—thrown among the stars for her vanity—sits in her golden chair with her head hung low, and the hares gather silent at her feet. They know winter will soon be here, with its cold and clacking finger bones. They know that this is the time for thoughtful preparation.

Choose an herbal-processing method you are unfamiliar with and spend the entire month learning how to perform it, back to front. Pick a family of herbs and study all you can, as much as you can hold at one time. Sing the song of the hare—never stop moving, never stop learning. Hares are swift on their feet; they pivot easily and never rest on their self-satisfied laurels. Stagnation is death come faster to your door. Hares know this. Do you?

Harvest the last of your summer herbs during the full Hare Moon. They won't survive the winter. String them in bunches and hang them together, away from the sun.

When the dark moon comes, prepare fresh wormwood, mugwort, catnip, lemon balm, and valerian in a dreaming tincture for use in later months.

October—Blood Moon

At the door of the western gate stands the Witch Queen, silent as the grave and moving through our breath with the stride of a primordial Titan. As October begins its slow turn from green to orange to black, so goes our glorious lady. Only at her whim does she open the door to the ancestors, and any fool too arrogant to know better soon finds what breathes dark and patient behind her skull-faced grin. What mother's mask is this? In her arms, we find the ability to let go of the security provided by the everyday walls we have constructed. In her embrace, we finally show our true faces.

The Witch Queen will whisper quiet to your heart on the night of the full Blood Moon, her voice like ragged casket velvet. Hide your face with cloth or paint or paper. Rub an ointment of wormwood into your skin and journey to her side.

When the dark Blood Moon comes, beg an audience with your queen and, with her, lay down your strongest apotropaic magicks.

Strengthen your wards, witch; the coming cold will surely test them and the walls are so thin right now, as fragile as aged silk.

November—Bone Moon

This is the bottom of the cauldron. From here, our dead stir and are restless to be heard. Their voices drift on the wind, twining through chattering branches. November is bleak, stark against the white winter sky—the beginning of the bare and barren times when the dead crowd around us, seeking the least bits of our warmth to burn off their chill. We call their names, we call them—the Mighty, the Beloved, the Honored. These are their names, we call them—the Forgotten, the Dishonored. We call them to us, we call them—the Untimely and the Nameless.

The full Bone Moon opens wide the West Gate and the dead pour into our hearts. At the pinnacle of the moon's luminosity, take a mirror outside and catch its light in your glass. Clear your ancestor altar of everything that normally sits there, then cover it with a white cloth. Set up this newly charged mirror in the center of the altar, with a single white candle. Burn the candle in front of the mirror for the next five nights, reading the names of your dead aloud.

On the dark Bone Moon, perform the necessary ritual acts to make contact with and name one of the Nameless Dead.

December—Toad Moon

Noticing things is only a trouble—isn't that what Toad says? But Toad does notice. He sees things, down in his mud, down in the dark. Toad burrows down deep; he closes his great, golden eyes. Toad sleeps and Toad dreams. The month of December is a drowsy time when everything is so cold, so cold. All the months have tangled together and now there's nothing left to do but watch the sun on its farewell journey. These are the nights and days to lay your cards and cast your runes. Sift through tea leaves; gaze into a crystal or flame. There is knowledge to be sought and found. This is the time for far-seeing.

During the full Toad Moon, divine what is coming using your favorite tools. Burn a combination of rue and hyssop until it smolders, then pass your tools through the smoke to reconsecrate them to their task.

On the dark Toad Moon, gaze into the depths of a black scrying mirror until faces and words and names rise to your mind's eye. If you do not have a black mirror, use this moon cycle to make one.

FULL MOON RITE

This is a basic Full Moon ritual that you can use in conjunction with the work of the moons given above. For a traditional Dark Moon rite, incorporate the Necromantic Spirit Summoning given in chapter 8, but forgo the spirit-scrying portion and the tripod setup, or follow it up with an additional working derived from the moon lore above, or one based on your needs.

Set up your working space as shown in chapter 2 and wear any protective jewelry you feel necessary for the rite. Add quarter candles, lanterns, or torches, as you desire, both for extra light and for additional warding of the space.

For the ritual, you will also need:

- An offering for the land (candy, coin, liquor, or something else suitable)
- A loaf of locally baked bread
- A bottle of locally sourced wine
- Your blackthorn cane
- A libation bowl

- A cauldron or fireproof bowl

- A bottle of Florida Water

- A drinking horn

- Separate bowls for salt and water placed on the sacrificial altar

Leave your stang lying down in the south of the space for the time being.

Ground and center, then go inside yourself and look for the small, still place you go to when you are preparing to enter a liminal space. When you are ready to begin, knock three times on either the floor, the ground, or your sacrificial altar (whichever applies to where you're performing the rite) with either the blackthorn cane or your knuckles. Say aloud:

May the spirits of the land be favorable to my work. Let us begin.

Make your offering to the land, either in the libation bowl or directly onto the ground itself, if you are fortunate enough to be outdoors. This act confirms your connection to the land, as well as to your Token of the Land. Light your incense and, if you have quarter candles, light them as well, starting in the east and moving in a clockwise direction. If you do not have quarter markers, simply stomp your foot in each quarter to set the compass.

Next, plow the space using the sword, starting in the east. Carve out the compass space in a clockwise direction as a declaration of your presence, and as your claim to the land and the work you are undertaking. Then purify the space with your incense in the same way you plowed with the sword—again, starting in the east. When you are done with the incense, add three healthy pinches of salt to the water, stir to dissolve, then bless the space in the same way you used the incense.

These three circumambulations about the space with steel, smoke, and salt physically ward the ritual area, and you can skip them if they are not crucial to the work you are doing. We feel it is always helpful to perform this portion of the rite, because it creates a quiet, focused time in which your brain can shift gears from ordinary space into ritual space—in other words, into an alpha state. Individual situations may demand otherwise, however.

When you are finished with the steel, smoke, and salt, perform the Crossroads Rite (see chapter 1), then move to the south to raise the stang (see chapter 6). After you have raised the stang, immediately begin to walk counterclockwise about the ritual space. Recite the Besom, Stang, and Sword chant given below, letting the words gradually overtake you as you spiral ever more quickly down on your journey to the Underworld.

Around, about, and throughout we go,
By serpent, by hare, by toad, and crow,
To seek the things that are yet unknown
From high above, to down below.

By bee, by cat—we unite the pack;
By our will and by our word,
We do the deed of six in one
By besom, stang, and sword.

By night, by moon, and compass round,
By devil and by whore,
We do the deed of six in one
By besom, stang, and sword.

We hail to you, beyond the veil,
Majestic Queen and great Horned Lord;

We do the deed of six in one
By besom, stang, and sword.

By tooth and word, and blood and might,
For all that we adore,
We do the deed of six in one
By besom, stang, and sword.

For furrow, for kin, for dead and gone,
We toil as we endure;
We do the deed of six in one
By besom, stang, and sword.

They heed our word, the deal is done,
And all that we implore;
We do the deed of six in one
By besom, stang, and sword.

We've laid the ground, down all around
Our covenant is born;
We do the deed of six in one
By besom, stang, and sword.

Now repeat the following three times:

We do the deed of six in one
By besom, stang, and sword.

At the chant's conclusion, you will have arrived in the Underworld. Call the ancestors and open the West Gate (see chapter 8). Be sure to share some bread and wine with the ancestors at this time. If your message box contains any notes from previous weeks, burn them in a cauldron on the sacrificial altar using an ounce of Florida Water as an ignitable spirit. When the fire has settled, proceed with the primary work for the night—a moon working, a spell, a journey, an activity, or something else entirely. When you are done with your primary work, then it's time for the Housel.

THE HOUSEL

The housel is a sacrifice and an offering akin to the concept of the Eucharist. Although it seems a very simple ritual on the surface, it is replete with profound symbolism. It reflects an extremely Old World custom—the breaking of the bread—and is used to extend trust, indicate welcome, and celebrate life. At their most primal essence, bread and wine themselves stand as the body and the blood of the land.

When you break bread in this rite, you do so with all the spirits and flesh-and-blood witches who have gathered for the rite. This ritual act is accompanied by sacred toasting, which can prove to be quite a magickal act on its own, as the simple act of toasting and asking for blessings during this rite frequently produces profound results in your life and practice. While performing the Housel, you are already in a ritualistic mind frame; your brain is revved up and running in the perfect gear for manifestation. Combine that with the focused intent found in the act of toasting and you have the beginnings of very effective spell work.

Begin by knocking three times with your left hand on your sacrifical altar. Lay your left hand on the bread and say:

> *This bread—forged from the earth,*
> *A sacrifice by the land itself.*
> *May it fill us with life and sustenance.*
> *Eat of it, eat of the land, and be as one.*

Break off a piece of the bread and, holding it in your left hand, raise it into the air and say:

> *I sacrifice this life to the Witch Father, the Witch Lord.*
> *I dedicate this death to his name, so I may*
> *walk within his wild power.*

Eat half of the broken piece of bread and drop the remainder in the offering bowl. Then break off pieces for everyone participating. As participants take bread and eat, they should also say the words given above.

When everyone has partaken of the bread, place your left hand over the wine and say:

> *This wine, forged from the earth,*
> *A sacrifice by the land itself.*
> *May it fill us with life and sustenance.*
> *Drink of it, drink of the land, and be as one.*

Pour a measure of wine into a drinking receptacle of your choice (we use a drinking horn), raise it into the air with your left hand, and say:

> *I sacrifice this life to the Dark Mother, the Witch Queen.*
> *I dedicate this death to her name, so I may know of*
> *all her unending Mystery.*

Take a drink of the wine, then pour some into the offering bowl. As participants drink the wine, they should each repeat the words you spoke to dedicate it. When all have finished, it's time to proceed with the honorary drinks.

HONORARY DRINKS

This rite, which immediately follows the Housel, can be done by anyone in the coven, but it must be done in the following order. Say:

A drink for the Witch King and Queen and the Mighty Ones.

All pass the wine and take a drink, then say:

A drink for the Mighty Dead and those who have gone before.

All pass the wine and take a drink, then say:

*A drink for the blessings we have received
and for those yet to come.*

All pass the wine and take a drink, then say:

A drink for friendship and a drink for life.

All pass the wine and take two drinks, then say:

A drink for love and a drink for joy.

All pass the wine and take two drinks.

You can add toasts to this list as long as they reflect things for which you are thankful, or people you honor, or things you may need help with or want to acknowledge.

Pass the cup from person to person as each toast is made and make sure that you have enough wine on hand for all the planned toasts. Depending on how many people have toasts to give and how much wine flows, this can be a merry time, full of love and laughter—and even perhaps some tears. Everyone should eat their fill of bread between toasts, as this can help keep everyone on their feet when the wine is particularly strong.

When everyone has had a chance to speak, conclude with the following toast:

And finally, a drink for you and a drink for me.

All pass the wine and take two drinks.

When everyone is done, pour whatever wine remains into the offering bowl and say:

Hear! Hear!

Close the rite in the same way you closed the Necromantic Spirit Summoning in chapter 8.

Your Tool Kit Complete

This chapter compiles much of our regular coven work, at least as it relates to the course of the year and keeping in mind that the name and work of the moons may shift, depending on what is going on in your life or environment. The Full Moon rite can be used as a framework for any other type of working, or it can be used in conjunction with other rites or activities described in this book.

By now, you have been given a comprehensive tool kit of rites and workings to employ in your craft as a witch. The variety of approaches and arrangements of specific ritual components we have discussed throughout this book can help you understand how these rites can be interchanged or used in different magickal agendas and pursuits. This ability to shift between traditions and paths specifically conveys that there is no "one true way" to work your craft. Having a structure and foundation you can fall back on is important and should always be treasured and respected. However, spontaneity and adaptability will always be your greatest allies in the work you do because of the inspiration they bring.

SUGGESTED READING

The Moon, by Michael Carlowicz.

The Moon Book: Fascinating Facts about the Magnificent, Mysterious Moon, by Kim Long.

Moon Lore, by Timothy Harley.

Moon Lore: Lunar Themes of Wisdom and Magic, by Elizabeth Pepper.

Goodnight Moon, by Margaret Wise Brown

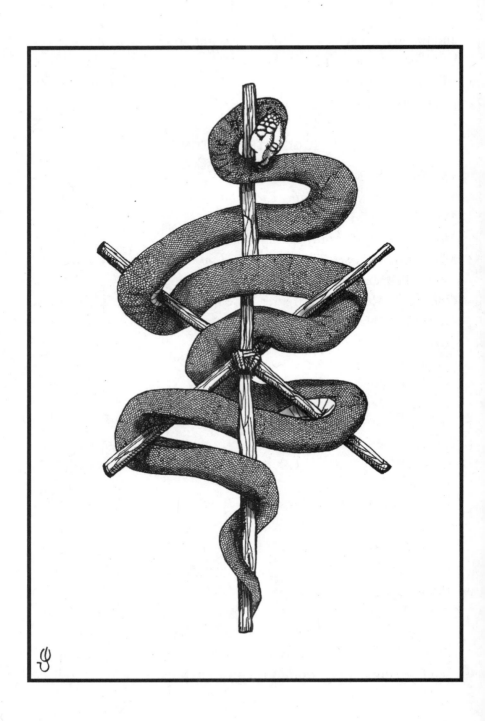

CHAPTER 12

The Crooked Path

And now our winding journey is about to end. As you near its conclusion, you may find yourself wondering where it has led. What is the ultimate goal of witchcraft? Is there anything more to it than self-governance and empowerment? One can never be quite sure.

Many paths, systems, traditions, religions, and schools of thought try to set some terminus to what they do—a proverbial finish line for your efforts, perhaps in the form of a special title, a sash, an outfit, a garter, or some other badge of honor. But after you collect the shiny trophy—what then? Where does the next step on your path lead? Unfortunately, the completion of a degree system is all too often treated solely as a destination rather than the beginning of a larger journey.

Further, no degree system should take a decade to complete. That's ludicrous! Yes, we are base creatures who are constantly learning and should always seek to view the world and our craft with fresh eyes, but how many points of reference do you need before you are permitted to fly free on your own? Blessedly, the witchcraft presented here is not of that ilk. In Blacktree, we give you the tools for practice and then send you out into the world to figure everything else out for yourself.

In Veritate Tua (To Your Own Truth)

If the ultimate goal of the study and practice of witchcraft could ever be expressed, it might include elements like testing the limits of your own reality, answering many if not all of life's greatest questions, gaining knowledge through exploring different beliefs, seeking a sense of enlightenment, researching the history of witchcraft, and understanding what witchcraft may be for others. All of these dwell within the heart of traditional witchcraft, when we distill it down to its most basic nature. We generally don't seek congress with deities, but rather with ourselves. We commune, not with some abstract divinity, but with the breathtaking land on which we live, with its myriad spirits, and with our ancestors. Traditional Witchcraft presents so few expectations; it holds so few limits. Where do we as witches sit in this grand theater, with little to constrain us but our own heads and hearts? How do we transverse the world?

It's simple. As witches, we walk this world via the Crooked Path.

What Is the Crooked Path?

We hear this phrase so frequently. But what is the Crooked Path? At its root, it is a delicate balance between left- and right-handed modes of thought. The left-hand path focuses on the needs of the self, while the right-hand path deals with the needs of others in light of the self. One is introverted; one is extroverted. One is selfish, while one is selfless.

The Crooked Path meanders back and forth between the two, acknowledging that there are no straight roads in life, no matter how much we may want there to be. In reality, compromise and conflict weave a funky tapestry of complicated decisions and resolutions. No one person has a perfect plan for governing and defining a completely flawless existence. Those who think they do are fools. Even the beloved Golden Rule found in so many of the world's religions—Do unto others as you would have them do unto you—still falls short of our expectations in the face of human depravity, ignorance, narcissism, and greed. Rules are rules, but we are still human; and humans are animals and always will be.

This is why witchcraft is a path of sovereignty with an undercurrent of self-exploration that flows beneath a strong pursuit of knowledge. Witchcraft makes no idealistic assumptions about humanity and the human struggle for peace and prosperity. Humans are of nature and within the balance of nature lie the ebb and flow of existence. We are nature personified and, like nature itself, we are inherently selfish and sometimes cruel in the face of personal risk and preservation. Proclaiming an oath of kindness, compassion, and love frequently only results in us making martyrs of ourselves or becoming gleaming targets for others.

Unfortunately, this often leads to shame and bloodshed when the inevitable exploitation comes. What we often fail to realize is that we only truly indulge in these emotions out of a strange sense of self-preservation. Deep within, anti-war sentiments, the crusade to end hunger and eliminate poverty, the quest for cures for disease, and other noble pursuits are undertaken only so we don't ourselves fall victim to these misfortunes.

The Inquisition, the Holocaust, sordid eugenics programs, and other historical acts of human cruelty are the children of allegedly noble virtues. All were committed in the pursuit of a stated desire for the goodness and benefit of a particular set of individuals. It is sadly just as easy to demonize one culture as it is glorify or uphold another, and the distinction between demons and angels really depends only on which side of the issue you occupy. The notions of greatness, triumph, and victory are all selfish and evil, because they usually (*usually*, mind you) rest on a high mound of human suffering. Success is always achieved at the expense of others; it never develops in a vacuum. A life raft can hold only so many survivors before it becomes useless; big business thrives because of a dependent and obligated working class. There are few exceptions to this reality. Witchcraft knows it. The Crooked Path reveals it.

Moving Forward

The Great Work often referenced in high magickal systems—the attainment of knowledge and union with the divine—does not apply in witchcraft as we have come to know it. Our craft contains no moment of divine spiritual ascension. These are the concerns of religion, not witchcraft. In witchcraft, you have lived either as someone to be remembered or as someone to be forgotten.

Don't be discouraged if your practice ebbs and flows, waxes and wanes, because it will. This is normal and natural. These periods of frustration and doubt may be difficult to get through, but allow them to happen. Despite how disheartening they may feel, these phases occur as a result of personal growth. Seekers of wisdom are often life's greatest skeptics—honest in their pursuit and observant about their findings. Life also has a tendency to get in the way when you least expect it. Not everyone can drop all of their daily responsibilities to lay out a Full Moon ritual with all the bells and whistles in the middle of a work week. Don't beat yourself up if this happens to you. You're still a witch; it's still within you.

To practice witchcraft in today's world is difficult. While the benefits of first-world living may save most from a fiery fate or the hangman's noose, there are those in the world who are not so fortunate. To know, to will, to dare, to grow, to keep silent, and to go. Silence is a witches' greatest advantage, as it denotes secrecy and privacy and working in the shadows, all of which are imperative to preserve the work and to insure survival. The road ahead is fraught with bumps and curves, but that's just how life is. At least with witchcraft, the bumps are less jarring and the curves don't seem as directionless.

In essence, one becomes a witch by choosing to practice witch-craft. You become successful at your craft through trial and error, not through someone else's will or selfless good grace. If you have been doing the work, and are finding some margin of success in what you do, then you are a witch through and through—a sovereign being—and no one can take that from you. You have the tools. Your eyes and heart are open. You have all the road maps in hand and waiting. Now—*fly*.

Bendith.

SUGGESTED READING

A Deed without a Name: Unearthing the Legacy of Traditional Witchcraft, by Lee Morgan.

Craft of the Untamed: An Inspired Vision of Traditional Witchcraft, by Nicholaj de Mattos Frisvold.

The Devil's Dozen: Thirteen Craft Rites of the Old One, by Gemma Gary.

Treading the Mill: Workings in Traditional Witchcraft, by Nigel Pearson.

Liber Nox: A Traditional Witch's Gramarye, by Michael Howard.

Acknowledgments

We are deeply grateful to the following people for all their inspiration, love, and support.

Mat Auryn

Byron Ballard

Amy Blackthorn

George Bowling

Star Bustamonte

Deborah Castellano

Corinne Castillo

Nathan Castillo

Cynthia Cole

Ivo Dominguez Jr.

Angelica Freeling

Will Guilford

Jeffrey Hill

Courtney Weber Hoover

Lauren Huchel

Devin Hunter

Cory Hutcheson

Judika Illes

Erik Johnson

Michelle Jones

Raymond Kennedy

Liana Kowalzik

Pete Kowalzik

Jenn Lane

Mia Lavorata

Sarah Anne Lawless

Nissa Lee

Polly Lind

Sarah Elizabeth Lyter

Cameron Aiden Mattei

Peter Paddon

Joanna Paparone

Erik Adriel Peterson

Alan Prachar

Robin Prachar

Jen Rue

Anthony Secreto

Stephanie Snow

Amie Tolomeo

Ricardo Urdinaran

John Taylor Williams

Katheryn Woodworth

Nancy Wykel

Laura Tempest Zakroff

And all of our *Down at the Crossroads* listeners and *Patreon* subscribers!

Bibliography

Agrippa, Heinrich Cornelius von Nettesheim, and Stephen Skinner. *The Fourth Book of Occult Philosophy*. Berwick, ME: Ibis Press, 2005.

Akhania, Hossein and Abdol Basset Ghorbanib, (2003), "*Mandragora turcomanica* (Solanaceae) in Iran: a new distribution record for an endangered species," *Systematics and Biodiversity*, 1(2):177–180.

Aradia, Lady Sable. *The Witch's Eight Paths of Power: A Complete Course in Magick and Witchcraft*. San Francisco, CA: Weiser Books, 2014.

Ballard, H. Byron. *Staubs and Ditchwater: A Friendly and Useful Guide to Hillfolks' Hoodoo*. Asheville, NC: Silver Rings Press, 2012.

Bodin, Jean. *On the Demon-Mania of Witches*. Toronto, Canada: CRRS Publications, 2001.

Broughton, Richard S., Ph.D. *Parapsychology: The Controversial Science*. New York: Ballantine Press, 1991.

Buckland, Raymond. *The Witch Book: The Encyclopedia of Witchcraft, Wicca, and Neo-Paganism*. Canton, MI: Visible Ink Press, 2002.

Carroll, Peter J. *Liber Null and Psychonaut: An Introduction to Chaos Magic*. York Beach, ME: Weiser, 1987.

Carus, Paul. *The History of the Devil and the Idea of Evil from the Earliest Times to the Present Day*. Chicago: The Open Court Publishing Company, 1900.

Cavendish, Richard. *The Black Arts*. New York: Perigee Books, 1967.

Chemonics International, Inc. (2001), *Biodiversity Assessment for Turkmenistan* (retrieved 05/10/17). *https://rmportal.net /library/content/118_turkmenistan/view.*

Chumbley, Andrew D. *Azoetia: A Grimoire of the Sabbatic Craft.* Chelmsford: Xoanon Publishers, 1992.

—————. *Three Books of Occult Philosophy.* London: Chthonios, 1987.

Crowley, Aleister. *Magick • Book Four • Liber ABA.* York Beach, ME: Red Wheel/Weiser LLC, 1997.

—————. *Moonchild.* York Beach, ME: Samuel Weiser, Inc., 1994.

Crowley, Aleister, and Israel Regardie. *Magick without Tears.* Phoenix, AZ: Falcon Press, 2001.

Cunningham, Scott. *Cunningham's Encyclopedia of Magical Herbs.* Second edition. St. Paul, MN: Llewellyn Publications, 2003.

Davies, Owen. *America Bewitched: The Story of Witchcraft after Salem.* Oxford, NY: Oxford University Press, 2013.

—————. *Grimoires: A History of Magic Books.* Oxford, NY: Oxford University Press, 2009.

Davis, Wade. *The Serpent and the Rainbow.* New York: Touchstone, Simon and Schuster, 1985.

d'Este, Sorita, and David Rankine. *Hekate: Liminal Rites.* London: BM Avalonia, 2009.

de Vries, Eric. *Hedge-Rider.* Sunland, CA: Pendraig Publishing, 2008.

Faraone, Christopher A., and Dirk Obbink, ed. *Magika Hiera: Ancient Greek Magic and Religion.* Oxford, NY: Oxford University Press, 1991.

Farrar, Janet, and Stewart Farrar. *A Witches' Bible: The Complete Witches' Handbook.* Custer, WA: Phoenix Publishing, Inc., 1981, 1984.

Frisvold, Nicholaj de Mattos. *Craft of the Untamed: An Inspired Vision of Traditional Witchcraft*. Oxford, UK: Mandrake of Oxford, 2014.

————. *Palo Mayombe: The Garden of Blood and Bones*. London: Scarlet Imprint, 2010.

Gary, Gemma. *The Devil's Dozen: Thirteen Craft Rites of the Old One*. London: Troy Books, 2015.

————. *Traditional Witchcraft: A Cornish Book of Ways*. London: Troy Books, 2012.

Ginzburg, Carlo. *Ecstasies: Deciphering the Witches' Sabbath*. Chicago: University of Chicago Press, 2005.

————. *The Night Battles: Witchcraft and Agrarian Cults in the Sixteenth and Seventeenth Centuries*. Baltimore, MD: Johns Hopkins University Press, 1992.

Guiley, Rosemary Ellen. *Encyclopedia of Magic and Alchemy*. New York: Facts on File, Inc., an imprint of Infobase Publishing, 2006.

————. *The Encyclopedia of Witches, Witchcraft, and Wicca*. 3rd ed. New York: Facts on File, Inc., an imprint of Infobase Publishing, 2008.

Harner, Michael. *The Way of the Shaman*. New York: Harper & Row, 1990.

Hauck, Dennis William. *The Emerald Tablet: Alchemy for Personal Transformation*. New York: Penguin Arkana, 1999.

Heselton, Phillip. *Doreen Valiente: Witch*. Centre for Pagan Studies Ltd, 2016.

Homer and E. V. Rieu. *The Odyssey*. London: Penguin Books, 1996.

Howard, Michael. *Children of Cain: A Study of Modern Traditional Witchcraft*. Richmond Vista, CA: Xoanon / Three Hands Press, 2011.

Huson, Paul. *Mastering Herbalism: A Practical Guide*. Lanham, MD: Madison Books, 2001.

————. *Mastering Witchcraft: A Practical Guide for Witches, Warlocks, and Covens.* New York: Putnam, 1970.

Hutton, Ronald. *The Triumph of the Moon: A History of Modern Pagan Witchcraft.* Oxford, NY: Oxford University Press, 1999.

Illes, Judika. *Encyclopedia of Witchcraft: The Complete A-Z for the Entire Magical World.* New York: HarperOne, 2005.

————. *Encyclopedia of 5000 Spells.* New York: HarperOne, 2008.

Irwin, Harvey J., and Caroline A. Watt. *An Introduction to Parapsychology.* 5th ed. Jefferson, NC: MacFarland & Company, Inc., Publishers, 2007.

Jackson, Nigel Aldcroft. *The Call of the Horned Piper.* Berkshire, UK: Capall Bann Publishing, 1994.

Johnson, Kenneth. *Witchcraft and the Shamanic Journey: Pagan Folkways from the Burning Times.* St. Paul, MN: Llewellyn Publications, 1998.

Jones, Evan John, and Robert Cochrane. *The Roebuck in the Thicket: An Anthology of the Robert Cochrane Witchcraft Tradition.* Edited by Michael Howard. Somerset, UK: Capall Bann Publishing, 2001.

Kieckhefer, Richard. *Forbidden Rites: A Necromancer's Manual of the Fifteenth Century.* University Park, PA: The Pennsylvania State University Press, 1998.

Kraig, Donald Michael. *Modern Magick: Twelve Lessons in the High Magickal Arts.* St. Paul, MN: Llewellyn Publications, 2011.

Lea, Henry Charles. *A History of the Inquisition of Spain, Volume IV.* Edited by Anthony Uyl. New York: The MacMillan Company; London: MacMillan & Co., Ltd., 1922.

Lecouteux, Claude. *Demons and Spirits of the Land: Ancestral Lore and Practices.* Rochester, VT: Inner Traditions, 2015.

—————. *Dictionary of Ancient Magic Words and Spells.* Rochester, VT: Inner Traditions, 2015.

—————. *The Return of the Dead: Ghosts, Ancestors, and the Transparent Veil of the Pagan Mind.* Rochester, VT: Inner Traditions, 2009.

—————. *The Tradition of Household Spirits: Ancestral Lore and Practices.* Rochester, VT: Inner Traditions, 2013.

Leland, Charles Godfrey. *Aradia or the Gospel of the Witches.* Newport, RI: Witches Almanac, 2010.

Levi, Eliphas. *The History of Magic.* Translated by Arthur Edward Waite. York Beach, ME: Samuel Weiser, Inc., 1999.

—————. *Transcendental Magic.* Translated by Arthur Edward Waite. York Beach, ME: Red Wheel/Weiser, Inc., 2001.

Lucan and Edward Riley. *The Pharsalia of Lucan.* London: Longmans, Green, and Co., 1896.

MacDonald, Stuart. *Witches of Fife: Witch-hunting in a Scottish Shire*, 1560–1710. (Google Books)

Masello, Robert. *Raising Hell: A Concise History of the Black Arts and Those Who Dared to Practice Them.* New York: Perigee Books, The Berkley Publishing Group, 1996.

Morgan, Lee. *A Deed without a Name: Unearthing the Legacy of Traditional Witchcraft.* Alresford, Hants, UK: Moon Books, 2013.

Ogden, Daniel. *Greek and Roman Necromancy.* Princeton, NJ: Princeton University Press, 2001.

Olmstead, R. G., C. W. dePamphilis, A. D. Wolfe, N. D. Young, W. J. Elisons, and P. A. Reeves, "Disintegration of the Scrophulariaceae," *American Journal of Botany.* Vol. 88, No. 2. 88 (2): 348–361.

Otto, Walter F. *Dionysus: Myth and Cult.* Bloomington, IN: Indiana University Press, 1965.

Paddon, Peter. *A Grimoire for Modern Cunningfolk*. Sunland, CA: Pendraig Press, 2010.

Penczak, Christopher. *The Mighty Dead: Communing with the Ancestors of Witchcraft*. Salem, NH: Copper Cauldron Publishing, 2013.

Pendell, Dale. *Pharmako/Dynamis: Stimulating Plants, Potions, and Herbcraft: Excitantia and Empathogenica*. Berkeley, CA: North Atlantic, 2010.

—————. *Pharmako/Gnosis: Plant Teachers and the Poison Path*. Berkeley, CA: North Atlantic Books, 2010.

—————. *Pharmako/Poeia: Plant Powers, Poisons, and Herbcraft*. Berkeley, CA: North Atlantic Books, 2010.

Pennick, Nigel. *The Eldritch World*. Leicestershire, UK: Earl Shilton, Lear, 2006.

—————. *Magical Alphabets*. York Beach, ME: Samuel Weiser, 1992.

Peterson, Joseph H., ed. and trans. *Grimorium Verum*. Scotts Valley, CA: CreateSpace Publishing, 2007.

Pócs, Éva. *Between the Living and the Dead: A Perspective on Witches and Seers in the Early Modern Age*. Budapest, Hungary: Central European University Press, 1999.

Preissel, Ulrike, and Hans-Georg Preissel. *Brugmansia and Datura: Angel's Trumpets and Thorn Apples*. Buffalo, NY: Firefly Books, 2002.

Robbins, Rossell Hope. *The Encyclopedia of Witchcraft and Demonology*. New York: Bonanza Books, 1981.

Roth, Harold. *The Witching Herbs: 13 Essential Plants and Herbs for Your Magical Garden*. Newburyport, MA: Red Wheel/Weiser, 2017.

Russell, Jeffrey B., and Brooks Alexander. *A History of Witchcraft: Sorcerers, Heretics, and Pagans*. 2nd ed. London: Thames and Hudson Ltd., 2007.

Schulke, Daniel A. *Veneficium: Magic, Witchcraft, and the Poison Path*. Richmond Vista, CA: Three Hands Press, 2012.

Scot, Reginald. *The Discovery of Witchcraft*. New York: Dover Publications, Inc., 1972.

Solomon. *The Lesser Key of Solomon: Detailing the Ceremonial Art of Commanding Spirits Both Good and Evil*. Edited by Joseph H. Peterson. York Beach, ME: Weiser, 2001.

Solomon and S. L. MacGregor Mathers. *The Key of Solomon the King: (Clavicula Salomonis)*. York Beach, ME: Weiser, 1989.

Summers, Montague. *Witchcraft and Black Magic*. Mineola, NY: Dover Publications, Inc., 2000.

Thompson, C. J. S. *The Mystic Mandrake*. London: Rider, 1975.

Thorsson, Edred. *Runelore: A Handbook of Esoteric Runology*. York Beach, ME: Samuel Weiser, 1987.

Valiente, Doreen. *The Rebirth of Witchcraft*. London: Robert Hale, 1989.

——————. *Where Witchcraft Lives*. 4th ed. The Doreen Valiente Foundation, 2014. Originally published in 1962.

——————. *Witchcraft for Tomorrow*. London: Hale, 1978.

Valiente, Doreen and Evan John Jones. *Witchcraft: A Tradition Renewed*. Custer, WA: Phoenix Publishing, Inc., 1990.

Waite, Arthur Edward. *The Book of Ceremonial Magic*. New York: Barnes & Noble Books, 1977.

Wilby, Emma. *Cunning Folk and Familiar Spirits*. Great Britain: Sussex Academic Press, 2010.

——————. *The Visions of Isobel Gowdie: Magic, Witchcraft and Dark Shamanism in Seventeenth-Century Scotland*. Brighton, UK: Sussex Academic Press, 2013.

Index of Rituals and Spells

Index of Exercises

CHAPTER 7—THE HIDDEN LANDSCAPE

CHAPTER 9—HEDGEWITCHERY

To Our Readers

Weiser Books, an imprint of Red Wheel/Weiser, publishes books across the entire spectrum of occult, esoteric, speculative, and New Age subjects. Our mission is to publish quality books that will make a difference in people's lives without advocating any one particular path or field of study. We value the integrity, originality, and depth of knowledge of our authors.

Our readers are our most important resource, and we appreciate your input, suggestions, and ideas about what you would like to see published.

Visit our website at *www.redwheelweiser.com* to learn about our upcoming books and free downloads, and be sure to go to *www .redwheelweiser.com/newsletter* to sign up for newsletters and exclusive offers.

You can also contact us at *info@rwwbooks.com* or at

Red Wheel/Weiser, LLC
65 Parker Street, Suite 7
Newburyport, MA 01950